ASLK-CGER, INCORPORATED IN 1865

Sûre,

fidèle...

et qui rapporte

SOCIÉTÉ NATIONALE DE

CREDIT A L'INDUSTRIE

N 1822

CRÉDIT À L'INDUSTRIE,
INCORPORATED IN 1919

The companies in the [...] for their strength in the fina[...] large. Some have more than a[...]

Fortis itself was created in 1990 by the combination of the Belgian insurer AG and the Dutch bancassurance group AMEV/VSB. It was the first cross-border alliance in the financial world. But the two parties were already well-known for their distinctive entrepreneurial spirit and innovative methods.

In the last century, AG 1824 was the first life insurer in Belgium. AMEV/VSB was the first bancassurance group in the Netherlands thanks to the merger between the insurer AMEV and VSB Bank.

Since its creation, Fortis has built up a unique organization that has grown in every respect. MeesPierson and ASLK-CGER joined Fortis. And recently the ranks were strengthened by the arrival of Générale de Banque, the oldest and largest bank in Belgium. The new combination with Générale de Banque makes Fortis one of the largest integrated financial service providers in the Benelux. A springboard for further growth in Europe, the United States of America and Asia.

From this solid base, Fortis' 58,000 staff are working hard on growing further and improving their services. It is a team made up of strong players that share their know-how and experience and make optimum use of each other's strengths. A group that has proven that it can respond promptly to developments in the market.

Wherever you see the Fortis name, you will find solid partners working on flexible solutions. We owe it to our roots and reputation. Fortis: another way of thinking about insurance, banking and investment.

FORTIS

Solid partners, flexible solutions

For more information on Fortis, telephone in Belgium 32 (0)2 220 84 53 or in the Netherlands 31 (0)30 257 57 77. Or visit our Internet site at: www.fortis.com.
regulated by the Securities and Futures Authority in the conduct of investments business in the UK.

WHO WOULD KNOW BETTER
HOW TO
MAKE YOU FEEL

WELCOME

ACROSS EUROPE
& FURTHER AFIELD

We have welcomed more travellers to more places in the world than anyone. And with all that experience, we know how to make you feel perfectly at home.

You'll always find comfortable rooms and quality service you can depend on. No matter where your travels take you, it's nice to know that we will be there, waiting to welcome you.

FOR RESERVATIONS AND MORE INFORMATION ON HOTELS IN EUROPE, THE MIDDLE EAST OR AFRICA
CALL TOLL-FREE FROM: UK 0800 897121, Germany 0130 815131, France 0800 905 999, Belgium 0800 199 77, Italy 1678 77399, Norway 800 11 33, Portugal 0800 831317, Spain 900 99 31 19, Switzerland 0800 55 11 75, The Netherlands 0800 0221155, From all other countries (NL) +31 20 606 0222 (not toll-free).

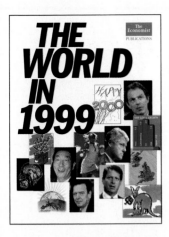

EDITOR: Dudley Fishburn

MANAGING EDITOR: Harriet Ziegler
DEPUTY EDITOR: Palash Davé
EDITORIAL ASSISTANT: Gemma Hyde
RESEARCHERS: Nicholas Harland,
  Lucy Tallon

DESIGN AND ART DIRECTION: Bailey and Kenny
DESIGN ASSISTANCE: Edgar Gonzalez,
  Nicola Bailey
CHARTS AND MAPS: Michael Robinson,
  Tim Carr, Carol Anderson
ILLUSTRATIONS: Derek Cousins,
  Geraldine Spence
PICTURE EDITOR: Juliet Brightmore

ADVERTISING DIRECTOR: John Dunn
CIRCULATION DIRECTOR: Des McSweeney
PRODUCTION: Laura Robinson,
  Andrew Rollings
FOREIGN RIGHTS: Hutton-Williams Agency

ASSOCIATE PUBLISHER: David Gill
PUBLISHER: David Hanger

ISBN 0 85058 475 2

PHOTOGRAPHIC SOURCES: Action Plus; Allsport; Associated
Press; Bridgeman Art Library; British Aerospace; Richard
Davies/Foster and Partners; Mary Evans Picture Library;
Stuart Franklin/Magnum Photos; Ronald Grant Archive;
IPG/Katz Pictures; Insight; Katz Pictures; Kos Picture
Source; National Trust Photo Library; PA News; Retna
Pictures; Rex Features; Frank Spooner Pictures;
Superstock; Sygma.

Printed by Polestar Ltd
(Bradford and Carlisle, England)
Reprographics by The Litho Origination Group Plc

THE ECONOMIST GROUP

25 St James's Street, London, SW1A 1HG
Telephone: 0171-830 7000
E-mail: theworldin@economist.com
Internet: http://www.theworldin.com

ECONOMICS '99

Europe's currencies become one, **John Peet**, *The Economist*, page 13. Why democracy needs economic transparency, **Jim Wolfensohn**, *World Bank*, page 78. Time for a trade round, **Leon Brittan**, *European Commission*, page 46. Tough times for the world economy, **Clive Crook**, *The Economist,* page 14. Britain will get through 1999 in good shape, **Anatole Kaletsky**, *The Times*, page 26. Capital markets will change with the euro's arrival, **Stefan Collignon**, *Association for Monetary Union*, page 134. The euro will be an essential capitalist tool, **Hugo Dixon**, *Financial Times*, page 128. But the Conservatives will have none of it, **William Hague**, *Conservative Party*, page 38.

POLITICS '99

China struggles with its 50th year of communism, **James Miles**, *BBC,* page 71. Bill Clinton struggles with his lame-duck presidency, **Morton Kondracke**, *Roll Call*, page 61. There will be new rules for diplomacy, **Fareed Zakaria**, *Foreign Affairs*, page 82. And old arguments in France, **Jean-Marie Colombani**, *Le Monde*, page 47. Expect regionalism to increase in Spain, **Juan Luis Cebrián**, *El Pais*, page 52. And in Scotland, **John Grimond**, *The Economist*, page 30. Australia will vote to be rid of its monarch, **Dennis Shanahan**, *The Australian*, page 77. Africa loses Nelson Mandela, **Patrick Smith**, *Africa Confidential*, page 84. A sane voice will be heard in Iran, **David Gardner**, *Financial Times*, page 80.

MANAGEMENT '99

The birth of the world stockmarket, **Richard Grasso**, *New York Stock Exchange*, page 138. The best management will migrate to the ether, **Michael Dell**, *Dell Computers*, page 124. How to keep up with the revolution in communications, **Michael Armstrong**, *AT&T*, page 116. Managing in a recession, **Edward Carr**, *The Economist,* page 102. British life will manage to bubble along, **Anthony King**, *Essex University*, page 25. How to cope with disruption in the financial markets, **Sandy Weill**, *Citigroup*, page 131. Which way will markets move? **Hamish McRae**, *The Independent*, page 127.

IDEAS '99

The arrival of interactive TV, **Bill Gates**, *Microsoft*, page 101. Britain will be full of creative ideas in 1999, **Martin Vander Weyer**, *The Week*, page 34. The dangerous idea that humans can be fixed like cars, **Alun Anderson**, *New Scientist*, page 141. Why fatalism is a bad idea, **Madsen Pirie**, *Adam Smith Institute*, page 19. America's love of size will grow, **Daniel Franklin**, *Economist Intelligence Unit*, page 16. New ideas about your brain, **Steve Connor**, *The Independent*, page 142.

HEADACHES '99

The nightmare of running Italy, **Beppe Severgnini**, *Corriere della Sera*, page 50. The world economy in 1999, **Pam Woodall**, *The Economist*, page 105. The spread of tuberculosis from Russia, **Kate Mallinson**, *Interfax*, page 144. More cheating by scientists, **Philip Campbell**, *Nature*, page 144. Raising money for the American election in 2000, **Charles Cook**, *Cook Report*, page 65. The headache of low commodity prices in Canada, **William Thorsell**, *Globe and Mail*, page 66. Getting Japan to get a grip of itself, **Nicholas Valéry**, *The Economist*, page 73.

The ThinkPad 600. It offers Intel's fastest processor. A huge hard drive. CD-ROM capability. A keyboard that feels so real you'll forget it's a notebook. Everything a mobile business professional could want. Yet, thanks to a great design team, the ThinkPad 600 still manages to offer a stunningly attractive, slim, elegant profile. It's a great mobile business tool. You know it. They'll know it too. Be gracious. For information, visit **www.ibm.com/pc/uk/thinkpad** or call **Tanya Proud** on **0870 601 0137**. In Ireland phone **1850 22 00 33**.

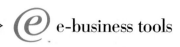 e-business tools

Travel the world.
Meet interesting people.
Make them jealous.

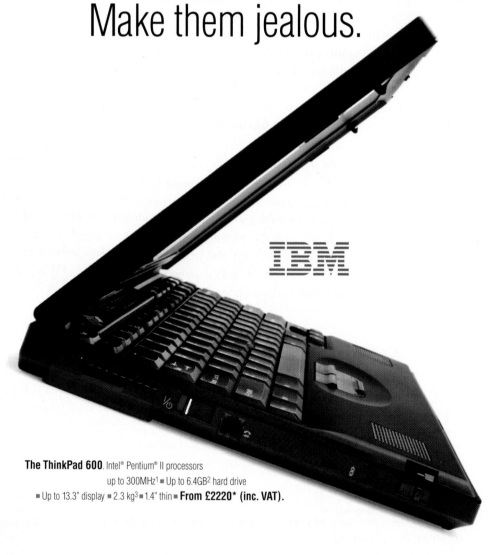

IBM

The ThinkPad 600. Intel® Pentium® II processors
up to 300MHz[1] ■ Up to 6.4GB[2] hard drive
■ Up to 13.3" display ■ 2.3 kg[3] ■ 1.4" thin ■ **From £2220* (inc. VAT).**

Dudley Fishburn: editor

1999 will be a thin year. Economic growth will slow right down. People the world over will save more and spend less. Anxiety will prevail over optimism. Will the financial turmoil of 1998 translate into carnage at your workplace in 1999? There will certainly be casualties: greater joblessness, lower corporate earnings, another round of cost-cutting. But do not expect a recession.

Everywhere there will be surpluses. Too much oil. Too many production lines. Too much food. This, despite the fact that some time in June 1999 the United Nations' computers will announce the birth of the baby who will take the world's population past 6 billion. She may well be Indian. (One new person in four will be.) She will be born poor but will die, as average lifespans grow longer, aged 90 and richer than today's westerners. Despite all the problems with emerging markets, India and China, with one-third of the world's population, will end the decade more than twice as rich as they started it: one of humanity's more remarkable achievements.

In Europe, on January 1st, a new currency arrives and eleven, once famous, old ones die. The euro will be born on time and in good order, a strong currency that over the next few years will change the way European business thinks and works for the better. This will thoroughly vex the "won't play" British, who will start to drop their objections. People will stop discussing the euro, just as they will stop discussing the Internet, in the future tense. It will become a daily reality.

America will enter its ninth year of continuous growth: the longest period of uninterrupted prosperity since the second world war. It will run a huge budget surplus and a huge current-account deficit: both healthy at this stage of the economic cycle. It will take in about 1m immigrants: also healthy. It will increase its spending on defence, thereby adding to its vast lead over the rest of the world and enabling it to broker another year of international peace.

The nation-state, always a more malleable thing than theory would have it, will change form in many places during 1999. Australia will vote to get rid of its monarch. Scotland will vote for its first national parliament since 1707. England will change its constitution. Germany will change its capital. A new Palestinian state may be born. Large parts of Russia will start running themselves with little regard for Moscow. And, as Nelson Mandela steps down, the world will see South Africa as a nation, not as a person. Regional power everywhere—from California to Catalonia—will be on the rise. Dictators, especially in Asia, will be in retreat.

The most memorable day of 1999 will be its very last. Book your party soon and make it a good one. The world will close down for three weeks, partly because of the celebrations, partly for fear of computer crashes. When it reopens for business early in 2000, fatter times will lie ahead.

These are some of the ideas to be found in *The World in 1999*, which will be circulated in 85 countries and 12 languages. As ever, a number of our predictions will be wrong but all of them will, I hope, be interesting.

Dudley Fishburn

LADIES AND GENTLEMEN,

Boeing is a world leader in satellite systems for guidance, surveillance and communications. Global Positioning Satellites built by Boeing provide pinpoint location accuracy anywhere in the world. Our DigitalXpress system moves mountains of information for leading businesses across North America

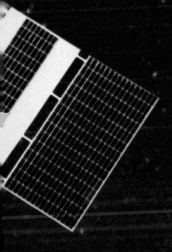

WE'VE REACHED OUR CRUISING ALTITUDE

OF 66,228,400 FEET.

And our participation in satellite-based communications systems, such as Teledesic and Ellipso, will bring affordable broadband and telephone transmissions to completely new markets. Boeing is the future of flight. And that includes space. For business opportunities in space, contact www.boeing.com/ics

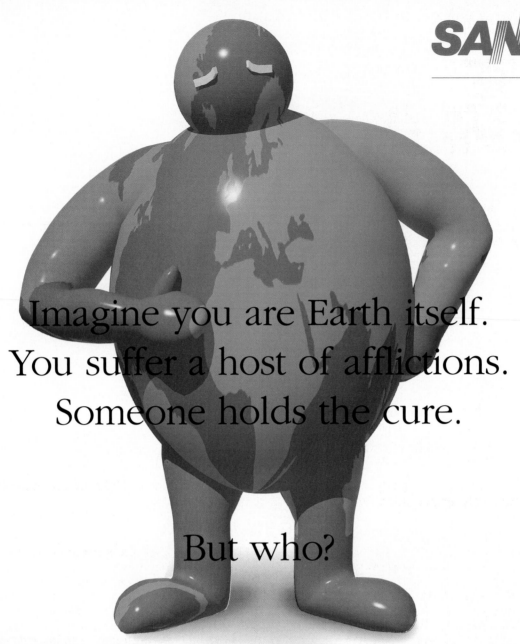

SANYO

Imagine you are Earth itself.
You suffer a host of afflictions.
Someone holds the cure.

But who?

When designing products that help protect the environment, our perspective at Sanyo is that we are Earth itself.

And you thought Sanyo primarily made consumer electronics. In fact, we're also known as a leader in solar technology development. The first amorphous silicon cells were brought to market by

Solar power is increasingly used in private homes

Sanyo. But then, imagining yourself as Earth has a way of heightening environmental awareness.

We've also eliminated harmful

Alkaline batteries with zero mercury content

mercury, a common environmental menace, from our alkaline batteries. Sanyo air conditioning systems are being manufactured so they don't emit fluorocarbons. And we're making CFC-free refrigerators.

Fluorocarbon-free absorption-type chiller/heaters

100% CFC-free 3-door refrigerators for residential use

The cure for environmental ills starts with lessening individual impact. It's the technology allowing you to do so that we develop at Sanyo.

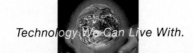

Technology We Can Live With.

THE WORLD IN 1999

The year of Europe

The arrival of the single currency in Europe will be the boldest stroke of 1999. Its undoubted success will not come easily, argues *John Peet*.

It will be a crunch year for Europe's Union, the most important since the Treaty of Rome was signed in 1957. The venture's biggest step yet, the single currency, arrives in the shape of the euro on January 1st. Last May, when Europe's leaders picked 11 countries to join the euro in the first wave, the mood was euphoric: economies were growing strongly, inflation had been tamed, unemployment was falling. The Brussels summiteers congratulated themselves that the timing set for the euro's birth was, perhaps fortuitously, the best they could have dreamt of choosing.

How times have changed. For a while, European politicians thought they were immune to the economic virus that first attacked Asia and then spread to all other emerging markets. Many even claimed that the euro was helping to protect them. Now it is clear that the euro will come into the world at a highly dangerous moment. The world economy is teetering on the brink of its worst recession since the second world war. The financial markets have taken collective fright at anything smacking of the remotest risk. Neither Europe, nor its planned single currency, will escape. Already, there are disturbing hints that the recoveries that began in Germany and France in 1997 may peter out swiftly. The euro could experience an unwelcome baptism of fire.

Yet although it will be singed in the process, it will not be destroyed. That is, not least, because so much political capital and practical business preparation have already been invested in it. A failure of the euro now would provoke such a crisis as to tear apart the European Union itself. That alone makes it unthinkable.

Even so, unless Germany, France and Italy, in particular, press ahead with structural reforms to their labour markets, they will find that the euro's impact on their economies is far more painful than they currently expect. Labour shakeouts and the competitive forces that the euro will unleash may increase unemployment, just when European voters, having put left-leaning parties in power in no fewer than 13 of the EU's 15 member countries, are looking for it to fall. Popular faith in the euro and in the new central bank will be tested to the limit. It will become clear throughout 1999 just how huge a change the euro will make in European business life: in marketing or in accounting, in purchasing or in pricing, in bond or stockmarkets, the euro will become ubiquitous. Its main impact, which will not be fully felt until the currency itself is in circulation in 2002, will be to increase compe-

John Peet: business affairs editor, *The Economist*.

tition, to narrow prices, to save costs. Combine it with the impact of the Internet, and European business is in for a revolutionary few years.

The arrival of the euro would occupy a fullish agenda for the European Union in any normal year. But in 1999, it will be only one challenge among several. By mid-year the Union is supposed also to have sorted out the farm-policy and budgetary reforms that are needed to prepare it for eastward enlargement. This is likely to occasion a fight over money between the Germans (with the Dutch acting as seconds) and the French (with Spanish support). The Germans hold that it is unjust that they, who have since unification been merely the fifth-richest people in the EU, should provide nearly 60% of all net contributions to the budget. The Dutch, who pay even more per head, are equally aggrieved. Expect this particular battle to end, after much shouting and table-thumping, with the Germans backing down. Germany will remain Europe's paymaster.

This row will further retard the Union's tortuous negotiations over enlargement. But these have anyway been proceeding at a snail's pace. The unpalatable truth is that, although all European governments subscribe to the strategic and moral case for admitting Poles, Czechs, Hungarians and the rest to their club, none is comfortable with the huge cost of such an expansion. And in the EU, money has always, in the end, counted for more than idealism. The chances of any aspiring country actually joining the Union before 2005 are slight.

There will be no idealism in the third big piece of EU business: the choice of new people at the top. A high representative for the EU's common foreign policy will be chosen by early 1999. Elections to the European Parliament will take place in June. And a new European Commission president and membership, picked by the 15 EU governments acting unanimously, will need to be in place by the year's end. This will see much nationalistic bargaining—far from the European dream.

Nothing to fear but politicians

The world economy will look after itself in 1999. There need be no recession, says *Clive Crook*, unless we go out of our way to make one.

The world economy will grow faster in 1999 than it did in 1998. Unfortunately, in Europe and America, it won't feel that way: growth is going to be a bit slower in Europe and a lot slower in the United States. The recovery will happen mainly in Japan, the rest of Asia and the other developing countries. The western industrial economies, preoccupied with their own slowdowns, will hardly notice that improvement. And the risk of a much worse outcome—that of an outright recession in the world economy—does for once need to be taken seriously. The danger is avoidable, but this is less comforting than it should be: governments have a proven ability to see a bad situation and steer straight for it.

The outlook and the risks turn mainly, as ever, on what happens in the United States. Growth there is likely to slow from this year's 3.5% to less than half as much in 1999. This is partly for cyclical reasons (after seven consecutive years of growth, the American economy has run out of spare capacity) and partly because of the financial squeeze that began in the fourth quarter of 1998. Lenders are shunning risk: the spread between what blue-chip companies must pay for their loans and the rates charged to less-safe borrowers is wider than for years. At least for the next few months, risky borrowers will find it hard to get credit at any price. This will hit personal consumption and corporate investment, the twin motors that have powered America's expansion during the 1990s.

If the fuel of easy credit has been cut off, why suppose that growth in the United States will be even as high as, say, 1.5%? The answer is that monetary policy

can be, and will be, eased by enough to keep the motors running, albeit more gently than of late. Growth in demand is going to slow in America, but if it slows too much, the Federal Reserve can keep cutting interest rates. For the time being neither the risk of inflation nor international considerations impinge on the Fed's freedom of action. In the unlikely event that monetary stimulus fails to buoy the economy, fiscal policy can be loosened. This is a rare luxury. America's budget is in surplus: cuts in taxes and increases in public spending, should they be needed, are readily affordable.

So far as the rest of the world is concerned, the more American interest rates fall, and the dollar with them, the better. This will allow greater scope for monetary easing elsewhere, without renewed pressure on currencies or debt burdens. Alan Greenspan, Chairman of the Federal Reserve, has already shown that he is willing to act. And Congress will not need to be told twice to loosen fiscal policy (always popular) should an abrupt slowdown require it. This blend of competence at the Fed and opportunism on Capitol Hill should be enough to keep American economic policy on about the right course. The main danger that governments will make matters worse, out of either neglect or stupidity, lies elsewhere: in Europe and Japan.

Henceforth interest rates for the 11 members of the euro system will be set not by national central banks but by the European Central Bank in Frankfurt. The new institution will want to establish its reputation as a fighter of inflation. Under ordinary circumstances it would be right to emphasise monetary rigour. But today's circumstances are extraordinary. Europe's stockmarkets are nervous and its banks are under strain. Undue con-

Clive Crook: deputy editor, *The Economist*.

cern for credibility may lead the ECB to err on the side of higher interest rates. It would be better in the first half of 1999 if it erred the other way.

And then there is Japan. Its irrepressibly incompetent leaders, having done so much harm to their own economy and to others in the region, may yet succeed in bringing on a global recession. Assuming the Fed does the right thing, Japan remains the biggest single danger in the global outlook. If the government had acted promptly to resolve its banking problems when they first surfaced years ago, the economy would have recovered already, and the Asian emerging-markets' slump would have been far milder. The illness might not have spread to Russia, and from there to other developing countries. The flight from risk worldwide, and the astonishing volatility in financial markets witnessed towards the end of 1998, might never have happened.

On balance Japan is likely to recover in 1999, assuming that the government does no more than muddle through. However, when the government at last comes to execute its plan, such as it is, for reviving the country's crippled banks, it may fumble. If the misplaced confidence of Japanese savers finally evaporates, and runs on the banks begin in earnest, the prospect of even a puny Japanese expansion will evaporate too.

In the balance lie not just the prospects for growth but a question that matters even more in the longer term: whether the newly established pro-market consensus in economic policy worldwide will be entrenched or swept away. The decade since the dismantling of the Berlin Wall has witnessed a shift towards liberal trade and market economics in Eastern Europe, Asia, Latin America, even in the once-socialist parties of the West European "left". Now, unconverted collectivists all over the world are rejoicing at what they see as the failure

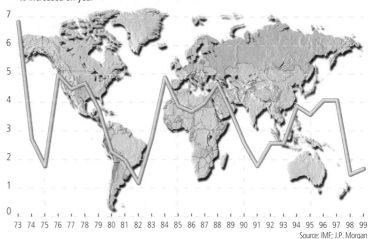

World GDP growth
% increased on year

Source: IMF; J.P. Morgan

of global capitalism. In a way, they are right. It is futile to point out that the forces causing the slowdown have been failures of government more than failures of the market: politically, that counts for nothing. If the present slowdown becomes the depression of 1999, watch out for a backlash against the liberal consensus.

It is surprising and encouraging that, so far at least, the collectivists have not been getting their way. Much of Asia has experienced a savage recession: only Malaysia has deliberately set its face against the new orthodoxy (by introducing draconian controls on capital flows). Elsewhere in the region, less government rather than more is still thought to be the best way forward. There are no signs yet of rising demand for protection in trade. Europe's "new left" governments remain—in some cases reluctantly, in others out of conviction—conservative pro-market governments cloaked in harmless "third way" rhetoric.

The empire of democracy

The Kosovo affair has given the world a new rule, asserts *Brian Beedham*: no undemocratic state can expect its sovereignty to remain untouched.

Slowly, nervously, as if it did not quite realise what it was doing, the NATO alliance has pushed its foot through one of the world's apparently shut doors. Because it was so hesitantly done, the Kosovo intervention of October 1998 was never likely to be the swift success it could have been if NATO had acted more decisively. Nevertheless, something big has changed. For the first time, a coalition of respectable countries has openly said that it is prepared to use force to stop the accepted ruler of a sovereign state doing bad things to his own people.

Ever since the League of Nations was created, 80 years ago this summer, the rules of the game had said that this was illegal. You could lawfully use force to de-

fend yourself or your allies against an enemy's attack (that is how NATO was born), or to rescue another country from unprovoked aggression (such as Kuwait in the Gulf war), or maybe to prevent some unmistakably imminent assault by the other man. If a country disintegrated, you might be entitled to send in your soldiers to feed the hungry. But so long as a government kept its control over a sovereign state, no matter how brutally it treated the people it called its citizens, you had to confine your intervention to words and perhaps economic sanctions; your gun had to stay in its holster.

Of course, the rules were not always obeyed. In the cold war, the Soviet Union sent its army into Hungary and Czechoslovakia to stop their peoples calling for democracy, and got away with it in the name of the

Brian Beedham: associate editor, *The Economist*.

"Brezhnev doctrine". The Americans sent their troops into a number of Latin American countries, though they usually found some sort of excuse. The Tanzanians marched into Uganda in 1979, they claimed, to prevent Uganda attacking them, but in fact to eject the Ugandan thug Idi Amin.

The Kosovo intervention, though, is different from all these. The NATO allies did not pretend that what Slobodan Milosevic was doing in Kosovo was a danger to themselves, or that they were chiefly worried about the safety of neighbouring Albania and Macedonia. They got their missiles and their bombers ready for action because they wanted to help the Kosovars. Yet they had long accepted Kosovo as at least loosely a part of Serbia, and Serbia as part of the sovereign state of Yugoslavia. Here was an alliance of the democracies defying the 20th century's sacred principle of sovereignty in order to insist that a dictator should not brutalise one part of his sovereign country; and, by way of insistence, the gun was out of the holster.

This is on the whole an excellent thing. The definition of "sovereignty" that allows dictators to get away with mass killings within their own borders has been a dark cloud hanging over the 20th century's theory of international relations. Other dictators, please note. But this undoubted step forward has its complications. NATO's intervention in Kosovo poses two large questions, which the alliance now has to answer honestly.

One is how to deal with the flood of applications for future interventions that will pour in if Kosovo proves a lasting success. Does the Kurdish part of Iraq qualify? Burma? Tibet? The imagination rapidly starts to boggle. The only serious answer is to say that any proposed intervention has to pass three tests. It must be manifestly wanted by, and be to the clear benefit of, a solid majority of the people in the area concerned. It must look as if it can be carried out reasonably quickly, and without too many casualties. And it should also, if possible, bring some benefit to the countries that carry out the operation. Only if these conditions are met will the case for trying to make the world at least a slightly better place carry public opinion with it.

Second, it must be made clear that the only legitimate intervention is one which has the clear support of the people at the receiving end. Anybody who ignores that rule must expect to find himself hauled before the United Nations and, when necessary, stopped by force. And that is the crux of the matter. If the democracies hope to encourage, however gradually, other people's freedom to decide how they should be governed—if they seriously want to widen the empire of democracy—they must back up their convictions with the necessary force of arms. The grim old reality is still with us: you cannot win justice unless you are ready to fight for it.

American upsizing

Here's a safe prediction. America's love of size will grow yet bigger in 1999, says *Daniel Franklin*.

Forget "downsizing", corporate America's buzzword of the 1990s. It is a deeply unAmerican concept: the country that invented the Big Mac, the jumbo jet and the mega-mall is at heart the Land of the Big. And bigness is back (if it ever really went away). Despite end-of-boom fears of a new round of corporate lay-offs, the new buzzword should be upsizing.

The fuss about downsizing was always misleading. Yes, there were high-profile examples of large firms that shed layers of labour, replaced men with machines and turned to outsourcing as corporate America restructured to gain competitive edge. But somehow the result of all the downsizing has been record levels of employment. Meanwhile, fledgling firms, such as Microsoft and Starbucks, have become giants. And in industry after industry, mega-mergers have created huge corporations with the muscle to match the demands of a globalised marketplace. Names like Citigroup, MCI WorldCom and PricewaterhouseCoopers tell the story.

And not just in business. In sport, baseball's sluggers smash decades-old home-run records. In philanthropy, benign competition breaks out between America's super-rich to make the fattest donations. Less virtuously, in politics candidates continue to raise and spend ever more obscene amounts of money for their election campaigns. It is safe to predict that in the coming year the upsizing trend will itself grow, in various directions.

Take government. In the mid-1990s Americans worried about irresponsible budget deficits and rebelled against Big Government. This brought a Republican revolution in Congress, a balanced-budget deal in Washington and boasts by Bill Clinton that government was at its smallest since the days of President Kennedy. But thanks to the strength of the American economy, the budget is now back in surplus, with the prospect of surpluses amounting to hundreds of billions of dollars in the years ahead. Despite vociferous demands by Republicans that these be used for tax cuts and debt-reduction, the overwhelming past experience in America and elsewhere suggests that much of the money will go towards expanding existing government programmes and creating new ones. Government will grow bigger.

So will people. Americans are notoriously large, and getting larger. About 90m of them, one-third of the population, are overweight. Extensive and expensive efforts to encourage downsizing—a multi-billion-dollar slimming industry, anorexic fashion models, fitness evangelism—have proved powerless in the battle of bulk. A backlash against the downsizers has even begun. In Santa Monica last August, outsized Americans demon-

Daniel Franklin: editorial director, Economist Intelligence Unit.

GET YOUR MIND WORKING WITH
PARIBAS

You arrive at a crossroads only to discover that the signpost has been blown down in a storm. You have no map. Which direction do you take?

fig. 1
You have no map.
Remember.

fig. 2
You lost your compass.

fig. 3
What good's a cellular phone if you don't know where you are?

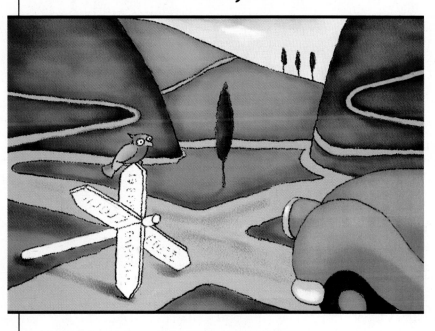

PARIBAS
No.1 IN THE EURO

Best Euro capital markets bank

First Supranational in Euro

First Sovereign in Euro

First Convertible in Euro

No.1 Euro Swap House

LEADING THE WORLD IN THE EURO

Today, it is easy to feel lost when confronted by the future. The financial landscape is shifting before our very eyes. Moving into new territory, as we are with the Euro, is fraught with uncertainty. What you need is a guide who's been this way before.

Founded 125 years ago simultaneously in 4 European countries, Paribas was the first bank with a truly European philosophy. Today, with an organisation based on banking activities and industrial sectors, no other bank can equal its experience in crossing financial frontiers.

In the 1998 Euromoney awards for excellence, Paribas was voted "best Euro capital markets bank". As we get closer to the "big bang" of 1999, the experience of Paribas as the lead Ecu bookrunner since 1981 puts the bank in a unique position of authority in all questions relating to the Euro. And it is, in fact, only by the application of experience that we can solve the problem of the crossroads with the fallen signpost.

How do you decide which way to go? You leverage your own recent experience. Since you do know where you've come from, you simply raise the signpost, point the relevant arrow in the direction from which you have come - and the way ahead is clear. *http://www.paribas.com*

∏ PARIBAS Thinking beyond banking

HOW MANY OF YOUR STAFF WOULD RISK THEIR LIVES FOR YOU?

It would be nice to think the question will never arise, but you need only look at recent events to see how close we can be, at any time, to a national emergency when our armed forces, including the reservists who work for you, are deployed.

Our forces may have reduced in size, but their commitments have not. That's why volunteers are increasingly important to us and why proper training is so crucial. In civilian life it makes them better employees; better motivated, more responsible and quicker to act on their own initiative. In an emergency this could make the difference between life and death. So, next time any of your volunteers need time off for military training, we hope you'll understand and support their commitment. After all they are prepared to risk their lives for you and your country.

N E L C

YOUR EMPLOYEES IN THE RESERVE FORCES WORK HARDER FOR YOU, HARDER FOR US.

Find out more, fax us on 0171 218 4888, e mail: mod.nelc@dial.pipex.com or write to NELC, Duke of York's HQ, Chelsea, London SW3 4SS. Issued by the National Employers' Liaison Committee on behalf of the Territorial Army, Royal Naval Reserve, Royal Marines Reserve & Royal Auxiliary Air Force.

strated with slogans such as "Don't diet, be happy".

The sheer size of people is one reason why cars in America will remain larger than elsewhere. Cheaper and cheaper fuel will reinforce Americans' taste for gas-guzzling designs. People-movers, pick-ups and sports utilities have been the fastest-growing segment of the light-vehicle market. What could be more American than cruising into the new millennium in a stretch limo?

Buildings are also upsizing. In Las Vegas, the first phase of the 6,000-room, $2 billion Venetian hotel will open in 1999. Built on the site of the old Sands hotel (of Rat Pack fame), it will be the world's largest resort hotel. In Chicago, developers will compete to produce plans for the world's tallest building. America being America, bigness—of the land, of ideas, of ambitions—belongs to the national ethos. Upsizing is America's manifest destiny.

Doomsday deferred

The world will enter 2000 in very much better shape than our predecessors predicted. Fatalism is out of fashion, argues *Madsen Pirie*.

It is because people invest numbers with magic that certain dates acquire momentous significance. At various times in our history, sections of the human race have expected the world to end, or, at the very least, for doom and disaster to unfold. Some thought at the turn of the previous millennium that one thousand years was the right date for the Second Coming. There have been other dates since, when faithful followers have sat on hillsides waiting for Armageddon, only to disperse disappointed until their leaders could recalculate the date.

As the calendar turns once more, there have indeed been wars and rumours of war, and earthquakes in divers places. Surprisingly, though, there has been no widespread "millennial movement" predicting the world's end. Indeed, large sections of humanity seem to be facing the new millennium with a degree of optimism that would have been alien to our forebears. What is missing is the sense of fatalism, the feeling that human beings are helpless objects to be tossed by fate like corks upon the waves. In its place is the widespread conviction that humanity is, to a great degree, master of its own fate, and that what happens to us will be the result of human action, even purposive action.

The doomsayers have found little echo to their apocalyptic alarms. The environmentalists have been confounded by evidence that so-called scarce resources are falling in price, indicating that supplies are outstripping demand. Most of the raw materials which were supposedly dwindling show greater reserves now than they did two decades ago. It seems that our ability to conserve and to employ substitutes is better than expected. Similarly, the talk of mankind poisoning the habitat has been difficult to reconcile with water and air that are becoming cleaner year by year, and with productive processes that visibly pollute less than their predecessors did a century ago.

Those who spent the century predicting the final demise of liberal capitalism were confounded when the system of collectivist central planning imploded instead. Even those who thought the British economy impossibly outmoded, and doomed to defeat at the hands of the "miracle" economies of Germany and Asia, have been confounded by a flexibility in the old-fashioned free-market model which has left it quite able to stand up against its rivals.

Other portents of doom have included a breakdown of social values and a so-called collapse of civil society. After decades of relentless gloom, the family remains the most popular of institutions. Most people settle down at some point with a partner of the opposite sex and raise children. A recent poll of the 16-21 age group showed that "to be happily married with children" was the most popular aspiration, coming out ahead of a successful business career.

The threat of the developed world groaning under the burden of an ageing population has been dispelled. People do indeed live longer, but their active lives are also prolonged, and timely pension reforms have ensured that most of the elderly in the early decades of the new century will be capital rich, not requiring support from taxpayers.

As the new millennium comes upon us, it seems that even the four horsemen have lost their thrall over us. Appalling famines still occur in localised conditions as a result of human folly, but Malthus has been confounded by a world food supply which has been increasing faster than the population which it has to support. War still occurs, also on a local scale, but no longer threatens the planet each day with nuclear annihilation. Pestilence is still there, but smallpox has been conquered, and polio subdued. Few doubt that the early years of the new millennium will bring victory over malaria, AIDS, and many forms of cancer. Although the fourth horseman, death, is still with us, advances in diet and medicine mean that each year he takes longer to catch us.

Dr Madsen Pirie: president of the Adam Smith Institute.

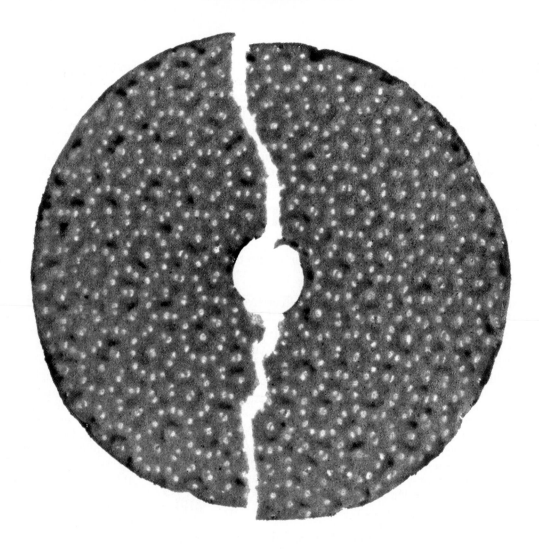

WILL YOUR FUTURE EUROBANK CALL THIS A VIKING SHIELD?

Anyone in the Nordic region could tell you straight away that the picture is not of a viking shield but of a traditional Nordic bread. The point is not to lose sight of regional differences when evaluating eurobanks. An inborn understanding of local and regional matters can be crucial to your success.

We have already been ranked as the best bank in the world for Nordic currency trading, according to Euromoney, May 1998. Now we are ready to offer the combination of unrivalled Nordic contacts and experience with unbeatable technology for euro transactions. Indeed, Euromoney places us amongst the five most technologically advanced international exchange banks.

Wherever you may wish to do business, S E B is ready to help, through our worldwide network of branches and established cash management relationships with 2,500 banks.

So we believe that the transition to the new currency will not be particularly dramatic, either for you or for us. Indeed, our currency and technology skills are ready to give the euro a warm reception. We have standard solutions ready to offer you – or we may recommend tailored solutions for your business. We are ready and willing to discuss the options.

Many things may change with the arrival of the euro. However, we do not intend S E B´s exceptional quality of service to its customers to be one of them. Just think of us as your Nordic eurobank from now on.

SKANDINAVISKA ENSKILDA BANKEN

Issued by Skandinaviska Enskilda Banken (publ) which is regulated by the SFA for the conduct of investment business in the U.K.

DIARY FOR 1999

January

The euro is born. The powers of the European Central Bank come into force. Goodbye to the D-mark, franc and nine other currencies

Germany takes on the presidency of the European Union

Weimar is European City of Culture

Superbowl XXXIII in Miami

Annual meeting of the World Economic Forum in Davos, Switzerland

February

EU electricity market liberalisation

Carnival time in Venice and Rio de Janeiro; Mardi Gras in New Orleans

Chinese around the world welcome in the Year of the Rabbit

Launch of the Stardust spacecraft mission to gather comet dust

Morse code dropped as the official channel of communication at sea. On-board satellite systems become a legal requirement

March

Annual meeting of the Inter-American Development Bank

The World Trade Organisation's multilateral agreement on financial services comes into force, opening 75% of the world's banking, insurance and asset management to competition

71st Oscars in Los Angeles

Elections in Finland, Fiji, Estonia, Tunisia

Presidential election in El Salvador

April

Hungary, the Czech Republic and Poland join NATO on its 50th anniversary

Election in Iceland

London Underground's Jubilee Line extension opens

May

EU-US summit in Bonn

German parliament moves to the Reichstag building in Berlin

Russian, French and German leaders meet at summit in France

50th anniversary of the 40-nation Council of Europe

53rd Cannes Film Festival

General Abubakar hands over power to a democratically elected government in Nigeria

Elections to the newly devolved assemblies in Scotland and Wales

Election in Indonesia

Presidential elections in Djibouti and Panama

The Italian Parliament elects its country's president

June

EU summit in Cologne chooses the next president of the Commission

G7 summit in Cologne

Tenth anniversary of the Tiananmen Square massacre in China

European Parliament elections in fifteen countries

World population reaches six billion

Elections in Armenia and Belgium

EU and Latin America summit in Rio de Janeiro

July

Finland takes on the presidency of the EU

End of duty-free concessions within the EU

Ninth annual Internet Society Conference

Final of Wimbledon

August

The total eclipse of the sun will be visible in parts of Asia and Europe (in Britain for the first time since 1927)

The World Monuments Fund releases its list of the world's 100 most endangered sites

Salzburg music festival

52nd Edinburgh festival

The Queen Mother is 99

Labour minister Tito Mboweni will succeed Chris Stals as governor of the South African Reserve Bank

September

New Zealand hosts APEC summit

IMF-World Bank meeting, Washington, DC

Jewish New Year 5760

October

50th Anniversary of the People's Republic of China

Elections in Botswana, Portugal

Presidential elections in Argentina and Ukraine

Annual Ibero-American summit in Cuba brings together leaders from Spain, Portugal and Latin America

November

Tenth anniversary of the breach of the Berlin Wall

Final, Rugby World Cup, Wales

The Russian government institutes a census. It will determine who is a true Russian and who is just a "foreigner" from the ex-Soviet empire.

The American South goes to the polls. Gubernatorial contests in Kentucky, Louisiana and Mississippi. Legislative election in Virginia

Presidential elections in Guatemala and Uruguay

December

The UN High Commission for Refugees is 50 years old

Macau returns to China after four centuries of Portuguese rule

The former Soviet Union goes to the polls, in elections to the Russian Duma, the Turkmen and Uzbek parliaments, and the Uzbek presidency

Presidential election in Chile

The Indonesian People's Consultative Assembly elects a president

Gabon, Gambia, Slovenia, Bahrain and Brazil end their two-year terms on the UN Security Council

The five-year term of the current European Commission ends. Jacques Santer gives way to a new Commission president

December 31st

Portugal takes on the EU presidency

The last US troops pull out of Panama

The Pompidou centre in Paris throws a massive re-opening party

Six British explorers return to Greenwich after achieving the first trans-navigation of the world by rivers, canals, inland seas and lakes

The world throws a party to see in the new millennium. The celebrations are spoiled as computers start to crash. Take an aspirin

Source: Future Events News Service. For tailored reports of future events and/or regular updates tel: +44 (0)181 672 3191 or http://www.hubcom.com/fens

BMW believes that driving should always be an entertaining experience. That's why, like every BMW, the new 7 Series has rear-wheel drive and near perfect front-to-rear weight distribution. Not only does this improve road-holding but it also makes handling exceptionally agile. VANOS and Double-VANOS have further refined the 8-cylinder and 6-cylinder engines to deliver the

Widescreen entertainment.

kind of performance you wouldn't normally associate with a luxury car of this size. While the

new chassis control systems ensure that the thrills of the road never turn into spills. In short,

the 1999 BMW 7 Series gives you the opportunity to take part in the action. Your screen test awaits.

The Ultimate Driving Machine

In an age of interchangeable businesses, how do you keep yours defiantly individual?

We can help you harness the power of information and technology to pull ahead of the competition. How can you get to market faster? How can you offer customers a benefit no one else can? How can you move ahead of the competition and stay there? One way is to call EDS. From management consulting to electronic business, our people have the experience and expertise to help you transform your ideas into reality. For more details, call: in North, South and Central America, 1-972-605-1422, in Europe, Middle East and Africa 44-181-754-4822 or in Asia/Pacific 852-2867-9883. Or visit www.eds.com. And discover how we can help you leave your mark.

▶ **A more productive way of working**

Systems & Technology Services   Business Process Management   Management Consulting   Electronic Business

John Bull's new face

Britannia bubbles

Anthony King

British society in 1999 will be open and bubbly and cosmopolitan—the most open and bubbly and cosmopolitan in Western Europe. It was not always so; Britain's reputation as a class-ridden and insular place with bad food and funny ideas about foreigners will only be buried with the century. But buried it will be, and will deserve to be.

Take British wealth, for example. In-herited wealth plays a lesser part in the economy than it does in France or Ger-many. Self-made millionaires abound. Brian Souter, son of a Scottish bus driver, is now a multimillionaire, head of Britain's fastest-growing transport busi-ness, with substantial stakes in Portugal, Sweden and New Zealand, as well as in Britain's privatised rail network. His sis-ter, Ann Gloag, is Britain's second-rich-est woman after the Queen.

Women will take two-thirds or more of professional jobs created in 1999. The typical young lawyer in Britain is now a woman. The typical young doctor soon will be. A mobile workforce means that employers are no longer reluctant to hire women on the grounds that they may go off to have babies.

The success of Asian incomers—

Anthony King: professor of government at Essex University; election commentator for the BBC and regular contributor to the *Daily Telegraph*.

mostly Indians and Pakistanis, many of them via east Africa—will make Britain in 1999 resemble California even more. The proportion of Asians attending Britain's universities and colleges will again be higher than the proportion of "indigenous" whites; and they will, on average, gain higher grades. The typical young British economist and business-school graduate will soon be Asian.

Their elders have already thrived. Waheed Alli, still only 35 but already worth £10m ($17m), adorns the House of Lords, put there by Tony Blair. Reuben Singh, still only in his 20s, has already made £45m out of fashion accessories. Lists of the richest Asians are published regularly. In 1999 Chinese immigrants and Asians whose families arrived in Britain via eastern or southern Africa will be better off than the average white.

Britain's Afro-Caribbeans used to complain that "there ain't no black in the Union Jack." There is now, at least in sport. England's 1982 World Cup squad contained no blacks. Its 1998 World Cup squad contained four: Sol Campbell, Les Ferdinand, Rio Ferdinand and the Liver-pool midfielder Paul Ince. Ince has al-ready captained England. He will again. In 1999 British athletics will again be dominated by black runners like Colin Jackson and Denise Lewis.

Despite the introduction of compul-sory tuition fees, the explosive growth of Britain's universities continues. The Scots have long prided themselves on their ancient universities, but for cen-turies the English showed scant regard for higher education. The upper classes thought a private high school, provided it was expensive enough, was good enough for their sons. The insulting phrase, "Too clever by half" spoke vol-umes. In 1850, the only universities in the whole of England were Oxford, Cam-bridge, Durham and the newly founded University College London.

All that has changed. England, Scot-land, Wales and Northern Ireland now have 124 institutions of higher educa-tion, and everyone who aspires to get ahead in modern Britain also aspires to a university degree. As in America, the Bachelor's degree has become the func-tional equivalent of a high-school diplo-ma. A university degree guarantees nothing. Not having one imposes a seri-ous handicap. The Blair government will

THE WORLD IN 1999

Britain will become one of the youngest countries in the EU. Only 15.4% of its population will be over 65.

create an additional 80,000 university places between 1999 and 2001.

Britain's increasingly open society will also be open to the outside world. The simple rule that allows any EU citizen to work wherever he wishes, without a nod to the authorities, is drawing tens of thousands of young continentals to Britain. High unemployment at home in France or Spain and a huge number of job opportunities in England pulls them across the channel. And they get a free course in English thrown in. Britain's universities are also now open to EU students: applications which were once a theoretical trickle are now becoming an actual flood.

In any case, the British were never as insular and self-absorbed as they were made out to be. If they had been, English would not be the world language it now is. It would be a strange blend of Anglo-Saxon and Norman French spoken on a small island moored off the north European coast. In 1999 foreign travel will also continue its upward trend. The British have always been travellers and explorers. The 18th-century Grand Tour was a British invention, and people from England, Scotland, Wales and Ireland famously settled Patagonia, the Antipodes and most of North America. The allegedly insular British have used their home less as a refuge, more as a launchpad.

Apart from business travel, some 40% of all Britons will take at least one foreign holiday in 1999, far more than a generation ago. A disproportionate number of those packing their sunglasses and suitcases will be professors, doctors, lawyers and business executives, but well over half will be bank tellers, shopkeepers, plumbers and lorry drivers. The holiday flight or cross-Channel ferry is a microcosm of modern Britain.

A quarter of those who travel abroad will sun themselves on Spanish beaches. Another quarter will fan out across France. Another quarter will travel elsewhere on the European continent. But, if the pound stays strong, nearly one in ten will take their holiday in the United States. A trip to America was once beyond most Britons' wildest dreams. Today taxi drivers discourse on their trip to Disneyland with the kids.

A young woman named Almut Geldsetzer is emblematic of Britain's more open society. She is German and a viola player. A year or so ago she saw a job advertised in an English newspaper. She applied for it, was given an audition and in 1999 will continue her career as a rank-and-file violist in the London-based Philharmonic Orchestra. The important thing is: no one will notice.

An economy that counts

Anatole Kaletsky

Tony Blair's windows of opportunity

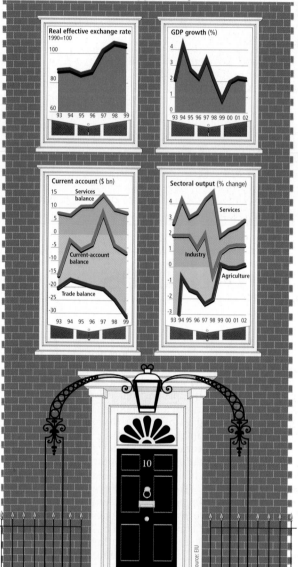

Source: EIU

Not many people have yet noticed, but Britain has regained its right to be considered one of the world's great economies. Britain has now conclusively overtaken Italy to become the world's fifth largest economy and in 1999, with a bit of luck and a few revisions of official statistics, it could be snapping at the heels of France. This is not the kind of news the average Briton could expect to hear from the country's businessmen and bankers, who spent most of 1998 predicting a recession and complaining

Anatole Kaletsky: columnist on *The Times* and director of Kaletsky Economic Consulting.

about the overvalued pound and its disastrous impact on manufacturing and trade. The facts, however, suggest that neither the predictions nor the complaints are likely to be justified by events.

The economy will most certainly suffer a slowdown—in fact it was already decelerating significantly by the autumn of 1998—but this slowdown has more to do with the crisis in Asia than with the supposedly overvalued level of sterling. In the event of serious financial contagion spreading recession to the United States and Europe, there would be little chance that Britain could resist the downward trend. But there is nothing in the British economy's domestic performance to justify headlines such as the one above a J.P. Morgan forecast published in the autumn: "UK manufacturing about to fall off a cliff."

Before looking at the prospects, consider the recent past. Although it was widely predicted that Britain would face the choice of either experiencing an inflationary collapse in the exchange rate or becoming the slowest-growing economy in Europe, neither of these events came to pass. The pound looks like ending 1998 at almost exactly its average level of the years before (£1=DM2.83). Yet the economic growth rate in 1998 is likely to have been around 2.5%, about the same as in Germany, well above Italy's 1.8% and only slightly below the 2.8% or so in France.

Even more surprisingly, the balance of payments, which had been expected to lurch deep into the red as a result of the "overvalued" exchange rate, actually remained in surplus in the first half of

At Orange we believe that no matter where you are in the world you should never be out of reach. Orange Answer Fax is your own personal fax service. It allows you to receive all faxes on one number, and then collect them on the nearest fax machine whenever it's convenient for you. For more information on Answer Fax or other Orange innovations call 0800 323 000. The future's bright. The future's Orange.

orange™

1998 and is likely to show just a negligible deficit in 1999. The upshot of Britain's unusual combination of full employment, a strong exchange rate and decent growth can be seen in the league tables of gross domestic product at market prices and exchange rates published each year by the OECD. These show that Britain's GDP of $1.29 trillion in 1997 had far overtaken Italy's $1.13 trillion and was only a little behind the $1.38 trillion reported for France.

Mere numbers are just playthings for statisticians, but those quoted above convey at least two messages which observers of Britain's economy should bear in mind.

When numbers count

The first is that the simultaneous strength of the pound and the British economy have defied the Jeremiahs for the third year running. This suggests that the now habitual year-end prophecies of doom may again prove wrong. Specifically, the evidence is mounting that, although many British companies are being forced out of business by an exchange rate anywhere in the recent range of DM2.70 to DM3, there are enough British exporters of goods and services that can compete at this level to balance the current account. Apart from the good current-account figures, the evidence for this contention comes from estimates of manufacturers' profit margins. These show that margins on exports remained slightly higher than on domestic sales in mid-1998 (and these domestic margins were, in turn, at record levels). Given that Britain is now at or near full employment, while the economies of its main trading partners in Europe remain cyclically depressed, Britain would normally be expected to have a big current-account deficit if sterling were at the "right" rate.

What is the practical upshot of all this theory? That Britain's exporters are likely to be disappointed if they are hoping for a free ride from a steeply devalued pound. Sterling will probably weaken somewhat, as the Bank of England eases interest rates in the year ahead. But the easing will not amount to more than 0.5% or so unless the United States and the world economies go into an improbable nosedive. As a result, the pound will probably spend most of 1999 in the lower half of its DM2.70 to DM3 trading range, but not any lower.

The main caveat relates to the European Central Bank (ECB). If the ECB defies all rational expectations and decides to throw Europe back into recession by allowing the euro to rise sharply against

Eclipsed

On the morning of August 11th 1999, the moon will cover the sun and the world will be in darkness. Or at least that is how it will seem for exactly two minutes and six seconds, if you stand somewhere between Penzance and Falmouth. The eclipse will be the first completely to block out the sun to Britons since 1927, when 3m people travelled north to experience the blackout. The "path of totality" will begin in the Atlantic and then cross Europe, the Middle East and India, where it ends at sunset in the Bay of Bengal. The greatest eclipse will be seen from

Romania, but a partial eclipse will be visible as far south as Kenya and as far north as Siberia.

Can Cornwall cope? At least an extra 1.5m people are expected to arrive to view the eclipse—six times the usual amount of bucket-and-spade holidaymakers. Cornwall is already packed full in August, so expect gridlock on the roads as 500,000 extra cars head for the county. Because the shadow of the moon moves across the Earth at 1,054 mph, the total eclipse will be over in minutes. The journey home will take somewhat longer.

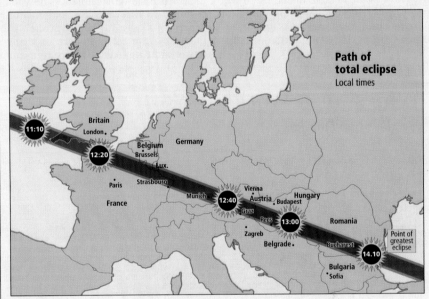

the dollar and yen, then all bets would be off. But even then, the expectation of Britain eventually joining EMU will start to put a floor under sterling at a level higher than many industrialists would like to see.

This leads to the second message from the figures. Although Britain is bound to suffer a substantial downturn as a result of the present turbulence in the financial markets, the outlook may not be as bad relative to the rest of Europe, as most conventional forecasts suggest. According to the IMF, for example, Britain will grow by only 1.2% in 1999, while Germany and France will each grow by 2.5% or more. But such comparisons may wrongly extrapolate recent performance. British industry cut back sharply from early 1998 onwards, responding quickly to the Asian crisis, the high level of interest rates and the high pound. Continental industry, by contrast, remained unrealistically upbeat about

emerging markets until much later and also benefited in 1998 from a weakening of exchange rates and the huge monetary easing in Italy and Spain. By 1999 several of these factors may go into reverse. By the middle of the year Britain should start pulling out of its slowdown, with interest rates and sterling declining, albeit slightly and with higher government spending boosting domestic demand. Europe could see exactly the opposite conjuncture. In all then, 1999 will be a tough year for Britain—but probably not much tougher than for Germany and France. The country will survive the year in much better economic shape than most pundits predict.

Two million British workers will get a 30% average wage increase as the National Minimum Wage becomes law.

A new constitution

Johnny Grimond

Among the events that will not take place in the United Kingdom in 1999 are the introduction of a new currency, the direct election of mayors in all large cities, the adoption of a new voting system, the abolition of the House of Lords, and the dissolution of the union. Scotland will not become independent. It will not therefore, in 1999, ask for membership of the European Union, pushing itself ahead of Cyprus and the five East European countries now at the head of the queue. It will not, in 1999, become the 12th country to join the euro. All these events are for another year, perhaps one in the near future, or perhaps never. They will, however, be very much on the 1999 agenda, if only because the next 12 months will bring a variety of changes to Britain's constitution unprecedented in their scope for nearly 300 years.

The changes have already started, notably with the devolution of power to Northern Ireland. Thanks to the 1998 Good Friday peace agreement, after 27 years of direct rule from Westminster, a measure of self-government is now to be restored to the United Kingdom's only province. Early in 1999, probably in February, the 12 ministers of Ulster's power-sharing executive are to assume their powers, taking responsibility for running the province's schools, hospitals, housing and other services. Regular cross-border meetings are to be held by Northern Irish ministers and their counterparts from the Irish republic, and a British-Irish council is to be set up to create links between Ireland and all parts of the United Kingdom.

That is the plan, anyway. In practice, the entire scheme could collapse into sectarian acrimony—as did the last significant attempt at power-sharing, in 1974—and thus return Northern Ireland to its more familiar state of violence and disputation. Two dangers are especially acute. One is that the executive, which will encompass some people dedicated to a united Ireland and others dedicated to the continuance of the union with Britain, will prove unable to devise a set of common policies, and fall victim to ancient animosities. The other is that the IRA, whose political wing, Sinn Fein, is a

Johnny Grimond: foreign editor, The Economist.

Who's for a World Cup?

Matthew Glendinning

Britain will provide the water not the winner

World Cup fever in 1999? Yes, if you are a fan of cricket or rugby, not that many Brits seem able to play either game with distinction. British cricket has an air of decay about it: local, amateur teams, which provide the green centrepiece for so many an English village, are in decline, usually having to scratch around for players. The Cricket World Cup (which runs from May 14th to June 20th) may give the game the spark it needs to revive. Certainly it will be well covered on radio and television. England, which won its first cricket Test series in 12 years against South Africa in 1998, will hope that luck will come to the tournament's host, as it did to France in football's World Cup (a victory predicted, incidentally, in *The World in 1998*). But the odds lie elsewhere: Sri Lanka and Australia will battle it out for the winner's spot.

The Rugby World Cup (October 1st to November 6th) will also be hosted by Britain, along with France and Ireland. Again, don't expect the hosts to do well (except at corporate entertaining, a pastime in which Britain is surely champion). The victors will come from the southern hemisphere: South Africa, Australia and New Zealand. Rugby makes a much better television spectacle than cricket. It is safe to expect the roads to empty and the pubs to fill in time for the 3 o'clock kick-off on Saturday November 6th, when the final is played in Cardiff.

Far more people sail than play rugby. (There are about 3m small boats and yachts around Britain's shores.) But sailing as a competitive sport, because it cannot be televised satisfactorily, has little following in pubs anywhere outside Cowes. Yet in 1999 Britain will again be the host to the nearest thing to a sailing World Cup, the Admiral's Cup (July 12th-25th).

The competition will involve some 12 national teams with three boats each. The favourites must be the United States and Italy. The Royal Ocean Racing Club will change the racing schedule so that, for the first time, the classic Fastnet race (a 605-mile haul around a rock off Ireland's west coast) will be excluded from the Admiral's Cup competition. The Fastnet race, the zenith of an offshore sailor's career, will still mark the end of Cowes week. But the organisers want to finish the grand prix competition before the amateur armada comes to Cowes. Even in the gentlemanly world of yachting, the professionals will in the end win out.

Matthew Glendinning: freelance sports and business writer.

signatory of the Good Friday agreement and is therefore committed to the disarmament of all paramilitaries, will fail to persuade the IRA to hand over enough weapons to keep the peace deal alive. It will be politically impossible for David Trimble, the unionist who is the province's first minister, to keep the support of his party if the IRA does not start to yield up its weapons and explosives.

So many people, British, Irish and American, have put so much political effort into this attempt to end the violence in Ulster that the prospects for a lasting peace there look better than at any time in the past 30 years. With luck, therefore, the executive will find its feet, the Northern Ireland Assembly elected last June will be made to work, and the paramilitaries' ceasefires will hold. But it is beyond doubt that there will be setbacks, possibly violent ones. The marching season—the four summer months in which 1,300 Protestant marches are held to commemorate the events of 1688-90, when King William of Orange established the Protestants' ascendancy in Ulster—will, as usual, be a time of particular tension. If all goes well, however, the new peace agreement will be fully in place, as scheduled, by May 2000.

Constitutional change will come to Wales, too, in 1999. On May 6th, Welsh voters will go to the polls to elect the principality's first parliament since the one set up by Owen Glendower in 1404. A few days later, it will hold its first meeting in the University of Wales Building in Cardiff (its own £17m—$29m—premises are yet to be built). It is a racing certainty that Labour will take charge, probably with an overall majority.

Conceivably, however, it may have to rule in coalition. The assembly will be elected under a system of proportional representation in which 20 of the 60 seats will be filled from party lists. It may turn out that the nationalist party, Plaid Cymru, will sweep up the second votes used to fill these seats. Even if it does, however, the assembly is unlikely to be a rebellious place. It will have power only to run the existing Welsh Office's £7 billion budget and to influence the detail of legislation affecting the principality. In Wales, at least, the whiff of secession is not in the air.

That is far from true in Scotland, which will also get its own parliament in 1999, its first since the Act of Union in

1707. This will have much more power than the Welsh assembly, including the right to vary income tax by up to 3%. And the party that takes office after the election, also on May 6th, in temporary quarters in Edinburgh could perhaps be the Scottish National Party, which is committed to Scotland's independence. Admittedly, that would be a surprise: Labour is traditionally the dominant party north of the border—it won 56 of Scotland's 72 Westminster seats at the general election in 1997—but support for the SNP has surged in 1998.

The Nationalists are unlikely, however, to be strong enough to take Scotland out of the union, maybe ever, certainly in

One man and his country

1999. For a start, their support does not rest on any serious sense of grievance, but rather, at least in part, on a romantic view of Scottish history. This is likely to diminish as Scots approach the polling booth and have to think about the consequences, notably the economic consequences, of voting for independence. Moreover, Scottish nationalism tends to rise with self-confidence. In 1999, Scotland's economy is likely to worsen, making voters more reluctant to take a leap into the unknown.

Support for the SNP will not fade away, though. The Scots are likely to vote Nationalist in significant numbers not so much to break up the United Kingdom as to protest against what they see as remote and insensitive government from Westminster. In theory, the new parliament will assuage their discontent. But it may do the opposite if it turns out to be no more than a gathering of windy incompetents. In that case, it could become

an escalator to secession. More likely, the Nationalists will keep the issue of secession permanently on the agenda, much as Quebec's separatists do in Canada. The ensuing uncertainty will do nothing to encourage investment and growth.

One imponderable will be the effect of these changes, especially the Scottish ones, on England. The English, long tolerant of greater public spending per head in Scotland and Wales than in England, of an over-representation of the Scots at Westminster and, some would say, of an excessive number of Scots in government, may get fed up with their Scottish and Welsh compatriots. Londoners do stand to get a form of self-gov-

ernment of their own: a bill to give them a directly elected mayor will go before Parliament in 1999. And in 1999 regional-development agencies will be set up in nine regions of England, drawing some civil-service power away from Whitehall. But, with the exception of London, England will not get regional assemblies for some time, if ever. A new voting system for the English also remains a good way off, despite the recent report of the Jenkins commission on electoral reform. As far as constitutional change goes in 1999, the English will have to content themselves with the removal of hereditary peers' voting rights and the incorporation of the European Convention on Human Rights into their law.

THE WORLD IN 1999

Expect not a dozen deaths from mad-cow disease. £3.8 billion of taxpayers' money wasted.

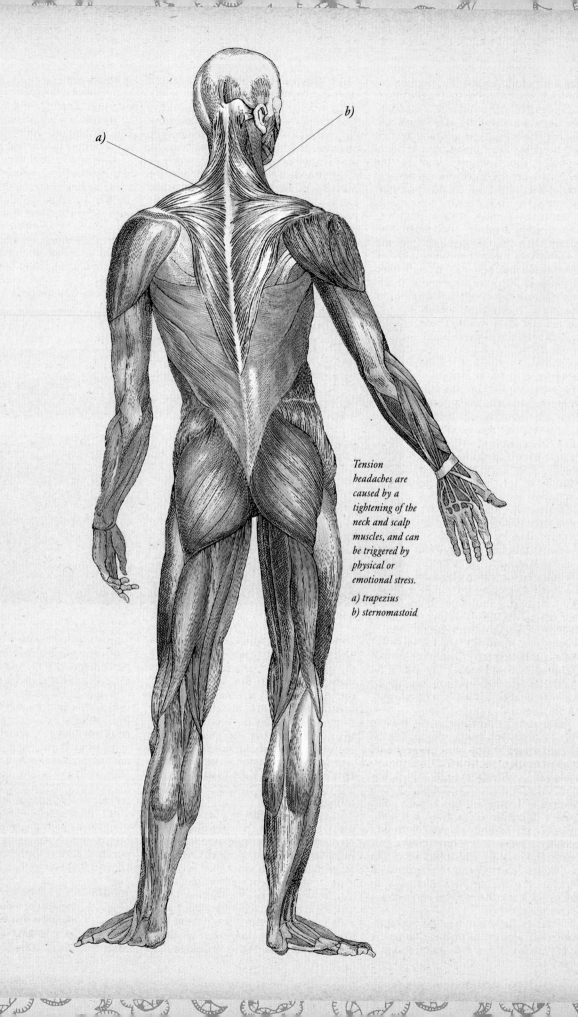

a)

b)

*Tension
headaches are
caused by a
tightening of the
neck and scalp
muscles, and can
be triggered by
physical or
emotional stress.*

*a) trapezius
b) sternomastoid*

Few things cause as MUCH STRESS as driving in the fast lane.

ESPECIALLY WHEN YOU'RE DOING TWO MILES AN HOUR.

I'T'S ONE OF THE MOST unnerving, stress-inducing sights you can encounter on the motorway. The scarlet glow of brake lights stretching away over the horizon. More often than not, this is usually the cue for your heart to start racing, your palms to moisten, and your muscles to bunch up. A predicament many of us suffer with astonishing frequency, if the statistics are to be believed. 50% of motorway drivers, for instance, experience hold-ups on a regular basis, while 20% claim that congestion adds more than four hours a week to their work-related journeys.[1]

Sadly, the signs point to these ailing, clogged-up arteries getting worse, rather than better. The RAC's prognosis is that by 2005, the average motorist could be spending the equivalent of two weeks each year stuck in traffic jams.[2]

Reason enough, we believe, to spend a few minutes reading about the Omega's helpful new navigation aids. We're not saying they can part the traffic and miraculously whisk you out of a snarl-up, but they can help steer you away from the trouble in the first place.

YOU MAY NOT HAVE HEARD THIS.

FINDING your way to an unfamiliar destination is a simple enough pro-position; you do your homework the night before with an atlas, and plot your course. But what if you wake the following morning to the news that a jack-knifed HGV has reduced your route to a single lane of misery? What then? You consult a reliable navigation aid called CARiN.[3]

CARiN is a satellite-based system which means it can accurately pinpoint the whereabouts of your car, and its progress along a given route. Punch in your destination, and it details the quickest way from A to B. It does this clearly and precisely, using spoken instructions and an LCD display. Should you take a wrong turn, or make a detour, CARiN quickly recalculates the quickest route from your new position.

ALL Omegas are also fitted with Traffic-Master Oracle, a dashboard-mounted device which provides up-to-the-minute traffic information. Not only does it tell you where to expect a jam, it even gives you the approximate length of the delay. Very handy if you need to phone ahead to the office to tell them how late you're going to be.

HOW TO COPE WITH A HOLD-UP.

* *If the traffic has come to a standstill, use the time to massage your neck and shoulders in slow circular movements. Better still, get a passenger to do it for you.*

* *Listen to some relaxing music, readings of poetry, or 'talking book' tapes.*

* *Take slow deep breaths for two to three minutes, then breathe normally again.*

* *Keep some aromatherapy oils in the car. Lavender and bergamot are well known stress-busters.*

THE VAUXHALL RELAXATION TECHNIQUE.

ALLOW us to point out the soothing qualities of the Omega to you in the calm, tranquil surroundings of your nearest Vauxhall dealership. Contact 0345 400 202 for more information,[4] and how to arrange a test drive.

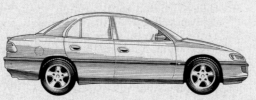

A Positive Aid To Relaxation: OMEGA

1). The Daily Telegraph, April 29th 1997.

2). The Daily Telegraph, ibid.

3). Standard on Elite 3.0i V6. Option on other models.

4). www. vauxhall. co.uk

VAUXHALL

An act of creation

Martin Vander Weyer

Can Lara Croft, computer superheroine, save the British economy? The downturn forecast for 1999 will take another bite out of Britain's traditional industrial base: 250,000 manufacturing jobs may be lost, many of them never to return. Once the world's industrial leader, Britain has been downshifting into post-industrial decline for the past 25 years. Manufacturing now accounts for only one-fifth of GDP, and many observers look despairingly at the low-skill economy of retailing and foreign-owned assembly plants that has replaced it.

But others, led by the Labour government's culture minister, Chris Smith, claim to have spotted a new force riding to the rescue: an unlikely line-up of computer-game characters, girl bands, fashion designers, software gurus and film actors. It is Britain's "creative industries", a flowering of native talent which could make Britain a world leader once again, in a 21st-century global economy in which leisure and entertainment will play a noticeably more productive part than old-fashioned industrial might.

The sectors concerned—computer software, music, fashion, design, film, broadcasting, publishing and the performing arts—will account for some £50 billion ($85 billion) of economic activity in 1999, and for more than a million jobs.

In software alone there are now around 50,000 businesses in Britain, any one of which might have the potential to become the Microsoft of 2010. More Britons now work in computer services than ever worked in coal mines. Here, says Mr Smith, "is where the growth is": activities that can harness the value-added of creative genius to generate high returns on capital and to nurture home-grown businesses capable of challenging multinational giants such as Time-Warner and Disney.

The British film industry, for exam-

Martin Vander Weyer: associate editor of *The Week*.

ple, once seemed little more than a special-effects workshop for Hollywood. But a string of successes from "The English Patient" to "The Full Monty", "Trainspotting" and "Sliding Doors" (though usually financed and distributed by American companies) has brought new vigour to the sector: production spend on British-made films has already multiplied five times since 1989.

Releases due in early 1999 such as "Little Voice", shot in Scarborough with Ewan MacGregor and Michael Caine, and "Mad Cow", with Joanna Lumley

An artistic temperament
Turnover by industry (£m)

Art and antiques sales 2,500 / 3,800
Architecture 1,500 / 2,600
Advertising 4,300 / 7,400
Computer games 890 / 1,800
Crafts 400 / 700
Design 13,200 / 21,000
Designer fashion 600 / 1,000
Film 2,000 / 3,000
Music 3,400 / 6,700
Performing arts 830 / 1,200
Publishing 17,500 / 27,300
Software 7,800 / 19,300
Television and radio 5,700 / 10,900

2007
1998

Source: Department of culture, media and sport

and Prunella Scales, will sustain international attention.

In music, Britain has been a leader ever since the Beatles and the Rolling Stones first toured the world in the 1960s. Even with 50% of the remaining Spice Girls (and at least one member of a rival girl band, All Saints) taking maternity leave, the output of British recording artists in 1999 will be more than twice the value of recorded music bought by British fans, creating a £500m-plus trade surplus which is comparable to the steel industry's.

British television has long been the

envy of the world for the quality of its documentary, drama and comedy output. Much of that reputation is attributable to the BBC as a non-commercial centre of excellence, but technological advance means that the fullest commercial possibilities of the genre are now well to the fore.

The big shift in late 1998 was the launch of digital broadcasting: BSkyB's 200 channels (one of them dedicated to BSkyB's latest subsidiary, Manchester United football club) are battling it out against OnDigital's 30 channels; by mid-1999 they will be joined by 200 more from Cable & Wireless.

Why is Britain's once bombed-out economy generating all this creative energy? The answer is partly to do with history—having lost so much of its traditional economic base, the country has fewer structured careers to offer, so more college graduates choose to survive by their own wit and imagination. And it is partly to do with national character: not for Britain the uniformity which underpinned Japan's post-war economic miracle, but which makes it so difficult for today's Japanese leaders to dare to back radical ideas. British education may fall short of the skills needed to beat German industrial productivity, but Britain has always nurtured original minds and treasured eccentrics.

In Britain, originality is commonplace, and has often attracted international recognition. In the world of stage musicals, Andrew Lloyd Webber and Cameron Mackintosh; in architecture, Richard Rogers and Norman Foster, in restaurateurship and household style, Terence Conran. And in computer games, there is the aforementioned Lara Croft, star of Tomb Raider and generator of over £300m in annual sales for Eidos, the British company which owns her; British-developed games account for 25% of world sales of computer games.

Until very recently, Britain's cultural self-image was more concerned with "heritage" than modernity, and our quintessential brand names—Rolls-Royce, Wedgwood, Burberry—spoke of old-fashioned craftsmanship rather than cutting-edge creativity. By drawing attention

THE WORLD IN 1999

The Royal Opera House remains shut. Curtain up, £214m later, at the end of December.

Britain turns to Europe

Anthony King

The Blair government in 1999 will edge Britain to participation in Europe's new single currency. The prime minister may go further and announce, in principle, that Britain would like to join. Tony Blair himself is relaxed about replacing the pound with the euro. His chancellor, Gordon Brown, is known to be keen.

The government's new moves towards Europe—whether tentative or bold—will owe nothing to the results of the June 10th elections to the European Parliament. Only about one-third of the British electorate will vote—and they will turn out not because they have any burning interest in European issues but because they are the sort of people who always turn out.

I bet it's cheaper in euros

The Conservatives will do tolerably well—or at least will appear to. They will benefit from the fact that the 1999 Euro-elections will be Britain's first-ever national elections under proportional representation. Five years ago, the Tories under Britain's traditional first-past-the-post system won more than a quarter of the popular vote but only a fifth of the seats. This time they will win more seats even if they fail to win many more votes.

They will then attribute this apparent improvement in their fortunes to William Hague's opposition to the euro in particular and his dubiety about further European integration in general. They will be wrong. Other things being equal, a clear majority of British voters would prefer to retain the pound. Few are "Euro-enthusiasts". Brussels interference in Britain's internal affairs arouses widespread resentment.

But most Britons are also pragmatists, more concerned about inflation and jobs than about an abstraction like sovereignty and the nation-state. They also have a secure sense of national identity and reckon, in the words of the song, that "there'll always be an England", even if the banknotes in their wallet happen to change colour. Europe anyway is no longer foreign. Thanks to the Channel Tunnel, frequent cross-Channel ferries and cheap holiday flights, it is fast becoming part of most Britons' patch.

The consequence is predictable. As the euro becomes established on the Continent in 1999, and as more and more British companies transact business in the euro, the British—in their usual phlegmatic fashion—will get used to the idea that the new currency is becoming a fact. Few of them will like it. Few will positively welcome the change. But most will accept it as inevitable—and come to fear the consequences of any British failure to sign up. Opinion in Britain in 1999 will gradually begin to shift in the euro's favour.

The scale of the shift will depend partly on the government. The Blair government is more widely trusted than any other in recent British history. If Mr Blair pronounces in favour of the euro, that in itself will have a major impact; so will the attitude of business leaders. A minority of businessmen in 1999 will campaign vociferously against the euro, mainly on the grounds that in time it will lead to more "federal" European institutions; but most of the big business guns will be fighting on the euro's side. A considerable number of companies will publish their 1999 accounts in euros. Anyone trading with Europe will have to make a major investment in computer technology that is euro-compliant. And millions of British managers will find daily decisions about pricing, sales, competitors—indeed the whole gamut of business—will have to take the euro into account. The Conservatives, once the party of business, will seem to these people to be, well, absurd. The City fears the loss of business to the Continent. Manufacturers fear the loss of exports. Both will say so more and more loudly—and be listened to. 1999 will certainly not be a good year for the Euro-sceptics.

to the data on creative industries, and by associating itself with them, the Labour government has deliberately set out to change that self-image.

Building creative might

But the question to be asked in 1999 is: how much substance is there behind the image? Can rock groups and digital interactive shopping channels really replace steel-mills and textile factories as the foundation of the nation's wealth? Or is all this just wishful thinking, encouraged by the propensity of media-business folk to talk about their own success, and by the urge of Labour ministers to be photographed with them?

In a recession, the disposable income that consumers spend on electronic entertainment and designer fripperies will wither away, taking many insubstantial businesses with it. In good times or bad, the British financial system is still ill-designed to support a "creative" economy: venture capital is notoriously hard to come by. It is for this reason that many gifted British software designers have chosen to make their careers in America, or simply to sell their designs to American firms. And the London stockmarket, always intolerant of the long-term investment horizons associated with new ideas and high technology, will be even more risk-averse in the bear mood of 1999.

For these reasons, much of the financial return on British creativity will continue to be enjoyed not by the British but by foreign investors. And much of it, incidentally, will also be lost to pirates: intellectual property, the essential asset of all these industries, is peculiarly hard to police. The owners of software, music and film rights will continue to suffer massive leakages of revenue through bootlegging.

The creative industries will stay in the news in 1999, and will dominate much of the rhetoric and style of the millennial celebrations. It would be premature to pin too much hope on their short-term power to revolutionise the economy. But with a few strokes of British genius, supported by intelligent investors and sympathetic governments, they will certainly make a vital and growing contribution to the prosperity of the coming century.

THE WORLD IN 1999

English banknotes will bear a woman's signature for the first time. The Bank of England's Chief Cashier, Merlyn Lowther, starts her job on January 1st.

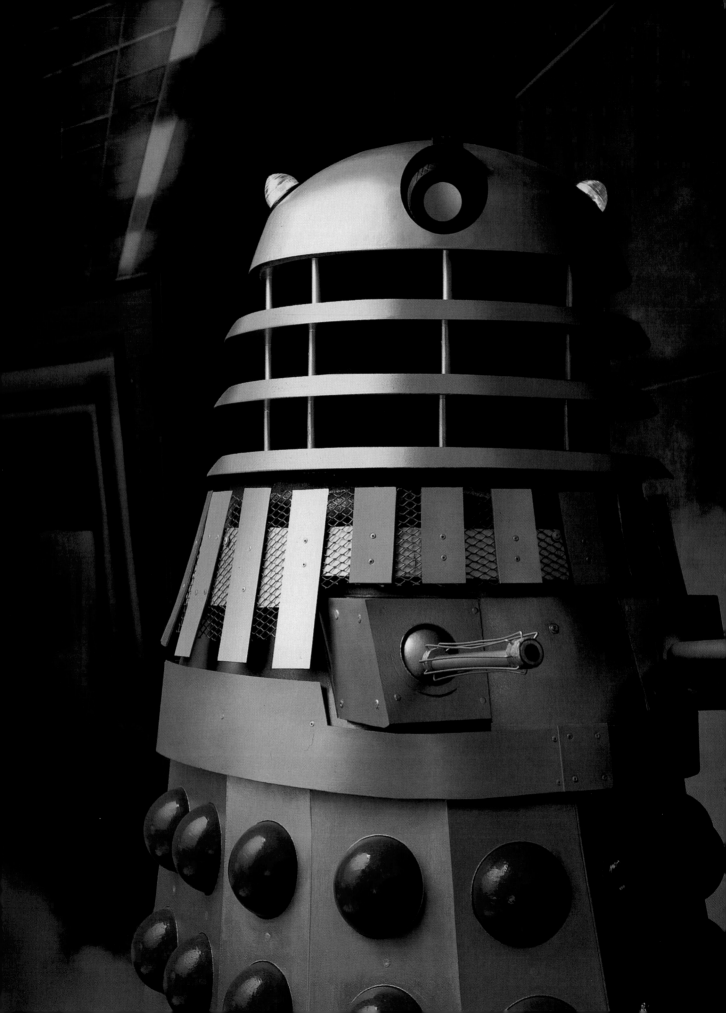

For people who've lost the power of speech, the voice synthesiser is a godsend.

You just type what you want to say on a laptop, and it automatically converts your words into sound.

But computerised voices have never been completely satisfactory. Simply because there's more to talking than just words.

When we speak, we use inflection and intonation to give extra meaning to what we say.

And it's hard to convey, say, urgency or irony if you can only speak in the same flat, measured tones.

That's why BT have developed the Laureate speech synthesis system.

Laureate actually allows the user to add emphasis to what they're saying.

And, while the synthetic voice that sounds completely natural is still some way off, the results are much closer to human speech than previous systems.

Not only that, people who use Laureate are able to choose a voice that's the same sex and the same approximate age.

In the future, we hope to be able to offer them the same regional accent as well.

After all, speaking with a dialect is much better than speaking like a dalek.

Laureate is just one of many BT projects that help people communicate more effectively.

Indeed, better communication can help people from all walks of life. If you'd like to know more, why not call us on **Free**fone *0800* **800 848**, or find us at www.bt.com

> Until now, people with computerised voices spoke in a rather distinctive way.

How right to be right

William Hague, leader of the Conservative Party, argues that
Britain's prosperity is at unnecessary risk in 1999.

1999 will be a tough year for political leaders. The after-shocks of the economic crisis in Asia and Russia will continue to reverberate around the world. If the prophets of doom who fill the pages of our newspapers are right, then further crises will develop. Those who believe that the western economies will be unaffected simply do not understand the truly global nature of the world in which our economy thrives.

Economic crises can quickly become political crises. Banks and businesses may bear the initial brunt of economic turmoil but that is soon passed on to individuals and families who see their jobs disappearing and their savings damaged. In such circumstances, political systems come under enormous pressure and governments fall.

In 1999 these problems will present the politicians of the West with a challenge unprecedented since the fall of the Berlin Wall a decade ago, and how we respond could affect the future prosperity and political stability of much of the world.

In Europe, centre-left and social democrat politicians will be singularly ill-equipped to provide the leadership that will be required. Although, politically, the left has been successful across the continent—and in 1999 almost every European government will be in the hands of left-wing parties—they have achieved that success by ditching conviction and consistency. Their political philosophy is bankrupt.

However much they dress up their philosophy in the language of the right, at the end of the day it amounts to a dangerous mix of government interventionism, expensive social costs, high taxes and high spending. Far from being the answer to the world's economic problems, it is precisely policies like these which are likely to make matters worse.

So in 1999 it will fall to the politicians of the centre-right to provide the kind of leadership which the left cannot offer. We must show that long-term economic stability depends on a genuine commitment to a free-market economy. We must fully support those governments which have the courage to

push forward with liberalising their economies and with difficult supply-side reforms.

Above all, we must unite in our opposition to protectionism wherever it rears its ugly head and drive ahead with the next round of the WTO talks. I believe that in 1999 we should set ourselves the ambitious goal of achieving global free trade by 2020. Governments in the European Union and the United States should start right now by creating a

"Watch out for the first clear sign in 1999 that the EU is headed for a single tax-structure."

joint free-trade area in services, removing industrial tariffs and liberalising investment. European businesses alone could benefit to the tune of a staggering £100 billion ($170 billion) a year from this initiative.

Politicians will owe it to those who elected them not to sit back, do nothing and see if the global economic situation deteriorates; we will have to be pro-active in taking the difficult decisions and confronting head-on the structural economic problems that lie behind the present uncertainty.

Whatever happens to the global economy in 1999, there is one event which we can be certain will dominate politics and economics in Europe. On January 1st, 11 European countries will abolish their national currencies and adopt a single European currency—the euro. With the world economic outlook so uncertain, there could hardly have been a more inauspicious time to have launched a project which brings with it so many economic and political risks. Are these risks worth taking?

Although Britain will not be joining the single currency, I sincerely hope that

it works. If the worst possible scenario happens and the money markets pull the euro apart, then British businesses and British jobs will be seriously affected.

Assuming the euro survives its launch, we will see what the longer-term advantages and disadvantages of the single currency are. For a start, we will begin to see whether the single currency really can work in good and bad times. We will see whether the euro brings with it dramatically lower interest rates, as its supporters promise. We will see whether having a single interest rate right across Europe will lead to overheating in some economies and hasten the onset of recession in others. It inevitably will do so, and those countries that suffer will need to decide whether the price is worth paying. And we will see whether being a member of the single currency leads to decisions about tax and spending being transferred away from elected national governments to the European Central Bank in Frankfurt, and what the political implications of that will be. Watch out for the first clear signs in 1999 that the EU is headed for a single tax-structure. Will national sovereignty be undermined? Will democratic accountability suffer? Does the single currency take us down an inevitable road to a United States of Europe? We do not know the answers to these questions now. Since the decision to take Britain into the single currency can be taken only after weighing a balance of interests, let us discover in the next few years exactly what those balances weigh.

Indeed it is precisely because we do not know now what the far-reaching economic and political consequences of joining a single currency will be that throughout 1999 I will be arguing vigorously that Britain should not even consider abolishing the pound until we see a single currency working in good times and bad.

We need to have a clear understanding what the implications for our democracy will be. This is not something to be rushed. That is not being anti-European, as my political opponents like to portray it. Britain must have the confidence to make the most of our membership of the EU without having to accept uncritically every idea labelled "European".

Reuters Business Briefing:
millions of news
items analysed and
targeted to your
precise needs.
www.reuters.com

Coccinella Septempunctata

We
know
what
you're
looking
for.

euro-dynamics:
exploring new horizons

The euro dawns, bringing the biggest transformation to global financial markets in our lifetime. Major investors, corporates and financial institutions turn to Deutsche Bank as a knowledgeable and trusted partner to help them profit from new opportunities – and avoid the pitfalls in a rapidly changing environment.

Euromoney has awarded Deutsche Bank "Best Bank in the euro zone" and "Best Bank in Western Europe". We listen to your needs and risk preferences and provide innovative and profitable solutions – using our breadth of experience backed up by our powerful balance sheet.

Whether your interests are financing or investments in the debt or equity markets, strategic or risk management advice or consolidation of financial activities, Deutsche Bank covers the full spectrum of your global financial needs.

Think euro, think Deutsche Bank.

Deutsche Bank

Gross debt
as % of GDP

Foreign direct investment
as % of world total

Protected environment
% of national territory

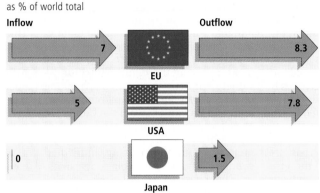

Sources: European Commission; UNDP

Lots to be doing in Europe

Robert Cottrell

BRUSSELS

The birth of the euro on January 1st will be only the first of several events to reshape the landscape of the European Union in the course of 1999. A new "high representative" for foreign policy should start work early in the year, raising the profile of the EU as a political actor. In June, voters will be invited to elect a new European Parliament: the British poll will involve, for the first time, a mechanism for proportional representation. Late autumn will be dominated by horse-trading for jobs by the next lot of European commissioners, who will take office in January 2000. By the end of the year final agreement should be reached on which applicant countries to admit next to the Union, and when. Reforms to the EU policymaking and decision-taking procedures will have to be adopted then or earlier, so that the Union can contemplate enlargement without inviting institutional gridlock. New budget rules will have to be set, especially for spending on agriculture. Managing such a busy year will be a test for the diplomatic skills of Germany and Finland, which will hold the EU presidency in the first half and second half of the year respectively.

The designers of Europe's monetary union seem confi-

Robert Cottrell: EU correspondent for *The Economist*.

Foreign aid
$ per person

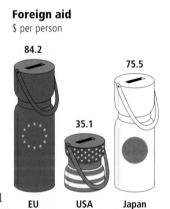

Armed forces
Thousands

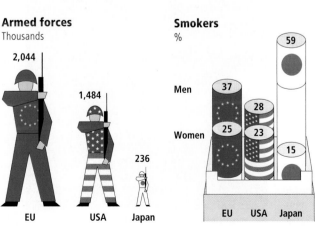

dent that no catastrophic surprises lurk among the legalities or the practicalities of the new system. If all goes according to plan, 11 of the EU's 15 countries will sink their national currencies into the euro on January 1st—but citizens in most of them will notice little change overnight. Notes and coins in national designs, denominated in national cur-

Cinema tickets
Average a year per person

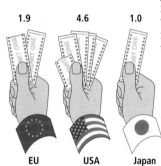

Smokers
%

rencies, will continue to circulate for at least three years. These will become mere façades for the euro, their value fixed permanently against it. Countries will not introduce new euro notes and coins generally until 2002, although some have already been minting coins in anticipation.

A successful launch for the euro will accelerate the general process of European integration. The more a common currency encourages convergence among European economies, the less distinction there will be between national economic interests. And the less distinction there is between national economic interests, the more reason there will be for EU countries to move towards a common foreign and security policy. Expect, therefore, to hear plenty in 1999 from the man (or woman) who starts work early in the year as the EU's first "high representative" for foreign policy—a European foreign minister in embryo.

Hitherto, most EU member states have been reluctant to pool their sovereignty into a common foreign or defence policy. But European impotence and disunity in the face of successive wars in the Balkans have brought about a change of mood.

The new grandee should be able to start work in the

new year—provided all EU countries have ratified the Amsterdam treaty of 1997, which created his post. He will be attached to the Council of Ministers, the EU's main intergovernmental institution. The job will be what he makes of it. He will have no military power directly at his disposal, but he will try to give early warning to governments that do, when he sees crises beckoning. He will help co-ordinate foreign-policy planning. He will appear on television giving "Europe's response" to this or that global crisis. By the end of the year he may be the EU's best-known public face. To perform plausibly he will have to advocate positions behind which a majority of EU countries can be relied upon to rally. If he does so, Europe will have an answer to Henry Kissinger's famous question, "Who do you call when you want to call Europe?"

If the EU has not been much involved in classic foreign policy until now, it has, arguably, played a triumphant role in its own region. By manipulating one main instrument, the prospect of EU member-ship, it has transformed and stabilised half Europe, with more to follow. In 1999 decisions will fall due about which countries to admit next, and precisely when. Most of the plausible candidates are countries that were Soviet-run until the fall of the Iron Curtain: Poland, the Czech Republic, Hungary, Slovenia and Estonia will start the year as front-runners. Malta and Latvia may creep up the list— as may Cyprus, if only a political fix can be found to the island's division.

The enlargement dossier is a sensi-tive one, in part because of the contra-dictory tensions it creates within Germany and Austria. In the long term both countries want stable and prosper-ous allies to the east. But in the short term both fear an influx of cheap labour. Austria paid a lot of lip-service to the subject when it held the EU presidency during the second half of 1998: it was keen to be seen as the country which got the process started, and keen to give a helping hand to its favourite protégé among the candidates, Slovenia. But ex-pect any final decisions on a timetable for enlargement to be pushed back to the end of 1999—when Austrian elections are past, and when Finland has taken over the EU presidency from Germany.

The prospect of enlargement will dic-tate another issue preoccupying the EU in

1999: how to reform the European Com-mission and the Council of Ministers, so that they can accommodate still more national voices and yet continue to func-tion. There is a broad acceptance of roughly how this can be achieved: it will mean reducing the number of commis-sioners who run the EU's policymaking bureaucracy, the European Commission; and it will mean allowing the Council of Ministers, the EU's legislature, to deal with a broader range of issues through majority voting, depriving individual countries of the right to block decisions.

The prospect of enlargement also raises budgetary questions: the countries

queuing up for admittance are relatively poor, giving them a strong claim on the EU's strictly limited development funds. They also have large farming industries, making further reform of the EU's com-mon agricultural policy more urgent still. Although the budget questions are sup-posed to be decided by April, the trick will probably be to sort out all these problems relating to enlargement and reform at roughly the same time, during the second half of 1999, thereby creating a negotiation so complex that every country will have a chance to win at least one battle it considers important.

Germany's chance to be different

Barbara Beck

For most of the post-war period, Ger-many has had a reputation for being re-assuringly boring. Governments came and went according to the rules; law and order generally prevailed; the economy mostly flourished; and the trains tended to run on time. Even the occasional world-shattering event—such as German unification in 1990—was soon stripped of its drama and translated into pro-

Barbara Beck: surveys editor for *The Economist*.

Mr Schröder moves to Berlin

grammes, budgets and bureaucracy.

But 1999, the Federal Republic's 50th anniversary, can hardly help being more exciting than usual. A new chancellor, Gerhard Schröder, fresh from his elec-tion victory in late September, will be leading a new government of Social De-mocrats and Greens, a coalition never previously tried at federal level. And no sooner will the new crew have settled into their offices in sleepy, provincial Bonn, the Federal Republic's enduring provisional capital, than they will have to up-sticks again. During the spring and summer, government and parliament will be moving to big, sophisticated, cosmopolitan Berlin, Germany's once and future capital.

That move hundreds of kilome-tres further east, a delayed result of unification, is likely to make a difference, both to the way the Germans see themselves and to how other countries see them; all the more so since it coincides with a generational change. Many of those serving in the old "Bonn Re-public" still remembered the sec-ond world war, and never quite stopped apologising for Germany's awful past; but very few of the ministers of the new "Berlin Re-public" are old enough to have any personal memories of their coun-try's darkest days. Some of Ger-many's partners worried at first that the return to Berlin would make Germany more conscious of its increased size and power, and less calculable, but such fears are

> The amount of arable farmland left unplanted in Europe will double to 10%. The countryside will look tatty and farmers poor.

now receding.

The first big official event to take place in Berlin will be the election on May 23rd of a new federal president. Given the political complexion of the new government, he or she is bound to be a Social Democrat, for only the second time in the country's post-war history. Although the head of state is meant to be above politics, both the current incumbent, Roman Herzog, and his predecessor, Carl Friedrich von Weizsäcker, have wielded considerable influence in the post, so the choice is not unimportant. The candidate most widely tipped is Johannes Rau, the long-standing premier of the large *Land* of North Rhine-Westphalia.

In European politics, the new government will be thrown in at the deep end. For the first six months of 1999, it will be Germany's turn in the presidency of the European Union. Many of the issues that will come up for discussion during that period are close to its heart; for example, enlargement of the union to the east, and reform of agricultural and structural policies, which between them eat up the bulk of the EU budget—at a time when Germany is arguing that its net contributions are far too high in comparison with other rich members, particularly France.

As it happens, Germany's new foreign minister, Joschka Fischer, is not a Social Democrat but a Green. A trainer-shod rebel in his youth, he might at first sight seem an odd choice, but at 50 he is now the most prominent representative of the realist wing of his party. His political career has included a spell as environment minister in his home state of Hesse, and according to Mr Schröder he has developed into an exceptionally rational person.

Still a powerhouse

For good measure, Germany will also hold the presidency of the G7 group of industrial countries for the whole of 1999, and will be in charge of preparing the G7's big annual meeting in June, in Cologne. That will provide an opportunity for Oskar Lafontaine, the powerful new Social Democrat finance minister, to air his ideas for exchange-rate target zones to limit fluctuations between the dollar, euro and yen.

The outlook for 1999 for Germany's own economy, as for other continental European countries, is relatively bright, though not quite as bright as before the Asian tigers caught flu. Russia's troubles have been unhelpful too, though German

economists point out that Germany's exports to Russia account for under 2% of its total exports, and those to all the sick tigers together for only 5%; so unless the contagion spreads far and wide, the damage to the German economy should be limited. Estimates for GDP growth in 1999, although slightly trimmed back, still range from 2.1-3.2%. And what growth there will be is likely to be better balanced than in the past couple of years, when a weak D-mark boosted exports and not much else. Private investment and consumption are beginning to pick up again, and even the construction sector, after years in the doldrums, may

The Reichstag will reopen in a blaze of light

be coming round. Inflation, which has recently been running at below 1%, seems well under control.

But that does not mean Germany has no economic worries. Its celebrated Stability and Growth Law of 1967 requires the country to aim for four targets simultaneously: steady growth, price stability, external balance and a high level of employment. On the last of these four, it is failing miserably. Unemployment is hovering around 4m, or about 11% of the labour force. Despite a slight decline recently, it is likely to stay at much the same level in 1999. And in some ways the figure is worse than it looks, because the bland average conceals huge differences between east and west.

In former West Germany the unemployment rate is heading slightly downwards, to about 9% in 1999; but in former East Germany it is still rising, and will be well over 19%. Meanwhile the east continues to cost taxpayers in western Germany lots of money. Since unification in 1990, a net sum of about DM1 trillion ($625 billion) has been transferred from the west to keep the east going, and annual net payments from the west still run at the rate of about DM140 billion a year.

Mr Schröder is fond of talking about

the "Neue Mitte", the new centre (or perhaps third way), an attractive-sounding mix of a compassionate society and a market economy, without quite specifying how the two are to be reconciled. Germans are ambivalent about their famously expensive welfare state, which pushes their public spending to over half of GDP. On the one hand they complain about their high taxes (for individuals, up to 53% of gross earnings) and their heavy social-security contributions; on the other hand they have come to rely on being looked after from cradle to grave, and would be appalled to be left to fend for themselves.

Mr Schröder is committed to undoing even the mild reforms to pensions, sick pay and job security introduced by Helmut Kohl's government; never mind that they had been intended to make Germany leaner, more competitive and therefore better at creating jobs. At the same time both he and Mr Lafontaine accept that there is an urgent need for tax reform (which the Social Democrats frustrated while in opposition), to lighten the overall burden.

Making Germany a more competitive, more flexible sort of place will require radical change, causing pain and upheaval. The year ahead will show whether Mr Schröder really has it in him to do it. If he wants to be brave, he has a good enough majority in both houses of parliament. If he shrinks back, the German people will find themselves with something they thought they voted against: the same mixture as before.

THE WORLD IN 1999

The German Mittelstand will be transformed as 120,000 of these family-owned small and medium-sized firms—the backbone of the German economy—progressively go public or are sold.

We'll never forget that communications isn't about Especially your people.

MCI WorldCom is the only provider of global telecommunications on a wholly owned, seamless network.

This gives unique advantages to you and your people.

You'll have one single provider for all your telephone, data and Internet traffic, regardless if it goes across the street, across the continent or across the Atlantic ocean.

You'll have one single technical platform ensuring quality, capacity and reliability.

Not to mention the cost effectiveness of having one partner instead of several providers, each one of them trying to build profit out of your communications.

You'll find MCI WorldCom in 65 countries throughout Europe, Asia Pacific and the Americas.

Would you like to know more about MCI WorldCom and what our people could do for your people?

Come visit our web site at **www.mciworldcom.com/1999**

technology, but about people.

The Millennium Round

Leon Brittan, vice-president of the European Commission, calls for a new round of trade talks to be ready by the end of 1999.

1999 will be a crucial year for world trade policy. Against the background of financial crisis in Asia and Russia, the role and importance of the global economy has never been more centre stage. As the next century approaches, no economy can remain insulated from the global market place.

But the answer is not to try to turn the clock back. Retreating behind protectionist barriers reminiscent of the 1930s is a sure-fire way to make a bad situation worse.

The crisis shows more than ever the need to look forward—and embrace further trade liberalisation. We must work together to keep markets open and to tackle global economic turbulence collectively.

The EU's commitment to a rules-based multilateral trading system is as strong today as ever. We are convinced that multilateralism is the best model for international co-operation and economic stability. An open trade policy leads to worldwide growth, prosperity and jobs. Comprehensive, multilateral negotiations are our best way of tackling the millennium's challenges head on.

In 1998 we celebrated 50 years of the multilateral trading system. We should rightly be proud of the achievements GATT has made in breaching protectionist walls. Eight rounds of major global trade talks have hammered at the boundaries of trade liberalisation to the benefit of business and consumers alike.

The last talks—the mammoth Uruguay Round—led to the creation of the World Trade Organisation (WTO) as a permanent body and a forum for settling trade disputes. In just four years it has made a significant impact, with the new dispute-settlement body successfully arbitrating trade quarrels across the globe.

Since then, agreements to open markets in information technology, financial services and telecommunications have been successfully negotiated. The WTO Telecoms agreement, which came into force early in 1998, covers more than 93% of world revenues in telecommunications. And the financial-services deal concluded in Geneva in December 1997 covers over 97% of the insurance premiums of WTO member countries. These agreements provide global rules in some of the world's most dynamic industries.

But much remains to be done. That is why the EU, Japan, Australia, Hong Kong, Singapore, Mexico, Chile and

"Exporters are being obstructed by a plethora of non-tariff barriers."

others believe the best way forward is to hold a new round of global trade talks starting on January 1st 2000—a "Millennium Round".

Only new multilateral negotiations on this scale, involving all industries and all trading countries, will enable every sector to say what it wants done and offer governments the chance to strike cross-sectoral deals. Nothing is agreed until everything is agreed. But everyone stands to benefit in some way from the final outcome.

Relying on sectoral or geographical agreements may offer piecemeal comfort in the short term but cannot provide long-term prospects for global growth. The benefits of comprehensive liberalisation will spread widely across the economy, and will not just benefit particular sectors or interest groups.

A built-in agenda for the new trade talks is already on the table as part of the Uruguay Round agreements. WTO members have already committed themselves to begin negotiations on agricultural subsidies and services by the end of 1999. The potential gains in these areas are huge.

But the EU believes these negotiations should be much broader. Trade and investment, and trade and competition rules are two areas that we cannot afford to ignore. Indeed the WTO has already set up working groups to look at both of these.

Open up, it's the WTO

The Millennium Round should push for a further liberalisation of industrial tariffs. It should spend time considering electronic commerce—an area which has expanded tremendously since the Uruguay Round. What rules, if any, should there be?

Exporters across the globe are being obstructed by a plethora of non-tariff barriers. There is a growing need to simplify export and import procedures; to focus on product standards and technical regulations; to strengthen intellectual property rights; to expand on the existing rules for public procurement; and to simplify complex rules of origin.

We must look at ways of ensuring that investment and competition rules do not amount to barriers to the free movement of goods, services and capital worldwide. These pressing issues cannot wait.

But although the new trade round should be market-driven it must reflect more than the interests of business alone. We need to look closely at the relationships between trade and the environment, labour standards, food safety and animal welfare.

Another challenge is to strengthen public understanding of, and confidence in, the multilateral system. To do this we must take steps to improve the transparency of WTO procedures and give greater weight to the consultation process. It is vital that we explain the economic and social benefits resulting from an expansion of world trade to interested groups and the wider public.

The world cannot afford to stand back at this critical moment. The Asian and Russian financial crises make it important that we act quickly. We must inject greater urgency into opening up world markets. And we must resist any moves to return to crippling pre-war protectionism.

If we are to enter the next century on a firm economic footing, it is imperative that there is further trade liberalisation leading to a truly comprehensive "Millennium Round".

France feels better

Jean-Marie Colombani   PARIS

Jospin has impeccable timing

With more growth and less unemployment, the French have begun to think that they are on the right track. Thanks to robust economic growth, supported by strong domestic demand and exports (witness the excellent results of its balance of trade), these are good times for France. The French seem to have regained confidence in themselves and in their leaders. The victory of its football team at the World Cup on its home turf was a blessing. It created a moment of national unity that will still echo in 1999.

The change in mood has come just in time. For many years France had been in a state of collective depression. This depression was nurtured by the slow erosion of the middle class's standard of living and by increasing inequalities, two of the principal characteristics of the Mitterrand era. France faced rapid growth in unemployment and social unrest in its suburbs, and these heated up an unhealthy debate over immigration.

Whether by coincidence or not, this change of mood started not with the election of Jacques Chirac as president in 1995 but with the appearance of Lionel

Jospin as prime minister in 1997. His government, a coalition of socialists, communists and ecologists has been remarkably popular. The continuing confidence of the French in their government after nearly two years is based on two factors: technique and substance. In terms of technique, with his propensity to listen and his pragmatism, Mr Jospin has worked out ways of putting back on track projects that had been at a standstill. Hence, a number of large state-owned companies are being privatised. Despite the fact that France Télécom and Aerospatiale are the largest French companies and are of strategic importance, they are heading for sale. The Socialists have privatised much faster than their right-of-centre predecessors. In terms of substance, the French have responded to a simple rallying call, even if it is a questionable one: make tomorrow better than today by combining economic growth with more social progress.

Encouraged by various fiscal measures, France is enjoying the strong rate of economic growth which has returned to Europe but it has also drawn up a law imposing a 35-hour limit to the working week, without any reduction in salary. Mr Jospin has, by this means, attempted to convince employees of the state and private sectors that growth can be synonymous with social progress. Presented as a tool against unemployment and as the promise made to companies to create more jobs, this law will be unevenly implemented. Certain sectors will be able to adapt to the new working-hour rules, others will not; all companies, both large and small, are displeased with this piece of legislation. Realistically, it will not be able to generate more than 50,000 jobs, a figure which does not come close to the government's promises. Nonetheless, the French public credits the government for the return of strength to the economy.

This renewed confidence is fuelled by something else: the worldwide financial crisis. As other currencies and economies have been toppled, the French have become convinced of the benefits of the euro. Perhaps they never

THE WORLD IN 1999

The French government will privatise Crédit Lyonnais, a bank whose losses none has equalled.

Jean-Marie Colombani: editor of Le Monde.

Portugal

After a year of exuberance (which began with money pouring into the Lisbon stockmarket and continued with visitors pouring into Expo '98), Portugal faces a year of reward. The reward for sound economic performance is participation in Europe's economic and monetary union. And the reward for sound stewardship of the country, the minority Socialist government hopes, will come in the general election due to be held by October.

Despite internal divisions, the Socialists' prospects are good, and will be boosted by a strong economy and falling unemployment. António Guterres, the popular prime minister, is expected to stand for re-election, although there is speculation that he has his eye on the top job at the European Commission, due to be announced by mid-1999, and may not be available for a second term.

The Socialists will also be keen to take the credit for overseeing Portugal's entry into the single currency in 1999, widely regarded as a symbol of the country's maturing status. (Portugal will nonetheless remain with Greece at the bottom of the EU league in terms of income per head.) The outlook for the Social Democrats, whose ten-year rule was ended by a Socialist victory in 1995, is more gloomy, though its chances cannot be dismissed out of hand.

Growth will slow to a more balanced 2.7% in 1999, still above the EU average. The economic cycle will remain out of step with France and Germany, and as the interest rate set by the European Central Bank is likely to reflect the benign economic conditions in those two countries, fighting inflation will be left to the Portuguese. Yet in an election year fiscal policy will remain slack, letting inflation edge upwards. That will leave the government to wrestle with public finances after the election, trying to reconcile the conflicting demands of EMU budget-deficit limits and under-investment in health and education.

KEY INDICATORS			
	1997	1998	1999
GDP growth (% pa)	3.7	3.8	2.7
Inflation (%)	2.1	2.7	2.9
3-month interbank rate (%)	5.7	4.3	3.6
Exchange rate			
Esc per DM	101.1	102.5	102.5
Esc per $	175.3	182.0	169.1
Current account (% of GDP)	-1.8	-1.7	-1.8

E·I·U EIU COUNTRY ANALYSIS AND FORECASTING

http://www.tntpost-group.com

IF THERE'S LIFE, THERE'S MA

If you have the feeling that the world is getting smaller, and the furthest corners of our planet seem to be get

closer, it's probably because our universe has expanded. The universe we are referring to is that of PTT Post (Du

Mail), and it expanded almost two years ago when PTT Post acquired TNT and was transformed into the TNT F

Group, the first organisation in the world to place Mail, Express and Logistic services of such a scale under

global roof and, in the process, brought all ourcustomers within easier and faster reach of each of

THERE'S MAIL, WE'RE THERE.

Post Group now operates in more than 200 countries with 100,000 employees. In 1997 our group impressed

economists when it recorded sales of NLG 15,3 billion (approximately USD 7,6 billion). A performance that in

hall way paved the way to Wall Street and beyond. TNT Post Group is listed on the stock exchanges of New York,

on, Amsterdam and Frankfurt. TNT Post Group envisages a world on which our fully

ated network for Mail, Express and Logistic services will have a great impact.

TPG
T N T P O S T G R O U P

THE WORLD BEHIND TNT & PTT POST.

Netherlands

A small country, an internationalist outlook, strong commercial interests but keen environmental concerns and a developed sense for the quality of life: all these Dutch characteristics hurtle together in the issue of the future of Amsterdam's Schiphol airport. Fast-expanding Schiphol, which alone accounts for about 2% of the Dutch economy, is Europe's fourth-busiest airport and, urged on by the airlines, it would like to expand faster still. But it faces constraints on capacity and environmentalists want to limit noise. How rapidly should Schiphol be allowed to grow? Should it expand at its existing site or on an artificial island in the North Sea? Should the noisier jets be restricted by taxes?

The Schiphol question is typical of the sort of intricate manoeuvring between interests that is the stuff of Dutch coalition politics. There will be plenty of manoeuvring in 1999. The second term of the "purple" coalition between Labour, Liberals and D66 promises to be more contentious than the first, as the two main partners (Labour and the Liberals) clash on a number of issues.

The Liberals are anxious to wipe out the government deficit and cut taxes; Labour is happy with the current deficit level and wants to use additional budgetary room to increase social benefits. Immigration could become a bone of contention if asylum-seekers keep arriving in the Netherlands in numbers.

Economic growth will slow in 1999 to less than 3% as the Dutch business cycle, which turned up in 1994-95, loses momentum. Business activity will nevertheless be strong enough to allow a further decline in unemployment while inflation is not expected to exceed 2%. With the economic basics nicely in order, the Dutch will be free to explore further the difficult balancing act between free-marketry and social policy for which their country is increasingly admired.

KEY INDICATORS

	1997	1998	1999
Real GDP	3.6	3.8	2.5
Consumer prices	2.2	2.0	1.9
3-month Aibor rate	3.3	3.7	4.3
Average exchange rates			
G:DM	1.12	1.13	1.13
G:$ 1.95	1.95	2.01	1.95
Current account (% of GDP)	5.9	5.6	5.5

E·I·U EIU COUNTRY ANALYSIS AND FORECASTING

Chirac's turning tough again

doubted them: a silent majority has always believed in the virtues of European integration, conscious that this process is being driven by a Franco-German community with a similar conception of European identity. However, everyone has become aware of the benefits of EMU as the financial crisis has deepened. Everyone has understood that if it were not for the euro, France would be facing severe monetary difficulties.

However, as America gains competitive advantage from the slide of the dollar, European countries feel more exposed: the euro is put under strain by its very strength. There are those in France who question whether Europe, especially the left-wing governments in Paris, Bonn and Rome, will be able to act together to maintain a grip on the situation. However, with the prospect of a 2.6% growth rate, France is not looking at a potential crisis in 1999.

Since June 1997, France has been in a regime of cohabitation: a right-wing president and a left-wing government. This system, which creates a balance between the two holders of executive power not stipulated in the constitution, seems to suit the French well.

But it is a perverse system. Lacking a majority, the president has his hands chained behind his back. However, having been the target of much criticism for two years, Mr Chirac's chances of being re-elected have significantly increased—thanks precisely to his passivity. Democracy is in theory a system that confers to a team the means to govern, and which enables voters to judge the latter's actions. The French constitution, by contrast, is a system that encourages idleness. And this hinders government action.

By 1999 Jacques Chirac will have recovered from the heavy losses inflicted by the voters at the last parliamentary elections. He will then launch an all-out war against the government. Mr Jospin had better keep a wary eye.

Who'll be who in Italy

Beppe Severgnini   ROME

Massimo D'Alema will spend 1999 on a roller-coaster. His new government has brought together his own Democrats of the Left (former communists), unrepentant communists, assorted (and assertive) former Christian Democrats, the odd technocrat, scattered greens and socialists. Will they all get along? And will they tackle some of the problems that have dogged Italy for years?

Mr D'Alema—who has never been elected but got his job after Romano Prodi committed political suicide (he miscalculated the votes to pass the budget)—is anxious to prove his worth, which is considerable. He will have his work cut out for him. Electoral reform is vital in order to reduce the number of parties and create more stable coalitions.

More privatisation is needed to bring better companies and competition to the market. Unemployment—on average 12%, but at least twice as much in the poor, crime-ridden south—must be tackled. Everywhere in Italy there must be a reduction in red tape. And immigration needs controlling.

Mr D'Alema will find out that many powerful lobbies will try to prevent each element of this programme. His allies in government, for instance, will bar any electoral reform which might reduce their power. The communists will push for a useless 35-hour week, and they will resist all privatisation, including Enel's, the state electricity monopoly. And banks, big business and the treasury ministry will try to maintain control of any privatised utility (as they have done in the case of Telecom Italia, with disastrous consequences). Civil servants will

Beppe Severgnini: columnist for *Corriere della Sera* and Italy correspondent for *The Economist*. His latest book is "Italiani si diventa" (Rizzoli).

oppose pension and welfare reforms. Environmentalists will stop the construction of much-needed roads (Autostrada del Sole, the main north-south thoroughfare between Bologna and Florence, will become a bottleneck). Well-meaning but unrealistic Christian pressure-groups will make sure that tougher immigration laws are not implemented.

Additional political turmoil is expected in May, when a new president of the republic will be elected by parliament, for a seven-year term, to replace Oscar Luigi Scalfaro. The job is mostly ceremonial, but does carry substantial powers (only the president can dissolve parliament). The front-runner for the Quirinale—the official residence of the president—is Carlo Azeglio Ciampi, a former central banker and prime minister, and now the treasury minister, widely respected for steering Italy into European monetary union. Among the hopefuls are Nilde Jotti, a *grande dame* of the Democrats of the Left, and the chairman of the Senate, Nicola Mancino. A possibility, if the popular election of the state president is close to approval by parliament, is for Mr Scalfaro to stay on as an interim solution. (He would be happy with that.)

Just after the president is chosen, Italians will vote on June 13th for the European Parliament. The vote will be the first test of Mr D'Alema's government. It will also be important for the opposition. Silvio Berlusconi, tycoon-founder of Forza Italia and leader of the centre-right Freedom Alliance, will invest heavily in the outcome. If he is successful, he is unlikely to give up his post as leader of the opposition, and we can expect more attacks on the magistrates who, in the recent past, have convicted him thrice for his actions as a businessman on charges of bribery and tax fraud.

A third election will follow. It will be a private affair among European heads of government and it will bring a new president to the European Commission. Italians believe they have a chance. After two northern Europeans (Jacques Delors and Jacques Santer), it may well be the turn of a southerner. There are Dutch, Spanish and French nationals holding important European jobs, but no Italians. A strong candidate is Romano Prodi. The former prime minister is keen to leave Italy behind, is known to be tempted by an EU job and has many friends among prime ministers. It is vital, though, that Mr D'Alema and Lamberto Dini (the foreign minister) back him wholeheartedly. They may not.

Expect much debate in 1999 to centre on amnesty. Attempts to find a way

out of the judicial tangle that followed *Tangentopoli*—a series of corruption scandals which erupted in 1992—have been met by public hostility. But the atmosphere of Christian forgiveness associated with 2000 and earthly pressure from Mr Berlusconi (who can offer his crucial votes to the new president), may bring, towards the end of the year, an amnesty for those who have not committed major crimes and agree to leave public office. The slow Italian system of justice cannot deal with hundreds of trials, which will soon be barred by the statute of limitations anyway.

The other key word of 1999 will be "Mezzogiorno". The poor southern part of the country has been the single biggest problem since Italy was united in 1861.

D'Alema's dilemmas

Trillions of lire have been wasted in useless schemes. The government is convinced that the small and medium-sized industries, which have made northern Italy one of the wealthiest parts of Europe, can be replicated south of Rome. Expect a slow start and more arguments.

Three men will cast their shadows on all these developments. The first is Umberto Bossi, the mercurial leader of the separatist Northern League; he believes that the north, not the south, needs help, as it is being suffocated by bad central government. The second is Antonio Di Pietro, a former prosecutor, now a populist senator with an adoring lower-middle class following. The third is Francesco Cossiga, a maverick former president with a kingmaker's qualities. In 1998, switching from the centre-right to the centre-left, he raised Mr D'Alema to the prime-ministerial throne; in 1999 he will exact a price for this support.

Greece

FORECAST

The government of Costas Simitis has set itself an ambitious goal: getting Greece into Europe's economic and monetary union in 2001. Will it make it? The verdict from fellow EU countries will come in early 2000, based on Greece's ability to satisfy the economic convergence criteria set out in the Maastricht treaty. So 1999 is a crunch year: Greece's performance will determine whether EMU membership can happen according to the Simitis plan.

To be sure of qualifying, Greece has to hit four targets. Inflation needs to be down to about 2.5% by the end of the year; ten-year interest rates should be down to about 6.5%; the government deficit must be below 3% of GDP; and the drachma must have held steady at or above the bilateral central rate against the D-mark of Dr180.54 in Europe's exchange-rate mechanism.

Greece has already made great progress in reducing the government deficit, which was down from 7.5% of GDP in 1996 to 4% in 1997. Despite high interest rates on the government debt (109% of GDP) the 1998 deficit should be down to close to 3% and, as interest rates fall, it will drop comfortably under 3% of GDP in 1999. Ten-year interest rates on government debt are also falling and likely to be well below the Maastricht threshold by end-1999.

There is one remaining criterion, inflation, that could still trip up the Simitis government. Inflation has remained stubbornly above 5%. It should fall gradually during 1999 and, with the help of cuts in indirect taxes, should just squeeze under the EMU barrier. There are dangers that tension with Turkey over Cyprus, or an escalation of the Kosovo conflict, could lead to a collapse in financial markets' confidence in Greece. But if luck and Mr Simitis's nerve hold, Greece will be ready to enter euroland, creating a feeling of local pride that will grow as Greece prepares for the Olympics, to be held in Athens in 2004.

KEY INDICATORS			
	1997	1998	1999
Real GDP	3.5	3.1	3.2
Consumer prices: year average	5.6	4.9	3.3
year end	4.7	4.6	2.4
12-month Treasury-bill rate	9.6	10.8	8.5
Average exchange rates			
Dr:DM	157.4	170.0	178.0
Dr:$	273.1	303.0	294.0
Current account (% of GDP)	-4.1	-4.2	-3.6

E·I·U   EIU COUNTRY ANALYSIS AND FORECASTING

Belgium

Even by Belgian standards, the country's convoluted linguistic politics is set to get messy. Parliamentary elections are due in June. The voters, weary of scandals and of a centre-left Christian Democrat-Socialist coalition that has been in power for longer than any other post-1945 government, will be keen to try some other combination of parties. But what exactly?

The right-of-centre Liberals and the moderate nationalists together can expect to win more than 30% of the votes, the largest share, in both Flemish-speaking Flanders and the French-speaking region of Wallonia. They would need to find another coalition partner to have a majority in parliament. An alliance with the Christian Democrats has been ruled out by the Liberals on the Flemish side and by the Christian Democrats on the francophone side. An alliance with the Socialists—which would leave the Christian Democrats out of government for the first time since 1958—is therefore looking likelier. Whatever the eventual outcome (and almost any permutation is possible), the negotiations to form a new federal government in 1999 will be arduous.

Tangled into these arguments are matters of money. Before and after the elections, tensions will resurface between Flanders and Wallonia over the Flemish community's drive for a revision in the financial arrangements between the Belgian regions; richer Flanders resents subsidising the social-security system in high-jobless Wallonia. Despite the squabbles, Belgians will unite over long-awaited reforms of the police and judiciary, giving greater independence to the justice system.

The economy will do well despite the political charades. GDP growth will tick along nicely. The general government deficit will dip below 1.5% of GDP. Inflation will remain below the EU average. And the current account will show a surplus that would sound healthy in any language.

KEY INDICATORS

	1997	1998	1999
Real GDP	2.9	2.8	2.4
Consumer prices	1.6	1.2	1.3
3-month treasury bill rate	3.4	3.7	4.3
Average exchange rates			
Bfr:DM	20.62	20.63	20.63
Bfr:$	35.77	36.77	35.79
Current account (% of GDP)	4.6	4.9	4.7

E·I·U EIU COUNTRY ANALYSIS AND FORECASTING

Any Spaniards left in Spain?

Juan Luis Cebrián
MADRID

Ready to charge at Madrid

One trend will be clear throughout Europe in 1999: regional voices will grow louder everywhere. Under the protective umbrella of the European Union, nation states are losing both power and independence, and provinces are seizing them—from Scotland to northern Italy, from Ulster to the many disparate regions of Spain. The paradox is that units of government are getting smaller at the very moment the overall government of Europe is growing more pervasive and more uniform.

Consider Spain. In October 1998 the Basque elections had shown a growth of radical nationalist votes after the unilateral ceasefire decided by ETA terrorists. And in 1999 the Catalonian elections, due to be held in March, will in large measure determine the timbre of national politics. The Socialist candidate, Pascual Maragall, is the man to watch. He is the former mayor of Barcelona and has been enormously popular since he organised the successful Olympic games in the city in 1992. If elections to the regional government, presided over for the past 18 years by the incombustible nationalist leader Jordi Pujol, produce a Maragall victory, it will mean an immediate change in the balance of power in Madrid. It will force the prime minister,

José Maria Aznar, to call early general elections (not scheduled till 2000) and throw out of joint many of the policies that have hitherto been thought of as the national policies of Spain.

The question of different nationalist movements within Spain is far from resolved 20 years after the belated adoption of a democratic constitution in the country. Spain's wholehearted acceptance of the European Union has made the need for a strong government in Madrid seem less urgent. Although the strong regional pride of Catalonia and the Basque country are well known, nationalist feeling in many other regions will be running high in 1999. Watch out for Galicia, for example, or for a coalition of nationalist parties in the Canary Islands. Indeed, in each of the 17 autonomous regions of Spain (with the exception of the two Castiles and Madrid itself), resentment towards the central government has led to small political groups claiming greater local power. Whereas in Catalonia and the Basque country the rallying call is often for independence from the rest of Spain, other regions which do not have this option are nonetheless smouldering with resentment against Madrid.

Since it is difficult for political parties to gain control in Madrid without regional support, Mr Aznar is having to

Juan Luis Cebrián: *founder and publisher of El Pais.*

give more and more ground in order to retain authority himself. The ruling Popular Party depends on Catalonian support to survive in power. And yet, in the past, this party has been much more opposed to greater regional autonomy than Felipe Gonzalez's old Workers Socialist Party. That is now changing. It will change further in 1999 because Mr Aznar knows he cannot get through the year unless he pays more heed to his regional allies.

Spain's paradox

The problem of balancing national goals with regional aspirations is a particularly hard one for right-of-centre parties: for the Conservatives in Britain, for the Berlusconi forces in Italy and for Mr Aznar in Spain. This is because in each case a substantial chunk of the conservative vote is attracted to the romanticism of regional politics: the desire to resurrect an old, historic national identity or a local language. So a right-of-centre government in Madrid will stay in power only if it cedes greater regional influence. But the ruling party of Mr Aznar is characterised by its ideological defence of Spanish unity in the face of regional separatist trends. This is the paradox of Spanish politics in 1999.

Language will be much argued about. In Catalonia, the language controversy has heated up in the past few months, and will remain one of the key issues in the election campaign. The relative advantage of Mr Maragall over his powerful opponent, Mr Pujol, is that he can obtain the vote of both linguistic communities—Castillian and Catalonian.

The Catalonian elections will be the first of a long series of elections which will end in June, during which votes will be taken in another 13 autonomous regions, for town councils and for the European Parliament. If these go against him, Mr Aznar may be tempted to call parliamentary elections. These would be the first real test of Mr Aznar's popularity, which over the past year has not stood particularly high in opinion polls. Mr Aznar's lack of charm is one of the reasons given for these polls not being too favourable, but he has the advantage of the excellent state of the economy and the disastrous position of the Socialist Party, which has not yet recovered from its last defeat.

THE WORLD IN 1999 Airfares will be quoted in euros, making it easy to decide whether your Paris-Rome ticket will be cheaper bought in Madrid.

Eastern Europe's sad duet

Matthew Valencia   BERLIN

A new curtain will come down across Eastern Europe in 1999. On one side will be those countries beckoned to join the European Union. On the other will be those which are to be left out in the cold for at least another decade—caught between the wealth of the EU and the chaotic misery of the old Soviet Union. This curtain will not be as rigid as the old one of iron. It may, however, seem almost as cruel. Unlike the old one, it does not run along the region's western borders, but down its middle; and it divides more by economic performance than political ideology.

The five countries in the leading pack to join Europe's political and economic club—the Czech Republic, Hungary,

get horribly tricky. For one thing, while the East European candidates desperately want the benefits membership would bring, they also fear the damage that it would inflict on large parts of their economies, as they are forced to adopt rules designed for wealthier countries.

Adopting EU laws on environmental and labour standards (just a small part of the Union's 80,000-page *acquis communautaire*, its body of law) will prove a hard sell to the myriad domestic business lobbies that stand to lose out from the changes. The squabbling has barely begun; in 1999 it is likely to turn nasty.

For its part, the European Union keeps saying how keen it is on eastern enlargement. But it knows that this

Poland, Slovenia and Estonia—will at long last, after countless delays, start bargaining in earnest with the EU, whose presidency for the first half of the year belongs to Germany, a keen advocate of moving the EU's borders east. These erstwhile satellites of the Soviet Union will be pulled into ever closer orbit around the EU: where they once looked to Moscow for guidance, from 1999 they will be looking harder than ever to Brussels. They won't like everything they see.

Agreeing the terms of entry will soon

Matthew Valencia: Eastern Europe correspondent for *The Economist*.

means upsetting some of its members and adding further pressure on its already stretched budget. Brussels wants the eastern hopefuls to join its single market straight away, in effect abolishing their borders with it; but it also wants to see slower integration in some areas, such as agricultural policy and the free movement of people, so as to ease the pain this would cause its bigger members. Reconciling these and other contradictions will take skill and patience. Do not expect negotiators to make more than the slightest headway in 1999. And there is still a chance, albeit a slim one,

VOLVO

ON THE ONE HAND,

I'M THE KIND OF DAD WHO CHECKS THE COT FOUR TIMES A NIGHT.

ON THE OTHER HAND,

I'M THIS FREE SPIRIT WHO LOVES WAFTING AROUND IN GREAT-LOOKING CARS.

JOIN HANDS.

THE NEW VOLVO S80
THE WORLD'S MOST EXHILARATING SAFE CHOICE

that public outrage in Eastern Europe could derail talks as opponents of EU membership make capital out of the club's double standards.

Poles apart

Of Eastern Europe's leading pack, Poland will remain the economy to watch. By far the biggest market for foreign investors in the region, it has also become the most dynamic. It recently overtook Hungary as the recipient of the most foreign investment in the region, and will continue to pull ahead of its neighbours as its economy motors on. Despite the turmoil in emerging markets, it will remain the region's tiger economy, though that is a label it may not care for any more: the economy will grow impressively in 1999, albeit not quite at the 6-7% rate it has registered in the past several years.

Poland's pervasive Catholic ethic has given the country a sense of morality that, though less than perfect, is sorely missing for so many other ex-communist countries. There is less dishonesty and cronyism than elsewhere. When Polish businessmen behave badly, at least they know it: not something that can always be said of Russians, for example.

The government's coffers will also benefit from a renewed bout of privatisation. Poland still has around 3,000 state-owned firms, employing over two-fifths of all industrial workers, and its poor privatisation record has been masked by high rates of growth.

Accelerated privatisation will be the top priority and the proceeds of such are hoped to be 10 billion zloty ($2.9 billion) in 1999. Among the sales will be the telecoms company TPSA, currently a monopoly; Pekao, Poland's largest bank; and LOT, the national airline. The man to watch is Leszek Balcerowicz, finance minister, deputy prime minister and author of many of the reforms that

THE WORLD IN 1999
Secret files from the communist era in Poland will be declassified. Many Poles will take legal action against named former agents.

New Millennium's Eve

On December 31st 1999, Christian nations all around the world will be in the grip of the biggest celebration in history. The best party will be in London, when the British tax-payer is putting on a dazzling display of fireworks and entertainment centred on the very spot where the millennium will start: the international time line at Greenwich. (It was here that the British, with a theatrical sense of empire, decided that the zero line of longitude should be struck.) The more quiet-minded could join the Pope's prayer vigil at St Peter's Basilica, to contemplate the horrors of the past 1,000 years and the hopes of the next. Both London and Rome will spend much of 1999 on public works in preparation for celebrations throughout 2000. There will be "silence audible" throughout the West from Friday December 24th until Sunday January 2nd. (Britain has a special holiday on both December 31st and January 3rd to keep people away from their offices.) Every airport in the world will be at a standstill on January 1st, as no one will want to fly on a day when the computers might fail. Spare a thought for those to whom this event has less significance: to Muslims for whom it will be the year 1420, to Jews for whom it will be 5760 and for 1.1 billion Chinese for whom it will be the Year of the Rabbit. No excuse for any of them to have a party.

had such a dramatic effect on Poland in the early 1990s.

In fact, 1999 will see the privatisation of much that had previously been considered family silver and kept in state hands, in Poland and elsewhere. In the Czech Republic, for instance, banks that the state has held on to, for fear of losing control over the economy, will go on the block. The Czech economy, once viewed as the region's shining star, has lost its lustre. In 1999 it will start to gleam once more, at least in parts—reaping the ben-

efits of improved financial regulations and of restructuring, forced on companies by a recent currency crisis.

If there is a fear, it is that the countries preparing to join the EU will be thrown off track by the economic turbulence in Asia and Russia. This fear will fade, however, as the reforms that the leading East Europeans have already put in place—such as strengthening their banking systems, making labour practices more flexible and clamping down on cronyism—offer some protection against the storms from the east. The Czechs, Poles and Hungarians have also, encouragingly, ended their reliance on Russia: they send on average only 5% of their exports there, compared with more than 20% in some countries to their east; and over 60% of Poland's trade is now with the EU. Now that the easterners have reoriented their economies westwards, their fate will depend on how immune the EU can remain from global turmoil and on the success of the euro, as much as on their own economies.

This contrasts with the bleaker outlook for the region's laggards (or the "pre-ins" as European Union officials have bizarrely named them). Romania and Bulgaria will continue to struggle with political and economic reforms, and much-needed international capital will give them a wide berth. With a new government, Slovakia, which once had high hopes of joining the EU quickly, will slowly start to throw off its image as the region's black sheep. Things will improve if (and that is a big if) the influence that government favourites have over the economy can be weakened, but either way the damage will be long-lasting.

Even those "outs" with better prospects, such as Latvia and Lithuania, have no chance of getting into the EU much before 2010, though officials in Brussels somewhat disingenuously insist they can overtake the leading pack in the next couple of years if they pull out all the economic stops. Eastern Europe will become a two-speed region, and everyone will know by 1999 just what side of the divide they are on.

Scandinavia's feeling of chill

Greg McIvor   STOCKHOLM

Scandinavians attach special importance to the seasons. The Nordic calendar is sprinkled with festivals to herald spring, celebrate midsummer and mark the onset of winter. In economic terms, 1999 promises to be a year of acute seasonal variation. While some countries, like Sweden and Denmark, will bask in the glow of steady growth, others—notably Norway—face an unwelcome chill.

After a decade of robust expansion, bulging current-account surpluses and low unemployment, Norway's oil-fuelled economy is on course for a bumpy landing. Falling crude-oil prices, a rash of over-generous wage settlements and the government's failure to cool an over-heating onshore economy portend a sharp economic slowdown in 1999.

Until now, Norway has confounded those who predicted dire repercussions from its rejection of European Union membership a few years ago. As the rest of Europe spluttered its way out of recession, Norway has averaged annual growth of 4% since its "No" in 1994. With no foreign debt to service, the state has pumped $17 billion into a Petroleum Fund to preserve the country's lavish welfare benefits once the oil wells run dry sometime in the next hundred years.

Enviable this may be, but ordinary Norwegians will be tightening their belts in 1999 as unemployment and inflation turn upwards. Against this background, Kjell Magne Bondevik's flimsy government coalition looks vulnerable. The three-party alliance, grouping Mr Bondevik's Christian People's Party with the Liberals and Centre, commands a mere 42 of parliament's 165 seats and has struggled to garner sufficient support to enact its policies. To its chagrin, and that of many Norwegians, it has been forced to cut deals with the Progress Party to push legislation through.

The strain is showing. The administration was the target of rare criticism from the central bank last summer for failing to implement a fiscal squeeze which would have cooled the economy before it blew a gasket. Foreign investors whisper that Mr Bondevik is weak and no longer enjoys their confidence.

Few would bet against the Labour Party of former premier Thorbjörn Jagland, by far the largest single parliamentary party, returning to power before

Greg McIvor: Stockholm correspondent for the *Financial Times*.

Europe gives it a tug

the year is out. For Mr Bondevik, who recently took sick leave to cure "depression from overwork", that really would be depressing.

Across the border, neighbouring Sweden and Finland will be spared such economic woes. Having endured deep financial crises at the start of the decade, they will end it with balanced budgets, low inflation and falling—though still high—unemployment.

Whether the benign economic legacy left by Finland's Social Democrat-led five-party coalition will secure a renewed mandate in March's general election is uncertain, though. Paavo Lipponen, the SDP prime minister, faces a determined challenge from the rurally based Centre Party headed by a former prime minister, Esko Aho.

Mr Aho has whipped up support with his criticism of the government's failure to reduce unemployment to single figures. But having unsuccessfully opposed Finland's entry into the European single currency, he will need partners to form a government. And even if he comes out on top in March's ballot, Mr Aho must then woo the influential Conservative Party, a bulwark of Mr Lipponen's pro-European administration for the past four years.

Finland will end 1999 holding the rotating EU presidency, the first time it has done so since joining the union in 1995. Expect it to promote two key areas: reform of EU institutions to give smaller states a greater say in decision-making, and enhanced trading links in the Nordic-Baltic-Russian triangle.

Given Russia's parlous financial state, the latter theme is particularly pertinent. As the only EU country to share a border with Russia, Finland gets understandably fretful over its big neighbour's bouts of instability. The recent collapse of the rouble immediately hit business activity across the border, underlining Finland's increasing reliance on its status as a trading hub for the Russian market.

Unrest in Moscow would doubtless raise calls for the Finns to tie themselves closer to western defence organisations,

The death of duty free

Say goodbye to comforting yourself with your favourite tipple, duty free. The decision to scrap duty-free sales within the EU, intended to be a stepping-stone towards a unified tax system, will take effect from July 1st 1999.

Duty-free shopping was introduced in 1947, and has become an accepted perk of foreign travel. The industry is worth £4.5 billion ($7.7 billion) in the EU alone. Much of the money which is spent at airports goes to subsidise running costs: so expect higher landing charges (paid by you, the passenger) at most European airports in the next few years. In place of duty free, airports will

have more ordinary high-street shops, places to pick up your groceries.

To have duty-free shops for people travelling within a customs union is plainly a nonsense. But abolition will produce its own nonsenses too. A passenger travelling by sea from Portsmouth to Bilbao may face four different charges for a drink, depending on when he orders it, as he sails through British, French, international duty-free and Spanish waters. Authorities worry about a business in "booze cruises" springing up, whereby passengers arrange trips to take advantage of these duty-free waters.

notably NATO and the Western European Union (WEU). Yet enthusiasm for NATO membership or full participation in the WEU remains thin in Finland. This stems partly from a deep-seated reluctance to antagonise Russia and also from the widely held sentiment that neutrality actually works. Or at least it has done so since the second world war.

Elsewhere, one Nordic NATO member—Iceland—will stage a general election before May. The ruling coalition of the Independence Party and smaller Progressive Party has seen its popularity tainted by allegations of financial sleaze. Nevertheless, pollsters suggest the government will again outscore the opposition Social Democrats and gain a fresh term to govern this tiny island.

Social democracy, traditionally strong across Scandinavia, is faring rather better in Sweden and Denmark. Both reelected minority governments. These will spend 1999 grappling with the perennial conundrum of how to improve welfare services without further inflating their bloated public sectors.

The Swedish prime minister, Göran Persson, will face a number of problems. A sharp fall in support for the Social Democrats in last September's general election will make it harder to secure majorities for his policies. During his last government Mr Persson was buttressed by the small Centre Party. Now he has been forced to turn to the anti-EU, former communist Left Party and the Greens. The question is whether their attachment to tax-and-spend economies will prove too much for the fiscally prudent Mr Persson to stomach. In this event, a snap election would loom unless Mr Persson could garner sufficient support among centrist parties. All have so far ruled out any formal co-operation with the Social Democrats.

1999 may be the year when Carl Bildt hands over to a new leader of the Moderates, Sweden's main opposition conservative party. Party leader since 1986 and prime minister between 1991 and 1994, Mr Bildt's interest in domestic politics appeared to wane after a two-year sabbatical as the international peace envoy to Bosnia in the mid-1990s. Aged only 49, he has been tipped for an international job should he decide to call it a day at home.

THE WORLD IN 1999

Watch out for trouble in Dagestan. Militant Islamists in this Russian state want to follow the secessionist lead of their Chechen neighbours.

Things fall apart; the centre cannot hold

Edward Lucas

MOSCOW

1999 will be the year of Russia's disintegration. It will not be complete. It is unlikely to be dramatic. But it will certainly be damaging, at least in the short term. For whatever happens in Moscow, whether Yevgeni Primakov survives, or Boris Yeltsin lives, whether elections are held early, on time, or at all, the big story in Russia will lie outside the Kremlin.

The reason is simple. Russia's central government (federal by name, but not by nature) is so corrupt and incompetent that all the things which help hold big countries together—patriotism, economic self-interest and, ultimately, force—have been weakening catastrophically. 1999 will be the year when regional leaders realise just how powerful they are, and how weak is Moscow.

Disintegration is already further advanced than the West realises. Most of Russia's 89 constituent parts have passed local laws which contradict, sometimes flagrantly, the Russian constitution. Their elected leaders already enjoy far more legitimacy in the public eye than the squabbling cronies and has-beens who dominate political life in the capital. In large chunks of Russia, the centre is at most a nuisance, in some cases all but irrelevant.

Russia's disintegration is driven not by nationalism, but by economics. When the central government is rendering the

Edward Lucas: Russia correspondent for *The Economist*.

currency worthless, extorting unfair taxes, confiscating export revenues and strangling imports, greater economic autonomy looks like the only solution.

The immediate effects will be bad. The dead hand of the centre will be replaced by a no less pernicious bunch of meddlers in regional government. One effect of 1998's financial crisis has been to speed up the balkanisation of Russia's internal market. Once a few local bosses start, for example, banning the export of locally produced food, others lose out if they do not follow suit. Why should Omsk send things to Tomsk, if only valueless roubles come back in return?

Trade between Russia's regions will therefore plunge—at least until they hit on a stable, trusted currency in which to do business. That is hardly likely to be the rouble, and the planned coupons and currencies which some regions have been planning look equally unattractive substitutes. How much would a Urals franc be worth in Rostov-on-Don, or a Saratov mark in Perm? Not a lot, at least at first. Eventually, trade will have to be cleared in dollars or euros, or even a newly stabilised rouble. But that will take time. Meanwhile, the Kremlin's tax revenues and importance will shrivel even further.

What will the centre do? Not a lot. The sinews of power are withered. The subsidies that Moscow pays to most regions have been devalued. Mr Primakov is trying to bring regional leaders into his government. That is splendid for them, less so for the centre's ability to act decisively. Last autumn's collapse has also loosened Moscow's chokehold on the financial system. The handful of banks with a nationwide presence have lost any credibility. Why transfer money through the centre if it risks being stolen? The collapse in the Kremlin's creditworthiness does the same for foreign loans.

The use of force looks ever more unlikely—what local soldier or policeman will risk death to restore the Kremlin's rule? And any appeal by the centre to Russians' national feelings will rouse nothing more than a cynical shrug.

Yet foreign invasion, albeit of a peaceful and benevolent kind, is exactly what Russia's regions should want. Foreign governments and companies already find it easier to deal with regional authorities than central government. Of course, there is greed and incompetence but there is also competition. Stroppiness or sticky fingers among local leaders mean that investment, or aid, goes elsewhere. Competition between regions will be the single most powerful force for better government. It will also bring a simplification of Russia's complicated structure. For small, impoverished bits of the country, cosying up to one of Russia's dozen or so rich regions is a better bet than hoping for help from the centre. Expect some mergers and acquisitions.

The next phase will be a clearer political engagement by the outside world. Foreign governments are already aware that they concentrated too much on the "centre" in the past. Now they are busy chatting up regional leaders, such as the go-ahead Vladimir Prusak in Novgorod, whose region is home to a promising cluster of new western factories.

For all the Kremlin's squawks, nothing is more natural. After all, foreign states dealing with Germany take the Bavarian government seriously; in the United States the governors of California and Texas are considerably more powerful and important than plenty of politicians in Washington, DC. Expect a crop of new consulates, and plenty of high-level visits to and fro as the world starts rethinking its political map of Russia.

And what will that map look like? Clearly, industrial countries neighbouring Russia, such as Japan and the United States in the far east, or Scandinavia in Russia's north-west, will be ever more heavily engaged with their next-door regions, both in trade and investment, and in strengthening democracy and civil society. Russia's core, the cold muddy places a long way from anywhere, risks

THE WORLD IN 1999

Russia will have hyper-inflation: one way to wipe out bad debts. 100% a year. Who said 200%?

being neglected.

That is a pity. Without the friendship of the outside world, or any restraining hand from the centre, some of Russia's new semi-independent regions will be pretty nasty places. The corrupt, lawless and impoverished Maritime Territory, in Russia's far east, is an ominous example. And there is the danger of ugly conflicts. These will not be full-scale wars—Russians' national feeling is still too strong. But there will be arguments about infrastructure ("I've got the pipeline, you've got the oil") which will be fatal for business confidence, if not for actual lives.

Most worryingly, these new games take place amid many dangerous toys—

Yeltsin's not needed anymore

tens of thousands of nuclear weapons, and a dozen or so rusty nuclear reactors. Keeping them safe and well-looked after as the country re-arranges itself is much more than Russia's crippled central government can manage. Outsiders have already put money and effort into this. More will be needed.

The probable decline in Russia's wealth in 1999 will be around 10%. Its banks are, without exception, bust. Its stockmarkets, down to about one-tenth of the levels reached early in 1998, are dead in the water. It will take far longer than the coming 12 months for Russia to win back the confidence of western investors or the IMF. So expect yet another bleak and miserable year.

Ireland

Exultant over the Northern Ireland peace process and flush with new-found affluence, the Irish have never felt better about themselves.

Ulster's peaceful settlement, the most important issue in the politics of the Republic, has advanced further than most people dared hope. Despite atrocities in 1998, appalling even by Northern Ireland's standards, the normalisation of life in the province will continue apace in 1999, with unionist opposition to the settlement waning and ultra-extremist republicans being further marginalised. The Irish government will not shrink from using tough new powers to mop up any remaining militants, most of whom are based in the Republic. Relations with Britain, uneasy since independence in 1921, will continue to improve.

At home, the prospect of further political graft being unearthed threatens the stability of the centre-right coalition of Fianna Fail and the small Progressive Democrat Party. The country's decade-old "social partnership" between government, employers and trade unions, universally accredited with moderate wage increases and enduring competitiveness, comes up for renewal in mid-1999. Negotiations will be difficult but ultimately successful, with labour representatives wresting more generous wage deals and further tax cuts from employers and government respectively.

Economic growth will slow in 1999 to just below 7%—still leaving most other countries emerald with envy. Slowdowns in Ireland's two largest markets, Britain and America, will halt the dizzying increases in Irish exports. But domestic demand will remain strong as EMU-induced real-interest rates drop below 1%.

Although this raises fears of inflation, the Irish are staying cool. An appreciating euro and deflationary pressures globally should keep inflation under control.

KEY INDICATORS			
	1997	1998	1999
Real GDP growth (%)	9.8	9.2	6.9
Inflation (average) (%)	1.4	3.2	3.4
Budget balance (% of GDP)	0.9	2.0	1.9
Current account (% of GDP)	2.7	2.0	0.6
Short-term interest rate (av; %)	6.1	5.1	4.3
Exchange rate I£:$ (av)	1.52	1.40	1.43
Exchange rate DM:I£ (av)	2.63	2.50	2.48

E·I·U EIU COUNTRY ANALYSIS AND FORECASTING

Now there's an easier way to accumulate miles.

Through the Star Alliance™ network and our partner companies, our Mileage Plus® programme offers more ways to accumulate miles than any other frequent flyer programme. Put it together with the most widebodies, a new business seat, freshest on-board air and over 250 worldwide destinations, and you'll understand why people who fly for a living fly United.

America worries itself

Morton Kondracke

WASHINGTON, DC

America, by its nature optimistic and self-confident, will have an unusually anxious 1999. There will be three major worries. Will the economy slow sharply? Will the presidency be so weakened by scandal as to paralyse American leadership? And will the troubles of the world—financial and political—all pitch up on America's doorstep looking for expensive and difficult solutions?

Most of these concerns will not cause deep furrows on the brows of the public. None of the potential troubles facing America is thought to have anything to do with the "fundamentals". Fifteen years of corporate conditioning and ten years of federal fiscal discipline have given the country the strongest economy in the world. America is the world's only superpower. Social indices that had been worsening ever since the cultural revolution of the 1960s—including crime rates, education test scores and the out-of-wedlock birthrate—have begun to level off, even improve. Public opinion polls show that record percentages of people, more than 65%, believe that the country is "on the right track". Support for Bill Clinton is strong despite the scandals surrounding him, as is support for Congress. Consumer confidence has dipped slightly as a result of stockmarket volatility, but not seriously.

And yet, there is a rough road immediately ahead. With only two years left in his second term, President Clinton would be a waning leader even if he were not beset by scandal. Resourceful as he has proved to be in many crises in the past, the impeachment process is of quite a different order.

Given the strong showing made by the Democrats in the November elections, an impeachment itself is most unlikely. But that will not stop the process being debilitating. The House Judiciary Committee, which is controlled by the Republicans, has begun hearing witnesses and considering articles of impeachment for referral to the full House

More hello than goodbye

of Representatives. The end of 1998 has been set as its target date for a vote on whether to proceed to impeachment. This deadline will probably slip and the full House will not vote until early in 1999, after the new Congress has convened. Mr Clinton has made it quite clear that he will not voluntarily resign. The most likely end-game will be the brokering of some form of official apology from, or reprimand to, the president.

The presidential scandal has proved a major cultural drama as well as a political one, with leading liberal intellectuals representing it in epic dimensions. In the pages of the *New Yorker* and the *New York Times*, writers have likened Mr Clinton's nemesis, the independent counsel Kenneth Starr, to a Taliban mullah and a Salem witch-hunter.

The public seems little agitated. Around 60% of Americans oppose impeachment but until he has this matter behind him, President Clinton will be distracted from his other duties, although in the past he has proved a ge-

nius at handling congressional negotiations, foreign diplomacy and scandal litigation all at once.

There are other problems. In 1999, Washington will try to fix the long-term solvency of Social Security. The nation's retirement programmes are projected to be in deficit around 2010 and will be unable to sustain current benefit standards for the giant baby-boom generation that begins reaching retirement age in 2001. Until the stockmarket began gyrating, a consensus had been developing around the idea of reforming Social Security by partially "privatising" it, either by government investment in the equity markets or by creating individual savings accounts. That consensus has been shaken by market instability.

Having failed to enact significant tax cuts in 1998 because of a threatened presidential veto, Republicans will use their power in Congress to get the job done in 1999. The task will prove easier if the economy softens. Debate will swirl around the merits of a "flat tax" and

---

Morton Kondracke: executive editor of *Roll Call*.

sales-tax substitutes for the current graduated income tax. No big policy changes can be made while a Democrat is in the White House.

Other issues on the Washington agenda include a rewrite of so-called "freedom to farm" legislation which has left American agriculture in crisis amid price deflation; a revisiting of "fast-track" trade authority for the president; and Republican proposals for increased defence spending. It is becoming dogma among Republicans that the military is being asked to do too many overseas jobs with too few resources.

Though the cold war is over, there is a world of trouble that the United States remains involved in. Some crises carry the threat of military involvement. Iraq will continue to play cat-and-mouse with the Clinton administration. North Korea teeters on the brink of collapse. Washington is constantly concerned that the Pyongyang regime will launch a desperate attack on South Korea or collapse into anarchy. Iran, thought to be showing sufficient moderation to be worthy of serious diplomacy, nevertheless continues working on weapons of mass destruction and is still deemed a threat to

American interests. And Russia's inability to establish a stable economy threatens a chaos that will undoubtedly enmesh Washington.

Watch out for a new worry: the conviction that the United States cannot remain immune from foreign terrorism. So far, due to the foresight of the intelligence services and a fair amount of good fortune, it has been all but untouched. Those who follow these things predict that it is only a matter of time before a terrorist group has access to chemical or biological weapons capable of wreaking havoc on an American city.

Whoa, there!

Zanny Minton-Beddoes

WASHINGTON, DC

For much of the 1990s America enjoyed a "Goldilocks" economy: hot enough to keep unemployment falling and profits high, but not so sizzling that inflation sparked. Buoyed by this magic combination, stock prices and consumer confidence reached unprecedented highs. That will all change in 1999, when Americans will be rudely reminded that Goldilocks was, after all, a fairy tale. Buffeted by turmoil abroad and tetchy financial markets at home, the economy will slow sharply. But only if American consumers lurch from irrational exuberance to an equally exaggerated pessimism will the country face a recession. And only if policymakers show an extraordinary ineptitude will the recession be a bad one. For America will be well placed to deal with the downturn.

Slower economic growth in 1999 was always to be expected. With unemployment at historic lows, America is simply running out of the workers required to fuel the 3.5% growth rates of recent years. A return to trend growth rates (2-2.5%), or even slightly below, would be a welcome relief. Unfortunately, 1999's slowdown will go much beyond that.

One big drag will come from the trade deficit. With much of Asia in economic depression and Latin America facing sharp recession, the demand for American exports will plummet. Imports from countries with cheap currencies will remain

Zanny Minton-Beddoes: Washington correspondent, *The Economist*.

strong. As a result, America's current-account deficit will balloon, perhaps reaching $300 billion in 1999, almost twice its level of 1997. This will hurt manufacturers of every stripe—from Coca-Cola to

Caterpillar. Although emerging markets usually provide only a small share of big corporations' profits, they helped underpin rosy forecasts. With recession across the globe, expect disappointing earnings and headline-grabbing lay-offs from big multinationals.

The rest of Main Street will also hunker down, as America's firms finally end the capital-spending spree that has characterised the expansion so far. Encouraged by easy access to finance and strong earnings, business investment rose by an average of 10% a year in real terms between 1993 and mid-1998.

Several factors will ensure that capital spending is, at best, flat in 1999. The prospects of a slowdown and lower levels of capacity use will limit firms' incentives for further investment. Even if America is spared a full-blown credit crunch, finance will be more expensive and harder to come by for all but the most blue-chip corporate borrowers. Declining profits will mean that firms have fewer internal resources to fund their capital spending. And then there is the millennium bug. Early in 1999, the Y2K phenomenon may buoy capital spending as laggard firms still race to get their computer systems in order. Towards the end of the year it will dampen investment as firms delay their spending until the millennium's uncertainties are over.

America's shoppers, fortunately, will do no such thing. The man from Peoria will react to the increasing economic gloom with prudence but with none of the panic that has afflicted the

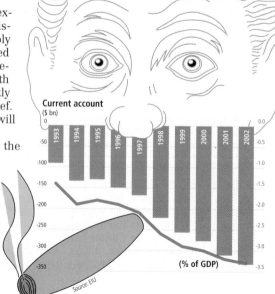

Federal government debt (% of GDP)

Unemployment rate (%)

Current account ($ bn)

(% of GDP)

Source: EIU

denizens of Wall Street. Consumer confidence will wane in 1999 but, judged by historical standards, will remain on the high side. The growth in consumer spending will fall back in line with growth in incomes. The saving rate will stabilise and perhaps rise slightly. But it will not shoot up. Most spending is done by the affluent, whose piggy banks—despite recent stockmarket losses—have still posted remarkable gains during the 1990s. The threat of joblessness will be too small to affect consumer demand, for even with a sharp slowdown the unemployment rate will barely top 5%. Throughout this decade Americans' appetite for consumption has exceeded expectations, and 1999 will be no different.

Led by Alan Greenspan, a man concerned about his place in history, the Federal Reserve will slash interest rates vigorously in 1999. With inflation regarded as a distant threat, the key short-term interest rate will be below 4% by the end of the year. This will shore up the financial markets.

It will, however, mean a more volatile and generally weaker dollar, as the credibility-conscious European Central Bank follows a stricter monetary policy than the Federal Reserve, and as investors fret about the size of America's current-account deficit.

1999 will also see much talk of tax cuts. As the economy slows, Republicans especially will be pushing hard to boost consumer demand through lower taxes. Although the Clinton administration will continue with the rallying cry of "Save Social Security First", it will be keen to boost the economy in the year before a presidential election.

Given America's labyrinthine budgetary system, it will be autumn 1999 before any tax cuts are enacted. Add this fiscal stimulus to the accommodating monetary policy and America will end 1999 with all the preconditions in place for a sharp bounce-back in confidence and spending.

Doing the unthinkable

Adrian Wooldridge   LOS ANGELES

Someone's paying attention to me at last

In one of her more cerebral moments Monica Lewinsky sent Bill Clinton a lengthy memo on educational reform. Her views on education are frankly rather less interesting than her ideas about Altoid mints. (For the record, the girl from Beverly Hills worries that teachers earn so little money that they can hardly keep themselves out of poverty.) But Ms Lewinsky was at least right about one big thing: that education is now firmly at the top of the policy agenda in the United States. If health care captured everyone's attention in 1994, and welfare reform in 1996, education will sweep all before it in 1999.

And not before time. America's schools (as opposed to its universities) are in a dismal state. The United States spends more per pupil than most advanced countries. But its schoolchildren get only middling results in international tests of scholastic ability—well below their peers in much poorer countries such as Hungary and South Korea. The United States is dedicated to the ideal of equality of opportunity. But its educational system is more corrupted by class than its rivals in Europe. In Ms Lewinsky's alma mater, Beverly Hills High, the most urgent question is providing enough parking spaces for the pupils' cars; in South-Central, a few miles away, the schools look as if they have been parachuted in from the third world.

Inner-city schools are little more than

Zero heroes

There is a new trend in American social policy which someone in 1999 might have the courage to debunk, if not the ability to stop: "zero tolerance". When you do not want something in your town—say, prostitution—you don't just restrain it but insist on stamping it out entirely. Sounds sensible? In fact, it disguises a move towards ever tighter control in the land of the free. The academic justification for this chilling absolute is the "broken window

theory"—the idea that small disorders lead inexorably to larger ones. But it also reflects a deep strain of puritanical bossiness in American life, a bossiness that is being fervently embraced by the very baby boomers who spent their youths flouting social conventions.

The mayor of New York, Rudolph Giuliani, has set the pace in this drive to turn the United States into a giant version of Singapore, with campaigns against everything from pan-handlers to

sex shops. But he has found plenty of imitators across the country. The result has been an extraordinary flowering of petty restraints on people's freedoms—from curfews on teenagers (which are now in force in 276 cities) to a ban on smoking in bars in California.

Zero tolerance is one of those classic ideas that seems so plausible in small quantities but is, in fact, fatal as an overdose. Expect a revolt to start some time in the coming year.

One for the history books

The world's foremost sportsman will stop playing in 1999. Basketball, a game which can bring Chicago to a halt and have millions of people who have never been to America glued to their television sets, will lose its greatest star at the end of next season: Michael Jordan. Mr Jordan, whom Chinese students once voted "the greatest man in the world" and who has won the championship for the Chicago Bulls six times, will be hanging up his shoes after the summer. "His Airness" is coming down to earth, and the Chicago Bulls, the NBA and Nike, a sportsgear company which has a $70m contract with Mr Jordan, will all feel the bump. Basketball will suffer. The NBA has focused its marketing strategy on star individuals—mainly Mr Jordan—rather than teams. Although young ball-players like Grant Hill of the Detroit Pistons and Kobe Bryant of the LA Lakers have been groomed as heir apparents, every pundit agrees: "Michael Jordan they ain't." The NBA must hope that Mr Bryant and the stylish LA Lakers come to the fore this season to add razzle to the league.

Sadly for the Chicago Bulls, Mr Jordan's retirement will spur a further exodus of front-line players like Scottie Pippen and Dennis Rodman. Without them the Bulls will be in trouble before 1999 is out. The city of Chicago can console itself by going ahead with plans to rename Lakeshore Drive, the highway along Lake Michigan, "Michael Jordan Drive".

Jordan puts the ball away

factories of failure: soul-destroying places where violence and drug dealing are routine and more than half the pupils drop out before graduating. Giving the poor such a dismal start in life was a risky enough policy in the days when there were plenty of blue-collar jobs to go round. But now that these jobs are being exported or mechanised out of existence it is a policy that guarantees the creation of a permanent and combustible underclass.

The good news is that the American political establishment has woken up to this dire situation. Throughout the country education dominated November's congressional races as it had never done before. And across the political spectrum candidates agreed that the only way to cure America's ailing schools was to give parents more choice.

Time to choose

Twenty years ago school choice was a creed that was confined to a few right-wing think-tanks and economic departments. The common high school was one of the great shibboleths of that United American society—along with cheap petrol and picket fences. Now school choice has gone mainstream. The first Democrats to break ranks with the teachers' unions (who are all implacably opposed to change) were black activists such as Polly Williams who refused to understand why the likes of Bill Clinton and Al Gore would patronise private schools while their children were trapped in ghettoes. Now they have been joined by mainstream Democrats.

The school-choice movement has also built up huge practical momentum. Seven million American children—a fifth of the total—have abandoned their neighbourhood schools for private schools or alternative public schools. And Gallup polls consistently show that two-thirds of the American public support giving parents greater choice over where their children go to school. In a society based on consumer choice people are increasingly unwilling to allow bureaucrats to force their children to go to inferior schools.

School choice takes two forms. The first emphasises the importance of increasing the variety of schools available through the creation of magnet and charter schools. Magnet schools, which emphasise particular subjects such as science or the performing arts, are now well established, educating more than 1.2m pupils nationwide, 60% of them from ethnic minorities. A quarter of all American children now have at least one magnet school in their district.

Charter schools are both newer and more radical. Their relative freedom from government control means that they can pursue a wide variety of approaches to education from ethno-centrism to tight discipline. But it also means that they can sometimes be captured by extremists. (One such school, in Washington, DC, was eventually closed down after the principal assaulted a journalist.) More than a dozen states, including California and Massachusetts, have sanctioned the creation of magnet schools. And President Clinton has proclaimed that he would like to see 3,000 of them in existence by the end of the century.

The second form of school choice is even more radical: vouchers that give parents the power to shop around among schools. Vouchers are anathema to both the teachers' unions and the Democratic establishment. (A couple of years ago the AFL-CIO spent millions of dollars to defeat a move to introduce vouchers in California.) But they are making converts by the day—particularly among the ethnic minorities that get the worst deals from America's schools. Support for vouchers is now de rigueur among minority activists in cities such as Los Angeles and Milwaukee.

Milwaukee has the country's most advanced voucher programme, with parents able to use their vouchers in private as well as public schools; other important pioneers are Cleveland and Wisconsin. But the movement is rapidly spreading to the rest of the country. There are more than 56 privately funded programmes around the country—and more are being added every month. When 1,000 scholarships were created in Washington, DC, 7,500 schoolchildren—a tenth of those enrolled in city schools—applied for them.

The voucher movement notched up some big successes in 1998, and could notch up even more in 1999. In June the Wisconsin Supreme Court handed down a landmark ruling that allows parents to use vouchers in parochial (or religious) schools—just as students can use public scholarships in religious universities such as Notre Dame. But the most important success of all is the pile of evidence showing that voucher schools are both more successful and more popular than their public-school competitors.

THE WORLD IN 1999

Big law firms will merge—across the Atlantic and within Europe. Fewer large firms, just as many large fees.

Who's in training for the next race?

Charles Cook

WASHINGTON, DC

The incubation period for the 2000 presidential campaign is already under way. The enormous fundraising demands on presidential hopefuls will force them to make their final "go-or-no-go" decisions during the first months of 1999. Potential candidates must weigh their chances of victory against the costs of running: an inhumanly exhaustive campaign schedule, endless grovelling for campaign donations and intrusive investigations into their personal lives. Campaign advisers grill their would-be contenders on whether they meet the *Washington Post* test, meaning whether they are willing to have anything and everything they have ever said or done splashed across the front pages of the nation's newspapers.

Those choosing to run cannot tarry in making up their minds: maintaining a winning pace means raising $20m during the calendar year 1999. The campaign kicks off with the Iowa Caucus in February 2000. But that will be only a few days before the New Hampshire primary election. This schedule means that candidates cannot rely on a bandwagon: money must be in the bag from the start.

Democrat hopefuls

Vice-President Albert Gore is the front-runner. From the beginning, the "inevitability" of Mr Gore's nomination and his chances of winning a general election were always contingent upon the success of the Clinton-Gore White House. President Bill Clinton's ethical problems and the spectre of a new independent counsel investigating the 1995-96 fundraising efforts by Mr Clinton and Mr Gore make things more difficult. He still remains the man to beat and a justifiably strong candidate.

The House Minority Leader, Richard Gephardt of Missouri has traditionally had strong ties to organised labour. This would be Mr Gephardt's second bid for the nomination. He ran in 1988, defeating the Massachusetts governor, Michael Dukakis, in the Iowa Caucus.

Senator Robert Kerrey of Nebraska is a winner of the Medal of Honor, the military's top award for courage under fire for his valour in a battle during the Vietnam war that cost him a leg. Recently he has been showing sure signs of making his second bid for the presidency. Mr Kerrey ran a rather disorganised and unfocused campaign in 1992, losing to Mr Clinton, but seems to be better prepared this time around. Whether he can raise enough money is doubtful. Though certainly left-of-centre, Mr Kerrey is very much a political maverick. He is an uneven performer—at times inspiring, other times distracted.

Senator John Kerry of Massachusetts is a classic left-leaning Democrat, though he has strayed in recent years on some education-related issues, embracing competency standards for teachers. Like Robert Kerrey of Nebraska, this Kerry is a decorated Vietnam war veteran, but on his return made a name for himself as a leader in the veterans-against-the-war movement. Although Mr Kerry is not expected to be able to raise enough contributions to be a potent force in this race, he could be financially viable if he decides to tap the personal fortune of his wife, Teresa Heinz, widow of Senator John Heinz, heir to the ketchup company fortune.

Senator Paul Wellstone of Minnesota is widely considered to be the most liberal member of the Senate. He served as state chairman for Reverend Jesse Jackson's 1988 presidential campaign. The former political-science professor pledged that he would serve only two Senate terms; he is scheduled to depart in 2002. Mr Wellstone has no chance of winning the nomination but his presence on the ballot in the early primaries and caucuses would undoubtedly syphon off liberal votes. His effort is a quixotic one.

Former Senator Bill Bradley made the transformation from professional basketball player to one of the more thoughtful members of the Senate but did not seek a fourth six-year term in 1996. Since that time, Mr Bradley has been writing, lecturing, travelling and contemplating a presidential bid. Aloof and an outsider even when a member of the Senate club.

Republican hopefuls

Governor George W. Bush of Texas is the front-runner. The son of former President George H.W. Bush (he is technically not a "junior"), the younger Bush was elected governor of Texas in the 1994 Republican landslide, unseating a popular incumbent Democrat. He accumulated a respectable fortune in the oil business and is a part owner in the Texas Rangers' major-league baseball franchise. He is considered more conservative than his father and more of a Texan. He has an appeal that seems to go down as well in corporate boardrooms and country clubs as among shopkeepers and farmers. Although he is far from being a live-wire, he has a knack of garnering people's trust: a nice man, not a particularly interesting one. Mr Bush can be expected to attract considerably more campaign contributions than any of his rivals and to draw on a base of his father's supporters in all 50 states. He must keep a close eye on a large crowd of other potential contenders.

Steve Forbes is a multi-millionaire publisher. By most accounts, Mr Forbes will be a far better candidate than he was four years ago, and seems to have learned from the mistakes he made in his ill-fated 1996 bid. He is smoother and more articulate, and espouses a broader message that goes beyond the flat tax. He has moved to the right on abortion in an effort to assuage the concerns of the right-to-life wing of the party. Most important, Mr Forbes has the personal financial resources to outspend any of the other candidates.

Former governor of Tennessee, Lamar Alexander, is another veteran of the 1996 campaign. Mr Alexander possesses a focus and strong discipline that are extraordinarily important in this race, but lacks charisma. Mr Alexander can raise money at an impressive rate, despite dismal rhetorical skills.

Former secretary of labour, Elizabeth Dole, is the wife of Republican standard-bearer, Robert Dole, and a woman of brains and charm. Mrs Dole heads the American Red Cross. She has been sending mixed signals about her intentions. While saying that she has little interest in running, her travel schedule seems to incorporate an inordinate number of visits to Iowa and New Hampshire. Mrs Dole's impressive speech on behalf of her husband at the 1996 Republican National Convention will long be remembered for its effectiveness, putting her on all the lists of potential heavyweights in the party. Mrs Dole is also the only prominent woman from either major party mentioned as a possible presidential candidate.

Expect a dark horse to emerge from the socially and religiously conservative wing of the Republican Party: a spoiler rather than a serious candidate. Although **former Vice-President Dan Quayle** starts out ahead and is surely the best known, **Senator John Ashcroft of Missouri** is energetically courting activists in this faction. **Gary Bauer**, head of the Family Research Council, is another important figure in the right-to-life and social conservative movement, with considerable grassroots support there. **Allen Keyes,** an eloquent former state department official and outspoken anti-abortion activist, may also run. The Republicans remain open to an ambush from any of these.

Charles E. Cook, Jr: editor of the *Cook Political Report*, and political analyst for the *National Journal*.

Eyes wide open

Adrian Wooldridge

LOS ANGELES

The empire strikes back and back and back

This will be the year of the prequel. "Star Wars: Episode One", which is made by Lucasfilm and distributed by Fox, is scheduled to open on Memorial day (May 21st 1999), exactly 22 years after the original "Star Wars".

Memorial day is traditionally the time when Hollywood makes its biggest splash, though the lame performance of "Godzilla" in 1998 showed that nothing is certain. But "Star Wars" was one of the most successful films of all time, turning phrases such as "feel the force" into part of the language. Rival studios are already steering well clear of Memorial day for the launch of their own offerings. Universal Pictures will release its big film, "The Mummy", about a French legionnaire who awakens an Egyptian mummy while on an archaeological dig, at least two weeks before the "Star Wars" frenzy begins.

George Lucas will not be the only director recycling old ideas. Warner Brothers has bagged the July 4th weekend slot—taken by "Armageddon" in 1998, "Men in Black" in 1997 and "Independence Day" in 1996—for its comedy-action hybrid, "The Wild, Wild West", a big-money version of the 1960s television series. "Runaway Bride" will reunite the team behind "Pretty Woman". "Austin Powers II" will re-spoof classic James Bond movies.

Walt Disney's annual animated offering will be "Tarzan", featuring songs by Phil Collins; Paramount/MTV will release a sequel to Beavis & Butthead; and Miramax is recycling a recent Japanese hit, "The Princess Monoke", which is now the biggest-selling movie of all time in Japan, with 12m viewers and ¥11 billion ($90m) in receipts.

At the more mature end of the market, the most anticipated film of the year is Stanley Kubrick's "Eyes Wide Shut", a Warner Brothers thriller starring Tom Cruise and Nicole Kidman. This inordinately delayed film is shrouded in secrecy, with senior executives at Warner Brothers unsure what it is about. Rumours suggest that it is a psychosexual thriller about two married psychiatrists who cheat on each other with their own patients.

Other serious films that will be released in 1999 include Spike Lee's "The Summer of Sam", about the "Son of Sam" murders in New York city in the summer of 1977; Michael Mann's "Man of the People", featuring Al Pacino as the tobacco executive turned whistle-blower, Jeffrey Wigand; and Martin Scorsese's "Bringing Out the Dead", in which Nicholas Cage plays a paramedic, based in New York's Hell's Kitchen, who has visions of the patients who have died in his care. Tom Hanks will also try to repeat his success in "Saving Private Ryan" in "The Green Mile", about Death Row inmates in a southern prison.

Adrian Wooldridge: West Coast correspondent for *The Economist*.

Canada's discomfort

William Thorsell

TORONTO

Canada is a member of the G7, and a leading light in a host of other international organisations. It sits on the edge of world events, in good seats to be sure, but seldom on the stage. Its population, after all, is less than that of California and it generates considerably less GDP per head. That Canada's pretensions exceed its ability to shape events will be all too apparent in 1999.

It will be a year when Canada takes its cue from external events, not internal politics. With more than 35% of its GDP generated by trade, Canada's economy depends to an unusual degree on market conditions in other countries (primarily the United States, which accounts for 80% of its trade). Commodities also constitute a good part of that trade, so a combination of foreign-market demand and external commodity prices determines much of what happens to Canada's economy, and thus its politics.

As the year turns, Canada will still be benefiting from the economic expansion in the United States that has pulled Canada along, with a lag of about three years, since 1992. The lag is explained by Canada's structural transition to free trade with the United States after 1989, and very tight fiscal and monetary policies in the early 1990s, adopted to fight large budget deficits and inflation.

As a consequence, the real after-tax income of Canadians declined over the first five years of the decade, showing signs of upward movement only in 1997. Unemployment fell below 10% for the first time in the decade only in 1998, as GDP growth reached 3% for the second year. And then came the external problem of world commodities. The fall in oil

William Thorsell: editor-in-chief of Toronto's *Globe and Mail*.

SIEBEL SOLUTIONS:
GLOBAL SALES EQUALS
GLOBAL SUCCESS

Sigrid Peterson
Vice President of Sales Process
APL

"APL's WORLDWIDE SALES FORCE NEEDED A POWERFUL CUSTOMER INFORMATION SYSTEM TO MANAGE OUR GLOBAL ACCOUNTS SUCCESSFULLY."

APL, a leader in container transportation and logistics services, wanted to increase its team selling efforts in order to win and manage global accounts. That's why APL chose Siebel, the leader in Enterprise Relationship Management software. With Siebel Sales Enterprise™, APL sales professionals from around the world share up-to-the-minute customer information that spans languages and time zones. The results? Truly collaborative selling and incredible productivity gains. To learn how Siebel can drive your global success, call +44 (0)01784 898403 or visit us at www.siebel.com.

SIEBEL
Sales • Marketing • Customer Service

SAN MATEO • CHICAGO • BOSTON • NEW YORK • LOS ANGELES • LONDON • SYDNEY • PARIS • MUNICH • TOKYO • MEXICO CITY

prices predated the Asian flu, which contributed to broader declines in metals, wood, paper and agricultural products. Canada is a big exporter of oil and natural gas, as well as the more traditional commodities, and declines in both prices and demand will hurt throughout 1999. British Columbia and Alberta will be especially affected because they are commodity-reliant economies dependent more than most Canadian provinces on Asian markets.

The offsetting wild card is the Canadian dollar, which has fallen dramatically against the American dollar in the latter half of the year (from more than 72 American cents to less than 65). Attrib-

uted to the general global "flight to quality" as well as declining commodity prices, the erosion in Canada's currency against the American dollar will help to sustain its share of exports to the United States.

Although the Bank of Canada came under increasing pressure to respond to the currency's devaluation with tighter monetary policy, it desisted until the autumn in the face of already high real interest rates, 1% inflation, moderate economic growth, reasonable capacity utilisation and high unemployment. Moreover, the Canadian federal government will run a budget surplus this year of perhaps 1% of GDP, based on rising tax

Canada's brain drain to the United States will accelerate. High taxes will push the best people south.

burdens built into an income-tax system that is not effectively indexed. Although some provinces—Ontario in particular—are cutting tax burdens as they move into balanced budgets, Canada's fiscal policy is still generally restrictive.

Despite an economic buffeting from abroad, Canada's politics will continue placidly. The prime minister, Jean Chrétien, is popular. His liberal government's mandate is modest. Both the official opposition Reform Party and the Conservative Party are lifeless. Mr Chrétien himself is expected to retire within the next 18 months, so a Liberal leadership contest will come to a head in 1999, pitting the finance minister, Paul Martin, against the health minister, Allan Rock, and the Newfoundland premier, Brian Tobin, among others.

Quarrels to come

The most contentious issue facing parliament will be proposals from four of Canada's six major banks to merge into two much larger institutions controlling as much as 70% of conventional bank deposits nationally. The banks' case for bigness, which includes an appeal to nationalist sentiment against foreign competitors, has played poorly in public opinion, which sees plenty of bigness already and believes that fewer banks will mean less competition and service.

Domestic political debate will centre on how to spend the budget surplus accrued in 1998, the first for 30 years. The surplus was achieved by a combination of tough spending cuts and sharply rising tax burdens, so pressures to restore both higher spending and lower taxes are vocal. Faced with growing volatility in world markets, however, the finance minister chose to devote all of last year's surplus to reducing Canada's federal debt.

The chronic and enervating question of Quebec separatism is never far off the agenda. In August 1998 the Supreme Court of Canada ruled that Canada would have a constitutional obligation to negotiate secession with Quebec if a request were made, based on a credible referendum result. The re-election in November of the separatist Parti Québécois under its charismatic leader, Lucien Bouchard, would give the next referendum campaign (expected by 2003) a much harder edge as a consequence. Some things just never seem to go away.

Northern talent

She has just won two grammies and sold over ten million copies of her latest album. Her recent tour of women in music sold out across America. But Sarah McLachlan will not be joining Joni Mitchell, Leonard Cohen and Neil Young in the gallery of Canadian musicians whom everyone confuses for Americans.

The coming crop of Canadian stars (Sarah McLachlan's international success in 1999 will follow Alanis Morissette's in 1997 and Celine Dion's and Bryan Adams's before that) is much more closely identified with the country that nurtured their talents. Canadian music has truly become a world star.

Government protection and promotion of the domestic music industry—as well as the benevolent cultural nationalism of institutions such as Much Music, Canada's answer to MTV—have transformed the Canadian music scene. What was a talent-feed for the United States in the 1970s is now a powerful and saleable brand. In fact, Celine Dion's new French-language album shows that the Canadians' ability to produce "pop without borders" transcends the American nexus.

"Canadian content" regulations insist that at least 35% of music played on prime-time radio must be Canadian. The government's arm's-length agency funding of the industry will increase by 50% in the coming year.

So watch out in 1999 for the following names to go international: a rock band, The Tragically Hip; The Barenaked Ladies; a soul-jazz diva, Diana Krall; a folk singer, Loreena McKennit. It will be a boom year for Canada's growing band of singing stars.

And just in the wings is David Foster, the master Canadian Hollywood producer of soft rock, who bathes the whole world in forgettable warming ballads incongruously rooted in the land of ice and snow.

Colour McLachlan Canadian

Making more of your capital doesn't necessarily mean taking more of a risk. As an issuer backed by the Federal Republic of Germany, KfW offers private and institutional investors AAA/Aaa security in a number of interesting **capital market products**. With attractive yields and high liquidity. Let us show you our safe and sound paths to a rewarding investment. **Kreditanstalt für Wiederaufbau.**

KfW WAYS AND MEANS

Palmengartenstrasse 5–9, 60325 Frankfurt am Main, Germany,
Tel. ++49 / 69 / 74 31-22 22, Fax ++49 / 69 / 74 31-21 93, Internet: http://www.kfw.de

Many paths lead to capital growth.

We get you there safe and sound.

MICRO-MANAGE.
MACRO-MINE.

A few minutes can mean a difference of thousands of tons in the mining business. But controlling the big picture, today, is often a matter of keystrokes. Komatsu, a world leader in mining hardware, created Komatsu Mining Systems (KMS) to tackle the software end. KMS enables mine operators to lower cost per ton at every step of production.

This total production partnership delivers the operational efficiencies of Modular Mining's DISPATCH® systems, monitoring and managing every aspect of mine operation in real time. Optimizing everything from dispatch and loading to monitoring equipment wear and setting maintenance schedules.

Every detail is backed by Komatsu's full range of mining equipment. Dump trucks, bulldozers and loaders that are world leaders in capacity, speed, reliability and, especially, size. Backed by Komatsu's on-site service, maintenance and local support anywhere in the world.

Not only is KMS optimizing mine productivity today, it's also laying the infrastructure for the potential gains of fully automated mines in the near future. Whether your business is mining, construction or demolition, Komatsu's expertise and equipment, hardware and software, will enhance your operational efficiency by the ton.

Head Office: 2-3-6 Akasaka, Minato-ku, Tokyo 107-8414 Japan. Tel: (03)5561-2617 Fax: (03)3505-9662 www.komatsu.com **KOMATSU**

China's communism, 50 years on

James Miles

China faces one of its most difficult years since it launched its economic reforms 20 years ago. Not only is the country struggling to avoid the financial chaos that has swallowed up many of its neighbours, but it is also trying to implement the most problematic phase of the reform programme, including sweeping lay-offs in the state sector. In October 1999, the Communist Party will celebrate the 50th anniversary of its coming to power in China, but the mood is unlikely to be one of unqualified joy.

Since the death of China's elder statesman, Deng Xiaoping, in February 1997, President Jiang Zemin has scored significant achievements in international diplomacy—overseeing the smooth transition of Hong Kong to Chinese rule and holding the first summit meetings with the United States in nearly a decade. But Mr Jiang's main concern during the year is likely to be affairs at home. These will especially preoccupy his prime minister, Zhu Rongji.

How China handles its economy will be keenly watched around the world. The rest of Asia in particular is looking at China as a bulwark against further financial instability. A sharp devaluation of the currency, the yuan, could destabilise other regional currencies. But the government is also under considerable pressure from domestic exporters to make their goods more competitive by adjusting the yuan's value. With overseas demand contributing a third of China's economic growth in 1997, the arguments of exporters will carry weight.

China has not said how long its promise not to devalue the yuan will remain valid. There are strong political as well as economic incentives for Beijing to maintain the currency's value. High among China's considerations is that de-

James Miles: China analyst for the BBC.

valuation could jeopardise the Hong Kong dollar and thereby undermine the goodwill that Beijing has built up in the territory since the handover. But continuing volatility in the region, including uncertainty over the Japanese yen, will make it difficult for Beijing to hold out.

In 1999, the impact on China of the Asian financial crisis will become in-

Zhu Rongji has his lighter side

creasingly evident. Funds from Japan, a major source of loans for China's infrastructure projects, will diminish sharply. Foreign investment will decline, particularly from the rest of Asia—a big problem in a country where nearly 30% of all investment involves foreign capital. Exports will decline too as the products of other Asian countries become more competitive thanks to devaluations. And cheaper imports from other Asian countries will present new dangers to some of

China's industries, for example the ailing steel sector, one of the pillars of the country's economy.

If there is any time that Beijing could do without such problems, it is now. China badly needs to reinvigorate its economy in order to provide job opportunities for the fast-growing ranks of the unemployed. In 1998 officials predicted the economy would grow by around 8%—an impressive rate by many countries standards but by China's reckoning only just sufficient to prevent unemployment from becoming a social problem. It is a much lower rate than the nearly 10% average annual growth recorded in the previous 18 years. The rate would be more like 6% if unwanted stockpiled goods were subtracted from factory output statistics.

Chinese economists argue that the growth rate should ideally range between 9% and 12%. But pushing it up to this level will require gargantuan efforts in the coming year. The government has announced plans to stimulate the economy through a massive increase in public spending on infrastructure projects such as roads, railways and airports. Some $750 billion will be spent in this way by 2000. Rehabilitating areas damaged by 1998's extensive floods, which caused damage estimated at more than $20 billion, will also boost expenditure.

In 1999, housing reforms will wind down the costly provision of state-subsidised housing to workers. Salaries will be increased and banks ordered to increase mortage lending in order to encourage workers to buy their own homes. The government hopes this too will invigorate the economy. The reforms, which were due to begin in mid-1998 but were delayed because of public concerns, are likely to arouse strong resentment among lower-income workers. Consumer spending, so sluggish that in

Soon it will be China's

At midnight on December 20th 1999, China will take back six square miles of land on the estuary of the Pearl River that have been in foreign hands for over 450 years: Macau. Once greater than neighbouring Hong Kong, this former Portuguese colony fell into decay in the 19th century, a decay that left it poor, degenerate but charming. Nothing is likely to change. A quarter of Macau's population of 400,000 have been offered Portuguese passports: a more generous offer than that made by the British on leaving Hong Kong. The handover will also remove the last speck of one of the greatest seaborne European empires. Portugal may allow itself a tinge of nostalgia, as it rushes headlong into Europe's monetary union.

late 1997 China began witnessing deflation, is expected to take a long time to respond to the government's initiatives.

The biggest concern during the coming months will be to avoid the kind of financial meltdown and explosion of social unrest that occurred in Indonesia in 1998. China's banks are as plagued with bad debt and political interference as many of their counterparts elsewhere in Asia. More than 20% of loans are estimated to be unrecoverable. With 50% of banking capital made up of deposits by urban residents, should public confidence collapse and a run on banks occur, the entire financial system would be in jeopardy.

China's leaders will have to make some extremely difficult choices in the year ahead. They know they urgently need to reform the banking system to make it responsive to market needs, but they know that to do so would exacerbate the problems of loss-making state-owned enterprises which are kept afloat by politically inspired loans.

THE WORLD IN 1999 Expect the Hong Kong dollar to devalue some time in 1999. China will lose face but gain wisdom.

The leadership's over-riding consideration will be the maintenance of social stability. There have already been numerous reports of isolated strikes, demonstrations and sit-ins by disgruntled workers. In the three years to the end of 1997, more than 6,000 such incidents occurred. Public anger is being fuelled by widespread corruption and cronyism in the government. As state-owned enterprises continue to shed workers in a bid to revive their fortunes, unemployment will continue to rise in 1999 and social unrest will become more common. Major plans unveiled in 1997 that allow the effective privatisation of most state-owned enterprises—and thus even more lay-offs—are likely to be implemented in fits and starts as the government tries to strike a balance between reform and stability. In some inland cities with large concentrations of state-owned industries, however, unemployment is already well over the government-declared danger level of 10%.

As of late 1998, there was no sign that China's economic difficulties were likely to have any immediate impact on the fortunes of any particular leader. Public discontent in China is directed more at policies and institutions than any individual. But Prime Minister Zhu

Rongji has been particularly prominent in promoting reforms, including sweeping cuts in the bureaucracy.

In the build-up to the Communist Party's 16th Congress in 2002, attention will focus on the choice of a successor to President Jiang, who is also the head of the party and military. Mr Jiang is widely expected to step down at the Congress, by which time he will be 76. A likely candidate is Vice-President Hu Jintao, who will be 59. Mr Hu has so far been a relatively low-profile leader without obvious political leanings, but it is possible that Mr Jiang will propel him more to the fore in the coming months.

There has been much speculation that Mr Jiang is planning to revive the idea of political reform that was raised by officials before the crushing of the Tiananmen Square protests in 1989. But this will certainly not be aimed at diluting the party's monopoly of power. Mr Jiang is expected to focus more on ways of developing the electoral system for grassroots leadership posts and streamlining the bureaucracy. In June 1999, dissidents will be marking the tenth anniversary of Tiananmen, and Mr Jiang does not want to give any encouragement to activists to press demands for more far-reaching political change.

Japan's unhappy introspection

Nicholas Valéry   TOKYO

Under Japan's historical calendar, 1999 will be the Year of the Rabbit—the year of the frightened rabbit, caught in the headlights of the world's disapproval. Japan dragged down the world's markets in 1998; it will do very little in the year ahead to help either others or itself. There is little chance that Japan will play anything more than a token role in world affairs during 1999 as it, finally and belatedly, begins to grapple with the self-inflicted problems that have brought its once-mighty economy low. Despite urgings from Washington, Brussels and Beijing, all of Japan's energies are going to be directed at internal matters. And yet there are worrying signs that Japan's political life could become dysfunctional in the year ahead.

Certainly, there will be a change of political leadership, if not an actual change of government. Since the breakup of Ryutaro Hashimoto's coalition government and his party's disastrous performance in the upper-house election last summer, the ruling Liberal Democratic Party (LDP) has seen to its horror that it can no longer ride roughshod over the opposition.

Making matters worse for the government, a more unified and assertive alliance across the aisles—with a rejuvenated Communist Party joining forces with the mainstream opposition groups now led by Naoto Kan's surging Democratic Party—is flexing its muscles ready for a final showdown. For the first time in living memory, the opposition parties have started to write credible legislation of their own, and will use their upper-house majority increasingly to get their own agenda adopted and win even greater support among the electorate. So expect to see lots of ugly knock-down, drag-out fights in the Diet during 1999.

Any one of these could turn out to be the wedge that splits the LDP. Unlike the rebellion by Ichiro Ozawa in 1993 that caused a 44-strong band of followers to split from the party, the putsch of 1999 will be for ideological reasons—and therefore more permanent and more damag-

Nicholas Valéry: bureau chief in Tokyo for *The Economist*.

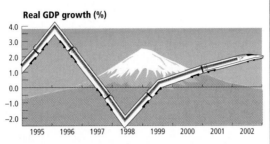

Real GDP growth (%)

ing. Mr Ozawa's move stemmed from an aborted power-play to take over the LDP's largest faction; most of his band of rebels eventually trickled back to the party mainstream.

But the internal strife that has rocked the LDP for the past six months concerns fundamental differences between the party's former chief cabinet secretary, Seiroku Kajiyama, and its current leadership under the less-than-charismatic Keizo Obuchi, who took over as prime

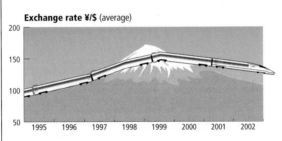

Exchange rate ¥/$ (average)

minister after Mr Hashimoto resigned. Mr Kajiyama, a feisty 72-year-old party hardman with little patience for the slow consensus-building negotiations behind the scenes, has campaigned vigorously for a more brutal and effective way of returning the country's debilitated banking system—with its estimated ¥130 trillion ($1 trillion) worth of dud loans—to health again.

The LDP has been ready to squander trillions of yen of taxpayers' money to effect a "soft landing" for the country's woefully mismanaged banks. As indicated by last autumn's attempt to salvage

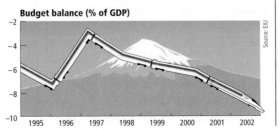

Budget balance (% of GDP)

Source: EIU

the Long-Term Credit Bank, the ruling party has sought to keep all 19 of Japan's major banks alive—whether they are viable or not. By keeping the insolvent institutions in business, the opposition has rightly accused the government of not only throwing good money after bad, but also threatening the survival of the better-managed banks.

Though ideologically to the right of the LDP mainstream, Mr Kajiyama and his 30-odd young party Turks have more in common with the opposition on this point. Both have criticised the government for seeking to use public funds to bail out ailing banks; and both, unlike the government, would cheerfully let insolvent ones go bust. Whether or not Mr Kajiyama and his "study group" bolt the party and align themselves with Mr Ozawa's Liberal Party and the rest of the opposition alliance, Japan's financial system is heading for a far harder landing in 1999 than the government would like.

That may actually be no bad thing. The economy is going to be mired in recession until the self-inflicted banking crisis is resolved. And the sooner that happens the better. By April, the opposition's more transparent laws for disposing of insolvent banks will be largely in place. That will not signal the end of Japan's financial woes; only the beginning of a long, painful process of cleaning up the mess left by the banks' over-exuberant lending during the bubble years a decade ago.

Most foreigners, and an increasing number of Japanese themselves, are now convinced that the only way to start the clean-up process is to let at least half a dozen major banks, and dozens of smaller ones, go bust. In turn, that will trigger the bankruptcy of thousands of marginal businesses which had previously been kept on life-support by banks terrified of calling in the bad loans and then having to take the liabilities on to their own balance sheets.

The knock-on effect will send Japan's bankruptcy rate through the roof. Soothsayers expect at least 100 of the 1,400 or so big household names listed on the prestigious first section of the Tokyo Stock Exchange to disappear during the year ahead. These will be merely the tip of the iceberg. And as people brought up on the myth of lifetime employment feel the sharp teeth of redundancy snapping at their heels, they will cease to spend on anything other than daily essentials.

Because individual consumption accounts for 60% of Japan's GDP, the economy—already on the ropes—can only deteriorate further in the year ahead. Real GDP is set to contract by around 2% in the fiscal year to March 1999 (compared with a 0.7% contraction in the year before). The best that can be hoped for in the year to March 2000 is that the contraction rate stays steady. Japan will begin 2000 at least 5% poorer than it ended 1996.

For the ordinary people of Japan, the pain can only get more acute. The good news is that, politics permitting, the measures to be adopted in 1999 should eventually leave the country's financial underpinnings in a far better state. That means, for the first time, people will be able to look forward to decent returns on their investments. Bank deposits will begin to pay more than the derisory rates of interest that Japanese savers have put up with for too long. And people will rightfully be able to enjoy some of the fruits of their earnings without jeopardising their savings for old age. That will be a revolution worth waiting for—and one certainly worth the pain.

Watch the Democratic Party grow in Japan. Founded in 1996, it will make its mark in the Lower House elections in 2000.

Rebuilding from Asia's rubble

Simon Long

BANGKOK

The past year was the most miserable that South-East Asia has suffered in a generation. 1999 could be worse; certainly it will be no better. It may be that the financial markets have seen their most panic-stricken days. The runs on regional stockmarkets and currencies that began with the devaluation of the Thai baht in July 1997 have given way to what looks almost like stability. But it is like the calm of a city devastated by an air-raid. The rubble keeps piling up even as rebuilding work starts. And there is still the fear of unexploded bombs. By late 1998, total market capitalisation on the Thai Stock Exchange was worth, in dollar terms, less than 15% of its value three years earlier. The Indonesian market had achieved a similar drop in little more than a year. Across the region, banks find themselves sinking under the growing weight of bad loans. Crippled by a collapse in domestic demand, high interest rates, and foreign borrowing made prohibitively expensive by currency devaluations, more and more companies are unable to pay their debts. Many banks have become insolvent.

1999 will be a year of overdue political change—throughout the region. In Thailand the fragile government of Chuan Leekpai is unlikely to wait until 2000 before calling polls under a new constitution that, in theory, should curb vote-buying. In Malaysia Mahathir Mohamad, the prime minister, is expected to call elections in late 1998 or early 1999, ahead of the triennial leadership contest in his own party. Having purged himself of his deputy, Anwar Ibrahim, who was also his most likely successor, Dr Mahathir's grip on power seems secure. But the reaction to Mr Anwar's dismissal, amid a bewildering array of allegations of sexual, financial and even treacherous wrongdoing, showed how even Dr Mahathir may have under-estimated the latent opposition to his rule.

The president of the Philippines, Joseph Estrada, elected in May 1998, may be wishing he had stayed in show business, where he made his name playing tough guys. The Philippines, initially among the more robust regional economies when the crisis struck, is looking weaker, partly because of doubts about Mr Estrada's own ability, and his apparent penchant for cronyism.

The poorest countries in the region—Vietnam, Laos, Cambodia and Myanmar—appear, on the surface, least affected by the economic downturn. They are less vulnerable to capital flight, if only because their opening to the outside world is so much more inchoate. But 1999 will be a disaster for them, too. Cambodia and Myanmar in particular,

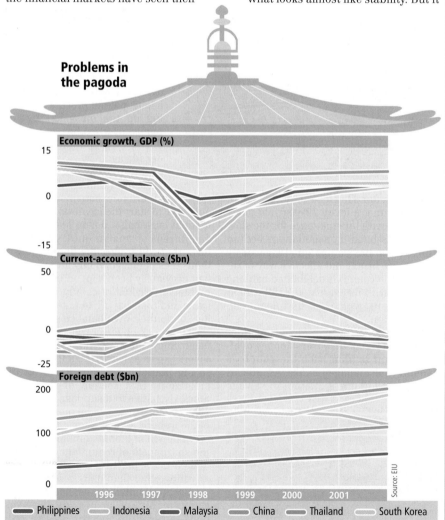

Problems in the pagoda

Economic growth, GDP (%)

15

0

-15

Current-account balance ($bn)

50

0

-25

Foreign debt ($bn)

200

100

0

1996 1997 1998 1999 2000 2001

Source: EIU

— Philippines   Indonesia   — Malaysia   China   Thailand   South Korea

---

Simon Long: finance editor for *The Economist*.

The biggest worry

It is Indonesia that has suffered the cruellest fate from the regional disaster, and that will evoke the greatest alarm among its neighbours over the next year. There, the sins that bedevilled other economies in the region—over-investment in property and other projects of dubious economic merit, lax banking supervision, corrupt links between business and politics, over-dependence on short-term foreign capital—are compounded by the most severe political upheaval. Confidence in the country's future evaporated in a few short weeks in 1997-98. The currency, the rupiah, fell by as much as 80% against the dollar. The country's foreign debts became unpayable. Most of the 240 banks and listed companies are technically bankrupt. Millions have lost their jobs. The number of people living below the poverty line, roughly defined as able to afford only one decent meal a day, will have jumped from 22m in 1996 to an estimated 90m people, 44% of the population, by the start of 1999.

The resignation in May 1998 of President Suharto, after 32 years of personalised, autocratic rule, was only the beginning of a period of political transition. His successor, B.J. Habibie, has promised a general election in May 1999, followed by a meeting in December of the assembly that elects the president. Already, some 90 political parties have sprung up. Some are organised on ethnic or religious lines. This is a worry in a country prone to racial violence. The ethnic Chinese minority—which numbers only about 4% of the population, but controls much business—has already been victimised in the looting, arson and mob violence of recent months. Many fear worse is to come.

Tensions will rise ahead of the elections in May. The strongest contenders will be Golkar, the political vehicle for Mr Suharto, and now

Now where did he put his chequebook?

President Habibie, and two opposition groupings. One is led by Amien Rais, a former leader of a large Muslim organisation, who, in the death throes of the Suharto regime, became its most prominent and outspoken critic. The other is an alliance between Megawati Sukarnoputri, the popular daughter of Indonesia's first president, and Abdurrahman Wahid, a Muslim leader.

There is a real fear in the region, especially in its closest neighbours, Malaysia and Singapore, that Indonesia will tear itself apart. The economic catastrophe could lead to ethnic pogroms, an exodus of boat people and an upsurge in piracy. It could delay the region's recovery for years. The outside world is also watching anxiously. Indonesia straddles shipping lanes vital to Japan. By far the biggest country in South-East Asia, its weakness debilitates the region, leaving it, in the eyes of gloomy strategists in America and Australia, vulnerable to greater Chinese influence. The role of the army will be decisive in preventing a slide towards anarchy. But many Indonesians fear that the military may use social unrest as a pretext for delaying elections and restoring dictatorship.

are governed by thuggish soldiers and bandits who face external revulsion and the loathing of many of their own people. In both places a confrontation between the state and the people is likely to erupt in 1999; an explosion made more likely by the drying up of foreign business interest and languishing economies.

Cambodia and Myanmar are also at the heart of a debate about the way countries in the region behave towards each other. The goal of expanding the regional club, the Association of South East Asian Nations (ASEAN), to include all ten countries of the geographical area may well be achieved in December 1998, with Cambodia's admission. But the coup there in July 1997, and Myanmar's international isolation, have raised questions about ASEAN's "cardinal principle": non-interference in other countries' internal affairs. At ASEAN's annual meeting in Singapore in July 1999, the more democratic members, notably Thailand and the Philippines, will renew their campaign for a less inhibited approach to other countries' domestic troubles. The more authoritarian members, such as Vietnam and Myanmar, will resist changing club rules so soon after their own accession.

But ASEAN is acutely conscious of its own failure to contribute to economic recovery—partly a result of its hands-off approach. It is galling for leaders who expected to be riding the crest of the wave of the "Pacific century" to find themselves reduced to international beggars, hoping the West, and the United States in particular, will rescue them. There is also, increasingly, the risk of a nationalist backlash. Already Dr Mahathir, its foremost spokesman, has imposed strict capital controls, in the hope of isolating his country from market forces, and forestalling a cap-in-hand call on the IMF. His experiment may succeed in the short term, by postponing, Japanese-fashion, a painful but essential economic restructuring. That will lead to mounting pressure for similar measures in those countries—that is, Thailand, Indonesia, the Philippines—which have adopted IMF orthodoxy, and have tried to combat collapse by opening, rather than closing, markets.

But in the whole region there is a feeling that recovery is now out of their own hands. The biggest threats lie in Japan, which may remain bogged down in its own financial quagmire; in China, where devaluation may be the only way to stimulate a moribund domestic economy; and in the markets of the West, which woke up belatedly to the deflationary forces swirling out of Asia.

THE WORLD IN 1999

Everywhere current accounts will be unbalanced. Expect big surpluses in Asia and a $300 billion deficit in America: the seeds of 1999's financial crisis. Protectionist noises grow louder.

One day the message will get through

India's happy chaos

Swaminathan Aiyar   NEW DELHI

Expect a government collapse followed by a general election in India in 1999. Expect too that a fresh election will leave politics as unstable and messy as before. The past two elections, in 1996 and 1998, were indecisive, leading to shaky coalition governments. The next one will be no different. Indian politics is now highly fractured. Regional and caste-based parties have become so strong that none of the bigger national parties can hope for an absolute majority. Unstable coalitions will be the norm.

In the 1998 election, the Bharatiya Janata Party (BJP) won the most seats (179 in a House of 543) but needed the support of almost a hundred more MPs for a majority, which meant cobbling together over a dozen disparate groups. The coalition was based on opportunism rather than principle. And opportunists make unreliable allies, constantly threatening to withdraw support unless their various demands are met. If even a handful of MPs switch sides, the government will fall. So its main ambition will be survival.

Waiting in the wings to take over is the Congress Party led by Sonia Gandhi, the widow of a former prime minister, Rajiv Gandhi. Congress is a fief of the Gandhi family, and when Rajiv was assassinated in 1991, the party leadership was Sonia's for the asking. But she de-

clared she had no interest in politics. She changed her mind only when defections threatened to decimate Congress in the run-up to the general election in early 1998. Her entry stopped the defections and raised party morale. Congress won only 141 seats, but is the largest by far of the anti-BJP parties, which control around 250 seats in parliament. So if the BJP coalition collapses, she is well placed to pick up the pieces.

After the last election, Sonia told impatient partymen not to try to topple the government quickly. She wanted to learn the intricacies of politics, and build a core group in the party she could trust. Besides, she felt it would be far better to let the BJP-led coalition collapse under the weight of its internal contradictions than try to buy over defectors immediately. She plans to let the coalition flounder on, plagued by dissension, and then strike at an appropriate time in 1999.

However, expect a new government headed by Mrs Gandhi to be as much at the mercy of opportunist minor allies as the current one, and as short-lived. Elections may become inescapable.

No party will come close to an absolute majority. The fate of the big parties will depend critically on the alliances they strike with regional ones. The BJP will make more progress than Congress in this. It will also gain something from its nuclear explosions, although the wave of popular support created by the blasts

ebbed rapidly. In any event, expect another shaky coalition.

The economy will keep chugging along despite political instability. India is no Asian tiger, and the half-baked nature of its economic reforms means its GDP is unlikely to grow faster than 6%. Yet this may suffice to make it the second-fastest growing country in the world (after China) in 1999, given the carnage in other emerging markets. Partial reform has denied India the advantages of globalisation, but spared it some of the tribulations too. Expect India in 1999 to be one of the few Asian countries that can raise large sums at reasonable interest rates. Foreign portfolio investment should pick up again.

There is a consensus across Indian political parties on economic reform, so this is in no danger of being reversed. Unfortunately there is also a consensus on keeping reforms half-baked. Powerful lobbies—trade unions demanding rigid labour laws, businessmen seeking protection, farmers wanting subsidies—will thwart radical reforms that are overdue.

Yet liberalisation will continue to creep forward, feeling its way into nooks and crannies where resistance to change is low. Non-tariff barriers will continue to be dismantled in keeping with India's pledge to the World Trade Organisation. Restrictions on foreign investment will be eased. Red tape will be snipped a few inches, but no more. State governments will reluctantly reduce totally unsustainable subsidies to barely unsustainable levels. Expect some small government companies to be privatised, but not the big ones.

Foreign sanctions will be less stringent in 1999. American economic sanctions imposed on India and Pakistan after their nuclear tests will be lifted totally. Expect India and Pakistan to accept some limits on their nuclear arsenals and missiles, sign the Comprehensive Test Ban Treaty, and join international negotiations to halt the production of fissile material. Non-proliferation protagonists in the United States and hawks in the sub-continent will oppose the deal, but it should go through.

Jingoism, which reached disturbing decibel levels in both countries after their nuclear tests, will become less noisy in 1999. The exchange of hostile fire in

THE WORLD IN 1999

America will import 300,000 highly skilled foreign workers over the next three years to work in the computer industry. Who will be left in Bangalore?

Swaminathan Aiyar: consulting editor of India's *Economic Times*.

Kashmir, which increased greatly in 1998, will diminish. New Delhi will press for a No First Use Treaty. However, progress on this will be slow since Kashmir will continue to be a highly contentious issue.

The American bombing of Osama bin Laden's training camps in Afghanistan in 1998 killed and injured many Pakistanis training there with the Harkat-ul Ansar, one of the most active Islamic militant groups in Kashmir. Expect India to try its hardest to have Pakistan characterised as a terrorist state.

Pakistan has a difficult act to perform. It needs to woo Washington to get

out of its current economic mess. Yet no Pakistani political party can afford to stop aiding the insurgency in Kashmir. Islamabad will claim it gives no help to the insurgents, amid hoots of derision from New Delhi.

India, which regards the sub-continent as its own stamping ground, has for decades opposed any American presence or intervention there. But the bin Laden affair has changed all that. In 1999, expect India to demand further American bombing of terrorist training camps in Afghanistan and even Pakistan, arguing that these jeopardise America's security as much as India's.

Australia will accept fewer refugees from Asia and more from Europe in 1999.

port for a republic. A majority of voters in four of the six states have to endorse any change to the constitution. This looks increasingly likely. So the betting has to be that the Republic of Australia will be conceived, though not born, in 1999.

If the referendum passes, preparations for the implementation of a republic on January 1st 2001, the centenary of Australia's federation, will begin immediately. But there will be no attempt to introduce a republic so that "an Australian head of state" can open the Sydney 2000 Olympics. A Labor government would have attempted to do so but the Liberal-National government, re-elected in October, has made it clear that Australia's constitutional changes will not be forced to satisfy a sporting event.

Of course, preparations are continuing apace for the Olympics, with stadiums and sports venues spreading inexorably through Sydney's Homebush area. Throughout 1999, the city's streets will look like building sites. The worst problem is traffic, which threatens to bring Sydney to a halt even before the Olympic rush begins. Nonetheless, the betting is that Sydney will look magnificent on the day.

Despite all the optimism of political renewal, civic pride and sporting ambition, the blight of the Asian financial crisis and attendant world gloom lurks on the Australian horizon. But after a raft of financial reforms and the return of a fiscally conservative government with an agenda for massive tax reform, the Australian economy is the best placed in its region to weather the storm.

Although the previous year's growth of 3.9% is likely to be halved to around 2% in 1999, inflation will remain at historically low levels. This will encourage further easing of monetary policy.

Mr Howard's election victory—despite the political baggage of introducing a goods and services tax—is likely to provide some stability of political leadership and constrain the leadership aspirations of the treasurer, Peter Costello. 1999 will be a year of anticipation and preparation for Australia, a year of national aspirations tempered by uncertainty.

Australia's choice

Dennis Shanahan CANBERRA

Australians will decide their future in 1999. They will face at the ballot-box a choice that has taken other nations to war. Despite the passion that discussions about the future of Australia's national character arouse, there is little likelihood that there will be a call to the barricades. The question the people will face, and answer, in a referendum in the second half of 1999 is whether to cut links with the British monarchy after more than 200 years, and become the Republic of Australia.

This chance that Australia has to declare its national independence will not be readily offered again should the referendum fail. A national constitutional convention early in 1998 decided to support "in principle, Australia becoming a republic" and to put such a referendum to the people. The prime minister, John Howard, has undertaken to "readily facilitate" the introduction of a republic if the referendum is carried, despite his personal preference for maintaining the monarchy as part of the constitution.

There is also the question of a "national statement" as the preamble to any revised constitution. Mr Howard's view is that the preamble would be a statement "of our history and of our being", including the contribution to modern Australia of the Aborigines, the British heritage and the waves of immigration. The preamble would also contain some description of the aspirations

Who will wear the crown?

Australians share for the future. It seems likely that, although Mr Howard may continue to oppose a republic, he would willingly grasp the initiative if the referendum is passed.

The likelihood of the referendum gaining both a majority of the Australian states and a majority of the people has improved with a combination of Labor governments in many states and a number of Liberal premiers declaring sup-

Dennis Shanahan: political editor of the *Australian*, based in Canberra.

A battle for corporate honesty

Jim Wolfensohn, president of the World Bank, asserts that the proper governance of companies will become as crucial to the world economy as the proper governing of countries.

Crises make us smarter. They make us fix things that we knew were wrong but were too busy to mend. As the battered economies of the emerging markets piece themselves back together in 1999 one lesson will not be forgotten: rotten national economies spring from rotten corporations; if business life is not run on open and honest lines, there is little chance that the wider economy can be.

Few recognised the profoundly corrosive effect poor corporate governance standards could have on seemingly vibrant economies. The cost has been enormous. In East Asia two-thirds of Indonesian and one-quarter of Thai companies appear insolvent. Cost estimates of financial-sector restructuring range from a low of 18% of GDP in Indonesia to 30% in South Korea and Thailand.

With hard work, we can take advantage of the current turmoil to construct a new business standard in all economies. The advantage will go beyond the corporate bottom-line. The World Bank has become acutely aware that strong corporate governance produces good social progress. The two go together. Western leaders have rightly kept up the pressure for democracy the world over; business leaders need to realise that a vital element in a modern democracy is modern corporate governance. Just as with governments, firms must be run transparently; management must be accountable.

Corporate governance has both internal and external dimensions. Internally, it refers to the checks and balances of power within a corporation; in particular between management, employees, the board of directors, shareholders and debt holders. It affects how vast amounts of capital are raised, where that capital is directed, the concentration of market power in the economy, and how firms interact with the state. Sickness in corporate governance is usually manifested in high debt-to-equity ratios, as firms are unwilling to undergo the scrutiny of the market, and insiders prefer to retain control. Again, look at Asia: in 1996, the ratio of debt to equity in South Korea

was 3.5 to 1, in Indonesia 1.9 to 1 and Thailand 2.3 to 1, compared with 1.1 to 1 in the United States and 1.4 to 1 in Germany. Perhaps most telling, in Taiwan, Singapore and the Philippines, economies relatively unaffected by the initial crisis, the number is no higher than 1.1 to 1.

Equally important, however, corporate governance determines how we on the outside—shareholders,

"Accountable business leadership is a vital element of modern democracy."

regulators, workers or citizens—are able to influence the conduct of these powerful actors in the global economy. Its significance goes beyond individual firms. Higher standards of corporate governance, by safeguarding transparency in commercial life, can form a democratic bedrock of rules.

We have been here before. In industrialised countries there have been battles over these rules between owners, workers and society, mediated by government, the courts and public opinion. These battles have eventually yielded societies that have helped produce a remarkable combination of social stability and economic progress.

If the rules of the game are not improved, economic growth will remain skewed to a small number of wealthy countries—a severe threat to all of us. Good corporate governance can make a difference by broadening ownership and reducing concentrations of power within societies. It bolsters capital markets and stimulates innovation. It fosters longer-term foreign direct investment, reduces volatility and deters capital flight. Moreover, it is only when high corporate

standards are adopted that the public will trust their savings to companies to provide their pensions. This is a daunting concern for countries with weak social-security systems.

Those with the highest standards will be the best rewarded. But markets cannot just expect better standards, they must build them. Although the age-old gambit of identifying balance between risk and reward will stay a central element of global investing, the calculus is changing. Investors will demand information more quickly, in more detail, and with greater certainty than ever before. Firms that respond will be rewarded. Those that do not will be punished. Investors, like voters, are decisive judges. The old suggestion that growth only comes about at the expense of openness is a nonsense. Free markets do not work behind closed doors.

Governments must build the right legal and institutional environments. International organisations can support change through lending technical advice. But it is business leaders who must lead the way by establishing tough rules of transparency and disclosure. They must see vigorous self-regulation and policing as part of their job. Good things are happening. The OECD, for example, has looked to business to help design an influential set of principles to guide corporate governance. Professional groups such as the World Congress of Accountants and the American Bar Association are identifying ways to harmonise professional standards.

The World Bank, a partner in many of these efforts, will play a unique role in these corporate reforms. In East Asia, for example, strict requirements for financial and corporate restructuring will be implemented alongside support for desperately needed social assistance.

It is a strategy that is taking hold. In Malaysia, the stock exchange and business leaders are working to improve on board independence, information disclosure and training; in South Korea, legislation has been passed to improve shareholder rights and access to financial performance data; and in Thailand, the Bangkok Stock Exchange is requiring the boards of directors of all listed companies to establish independent auditing capacity. This is just the start.

The multilateral muddle

John Micklethwait   NEW YORK

The United Nations and its sister institutions will face a period of harsh reform. Most of the global organisations set up at the end of the second world war are held in low esteem: politicians around the world have made the IMF and the World Bank the whipping boys for the Asian contagion. The World Trade Organisation has more to boast about—but it also comes under attack (usually unfairly) from the Left for not doing more to prevent child labour.

This is odd. The end of the cold war—and especially the economic integration since—has accentuated the need for global institutions. The world has been confronted by a wide range of challenges—from long-term problems such as the environment to individual crises such as Rwanda—that have outstripped the capability of national governments.

Unfortunately, global institutions have not risen to the task. Consider the two most prominent organisations. The IMF's bail-out of Mexico was a success; but its record in dealing with Asia's economic mess has been patchy—and its methods are opaque. The UN has been hustled out of places like Bosnia, partly because few national leaders trust it enough to hand over power to it. Feelings about the UN are particularly strong in America, where Congress has unilaterally (and unjustifiably) decided to stop paying its dues.

Some kind of explosion on the question of American dues is likely to happen in 1999. The UN like any other club has its rules; according to those rules the United States will lose many of its voting rights if it does not pay up—perhaps as early as January 1999. But that should only spark a wider debate over what kind of UN should exist.

In his first two years in office as secretary-general, Kofi Annan has cut costs, introduced cabinet-style government to the top of the organisation and tried to co-ordinate the various UN operations on the ground. But the basic structure of the

John Micklethwait: New York bureau chief for *The Economist*.

Kofi Annan's got a point to make

UN remains unchanged. His organisation remains a hotchpotch of agencies, funds and programmes, many of which have their own independent governing bodies.

This is not Mr Annan's fault: he is, famously, more the secretary than the general of his organisation. The General Assembly, where each of the 185 members has an equal vote, has shown little appetite for change. The UN, quite simply, looks out of date. By trying to do everything, it rarely does anything very well. In particular, most of its money goes into social and economic development. These activities appeal to the poorer "southern" states that have such a grip on the assembly. But government aid now accounts for only a tiny proportion of the money flowing to developing countries. And much of the UN's development work has been superceded by leaner, non-governmental organisations, such as charities.

If the UN were to put itself through the same sort of process that plenty of private-sector organisations do and ask

what exactly it does that nobody else can, it would discover an interesting list of "core competences". On issues like drugs and the environment the UN is certainly the logical forum for debate. It is also the natural place to deal with the politically sensitive problems of refugees and human rights. The case for the UN having a small standing army is a strong one: many of the world's nastiest conflicts could have been nipped in the bud if troops were put on the ground quicker.

This narrower, deeper UN would not need much of the fluff that it has accumulated. Most of the semi-autonomous agencies could be given a choice: either submit to Mr Annan's will or leave the system. And rather than each committee

THE WORLD IN 1999 The world's population will hit six billion in June. This is double the 1960 level and approaches the total number of people who have lived on earth until this century.

being created in perpetuity, each part should be forced to justify its existence at least twice a decade. All these reforms could be part of a bigger package for the special millennium assembly in 2000.

This sort of thinking is regarded as dangerous by many. But the current alternative, of slowly withering on the vine as its richer backers get ever less impressed by its inefficiencies, is not an attractive one.

The IMF, which is technically a UN agency, is in a similar position. It has already come under fire from creditor nations, reluctant to cough up their share of its funds. It may also face, in 1999, a challenge from a debtor nation that refuses to accept its terms. Both Bill Clinton and Tony Blair have been muttering about the need to modernise an organisation which was set up to monitor the post-war fixed-exchange-rate system.

Libertarians argue that the Fund's mere existence helps cause the crises it then has to solve. There is something in this: at one point Ukrainian bonds were being touted as a "moral hazard play"—meaning that investors could count on the IMF bailing them out. However, the arguments for having some sort of lender of last resort are strong. Crudely speaking, the prospect of a systemic failure of the world's financial system is sufficiently horrifying that it is worth taking precautions against it. The world needs some form of financial overseer.

The problem is that the IMF does not fit the bill on either count. The fact that it cannot print money makes it an unimpressive lender of last resort. It also lacks both the staff and the information to be a global financial regulator.

One answer would be to leave the IMF to concentrate on emergencies and set up a new global watchdog for financial firms, such as a beefed-up version of the Bank for International Settlements in Basle. This could force more transparency in the market by, for instance, restricting lending by foreign banks in countries which fail to modernise their financial systems.

There are three common themes that both the UN and the IMF must confront over the next few years. The first is that they are both trying to do too much; both need to be more precise as well as more modern. Second, nothing will happen unless the richer, western nations put their shoulders to the task. The United States, in particular, has done little to encourage or pay for change. The final point is that reform does not mean emasculation: the more efficient the two organisations become, the more powerful they will be.

Will Iran change?

David Gardner

On the face of it, the Middle East looks as benighted as ever, moving into 1999. It remains governed by autocrats still undecided whether to crush, or temporise with, the Islamist revival. It is still trapped in the coils of the Arab-Israeli conflict. In Iraq, the erstwhile industrial and cultural hinterland of the Arabs, the hope of future generations is bleeding away under Saddam Hussein and sanctions. And the only reason the region's economies have been spared the world's financial turmoil is that they are not developed or globalised enough for anyone

Khatami is a rarity in the Middle East

to notice them.

The bitter stand-off between Israelis and Palestinians over how to share the historic land of Palestine will certainly continue—and postpone indefinitely any hope of a comprehensive peace deal in the region.

If Yasser Arafat, the Palestinian leader, carries out his threat to declare a Palestinian state on May 4th—the date the "interim" period of Palestinian self-rule is supposed to end—Israel may attempt a foreseeably bloody operation to retake Palestinian towns. Just as likely, the hardline government of Binyamin

David Gardner: Middle East editor for the *Financial Times*.

Netanyahu will implement piecemeal measures already agreed by its Labour predecessors in the three Oslo accords of 1993, 1994 and 1995. These "concessions" will then be offset by real gains for Jewish settlers in the West Bank, and their religious and nationalist supporters who shore up the government.

Mr Netanyahu has authorised further settlement-building during 1999 in occupied Arab east Jerusalem and in Hebron, where 400 Jewish colonists live surrounded by 130,000 Arabs. He has also approved a plan to annex the settlements ringing east Jerusalem, amounting to 8% of the West Bank.

Mr Netanyahu is unpersuaded that Israel's security requires a fair and balanced settlement with the Palestinians. Instead of Palestinian self-determination, he envisages administrative self-government on, at most, half the West Bank or a tenth of historic Palestine, broken up by Jewish settlements into isolated Bantustans with Arab east Jerusalem under Israeli sovereignty. This is a blueprint for another generation of strife. It will ensure that no Arab government can build normal links with Israel.

1999 could prove particularly difficult to manage if any of the region's many ailing leaders dies. Mr Arafat's health is deteriorating rapidly. King Hussein of Jordan is struggling against a second bout of cancer. President Hafez Assad of Syria is subject to four different medical regimes, according to western diplomats. All these leaders are part of any eventual peace equation; and all are, to a greater or lesser extent, holding at bay forces inside their countries inimical to a settlement. Mr Saddam, by contrast, appears in robust health and has seen his grip on power strengthened, partly as a result of the Arab perception of America's pro-Israel bias.

So, is there no beacon of light? Perhaps. Iran, under the reformist presidency of Mohammad Khatami, is pressing to make government accountable to the rule of law and the assent of the governed. There is no guarantee that he can overcome the hardline theocrats

A surfeit of surplus

Expect raw material prices to fall in 1999. They have already declined steeply, at a time when the world economy was expanding. So with things slowing in the year ahead, prices will drop further.

Huge increases in the yield of almost all crops are certain in the years ahead, the result of genetic engineering and computer-based, precision farming. A world of six billion people will have to struggle with the political problem of food surpluses: a prediction that would have been laughed at a few years ago. Oil prices will stay low—unless there is war in the Middle East—because deep-drilling technologies have made markets afloat with the stuff. The cost of filling the tank of your car in America will be lower in 1999 than any time in living memory. And who, in an information-driven world, needs all those heavy industrial metals?

One commodity worth watching is unfashionable gold. If central banks respond to the many financial crises of 1998 by pumping out liquidity, that means inflation will follow and gold will look cheap. Don't bet on it.

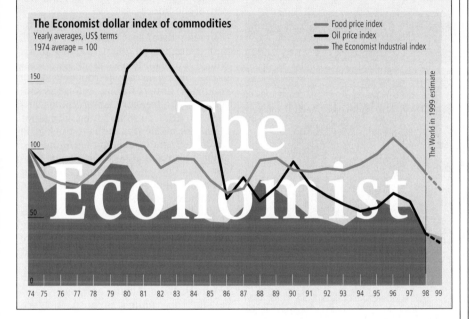

The Economist dollar index of commodities
Yearly averages, US$ terms
1974 average = 100

- Food price index
- Oil price index
- The Economist Industrial index

The World in 1999 estimate

74 75 76 77 78 79 80 81 82 83 84 85 86 87 88 89 90 91 92 93 94 95 96 97 98 99

whose material as well as spiritual interests this project threatens. They are grouped, in myriad power centres, around Ayatollah Ali Khamenei, the Supreme Leader who still controls defence, foreign policy, the Revolutionary Guard and the judiciary.

Yet Mr Khatami, who was elected in 1997 with over 70% of the vote on a 90% turnout, has overwhelming popular legitimacy, while Mr Khamenei (also believed to be ailing) has had his theological credentials and fitness to govern questioned even by the Shi'a Muslim hierarchy. Mr Khatami is no political novice. Well known to be an admirer of de Tocqueville, it is less known that he is also a translator of Machiavelli. He has quietly replaced all Iran's provincial governors who will control the forthcoming municipal polls and the next election to the now conservative-dominated *Majlis,* or parliament. Mr Khatami has also purged the civil service of political appointees. Realising, too, that the vast majority of the Revolutionary Guard voted for him, he sacked its commander.

Under Mr Khatami, Iran has forged a rapprochement with Saudi Arabia, mended fences with Iraq and Turkey, and will this year re-establish full diplomatic relations with Egypt. A dialogue with the European Union has resumed, helped by putting to one side the Salman Rushdie affair. There is even a cautious rebuilding of links with the United States.

Mr Khatami may stumble yet. But if he succeeds, Iran could have a profound influence on the Middle East. Post-revolutionary attempts to export essentially Persian and Shi'ite radicalism were always going to have a limited market. But Mr Khatami's Islamic democracy project is much more exportable and, in 1999, will challenge the fossilised despotism of the Arab world.

Saudi Arabia

FORECAST

With oil prices weak and likely to stay that way, the ruling Al-Saud family faces a tough year. As pressure mounts to curb state spending further and push ahead with economic reforms, including the removal of subsidies, popular discontent is likely to resurface. This may spill over into isolated acts of violence against American targets by radical Wahabi Islamic dissidents, who continue to rail against the presence of American troops and the lack of progress in the Middle East peace process.

The succession issue may also come to a head in 1999. King Fahd's ailing health and more frequent hospitalisation suggest that the formal transfer of power to Crown Prince Abdullah is imminent. Although Abdullah is the accepted heir apparent, there is no guarantee that the next Crown Prince (and hence second in line for the throne after Abdullah) will be Prince Sultan as widely assumed. Tensions, even a serious family rift, could flare if Abdullah, as king, seeks to relieve the so-called Sudairi Seven (King Fahd's full brothers) of some of their power.

As king, Abdullah will take more interest in Arab affairs, and will play down relations with the United States. However, the American alliance will remain strong and, although Abdullah is often painted as less friendly to Washington than King Fahd, it should be remembered that he is head of the National Guard, which has very close links with America.

Lower oil revenues and low private-sector confidence suggest that the economy will at best stagnate during 1999, while the current-account deficit will remain large. Inflation will experience a "one-off" hike, denting the country's reputation as a low-inflation economy, as subsidies are cut. Economic pressures will once again bring privatisation of state assets on to the government's agenda. The Saudi riyal could come under increasing pressure.

KEY INDICATORS			
	1997	1998	1999
GDP growth (%)	3.0	-2.0	-2.5
Inflation (%)	0.1	-0.5	4.0
3-month money market rate (%)	5.8	5.9	5.2
Exchange rate			
SR per $	3.75	3.75	3.75
SR per DM	2.16	2.10	2.27
Current account (% of GDP)	0.2	-11.7	-15.7

EIU COUNTRY ANALYSIS AND FORECASTING

The future of statecraft

Fareed Zakaria   NEW YORK

Despite all the turmoil in the developing world, the major industrialised nations continue to move unavoidably into the world of globalism, technology and cyberspace. Ironically, in this futuristic age, diplomacy is returning to its roots. Don't think of Edwardian toffs in striped pants and bowler hats passing cables to one another in Whitehall or of 19th-century statesmen meeting in a baroque ballroom to redraw the map of Europe. These are variations on the way diplomacy is often still conducted—in summits, governmental conferences and bilateral talks. The diplomacy of tomorrow will resemble an even earlier period in history—the Renaissance.

The one trend that is sure to dominate the coming year, decade, and even quarter-century is the decline of the power of the state. The state has had a good run for a couple of centuries. But before that, from the late Middle Ages to the Napoleonic era, it was one entity among many, competing with others for loyalty, legitimacy, money and armies. Over the past two centuries the central state wrested authority from the hundreds of duchies and other principalities on its terrain that once fielded armies and collected taxes. It took over from the church that crucial function, the education of the young. It turned nationalism, rather than religion, into the coin of legitimate rule. And it became—through taxation and regulation—the most important player in the national economy.

This dominance will not disappear, but it will wane. The balance of power between the state and other elements of society has been shifting for the past quarter-century. The rise of fluid capital markets, information technology, global media, the end of communism, the inefficiencies of government regulation all point in the same direction—against the autonomy and power of the state. Diplomacy is already reflecting that change.

Consider the Renaissance prince. To wage a war he would first need a *causus belli*—recall Shakespeare's "Henry V" asking his priests to find a legal claim so that he could invade France. Next he would need troops and money. For the former he would haggle with his counts and earls—some of whom would become dukes in the process—and for the latter with private bankers like the Salimbenes

Fareed Zakaria: managing editor of *Foreign Affairs.*

or the Hochstetters. Lastly, he would need legitimacy, for which he would send emissaries to Rome, seeking papal sanction. Describing this process Michael Lind, an American writer, points out that the most successful Renaissance statesmen were impresarios, "political Zeigfelds", who orchestrated these disparate forces to serve their interests.

Now think of the Gulf war, which was unwittingly fought using Renaissance methods. Saddam Hussein's invasion of Kuwait gave a clear legal case for inter-

A good model for Greenspan

vention. But the Bush administration knew that it needed to assemble an international coalition for political legitimacy and effectiveness. It asked the major Arab states—Saudi Arabia, Egypt and even Syria—for troops for symbolic reasons. It got the backing of NATO, whose troops, equipment and command structure made the military aspect of the intervention much easier. The United States was broke, so James Baker went on a round of "tin cup diplomacy", gathering contributions from wealthy countries like Japan, Saudi Arabia and, of course, Kuwait. Finally, to enhance the legitimacy of the enterprise the United States took its case not to Rome but to Atlanta, Georgia. Public opinion today is the equivalent of a papal edict and CNN's world headquarters symbolises the site

where people struggle for that sanction.

Contrast this method of waging war with that of Churchill and Roosevelt, or for that matter Stalin and Hitler. Having declared war, they drafted all able-bodied men in their country, nationalised or commandeered all relevant industries to produce munitions and equipment, and spent whatever they needed running up a vast national debt. Such legitimacy as was necessary was provided by government propaganda. It was a mass-production, command model like that espoused for corporations by Frederick Taylor, a management theorist, early in this century. The Gulf war, by contrast, was waged with all the flexibility, horizontal structures and co-ordination that today's management gurus insist is the way of the future.

It is not just war that is going the way of the Renaissance. Consider the turmoil and contagion in the world economy, whose immediate cause is the withdrawal of private capital from developing countries. Robert Rubin, America's secretary of the treasury, co-ordinates rescue activities, but he must get other members of the G7, the IMF, the World Bank, the Asian Development Bank and other international organisations to support his efforts—all of which are aimed at luring the foreign investor back into the affected markets.

Non-governmental actors play a crucial role in this process. The risk-rating agency, Moody's, for example, can save or sink a country. A currency trader, George Soros, has been credited with breaking the European Exchange Rate Mechanism, attacking Malaysia and causing the rouble's collapse. A figure like Mr Soros can also provide legitimacy; South Korea's markets rose sharply after he visited and approved of its reform programme. To gain support for its policies, pressing change on Japan for example, the American administration often wheels out another respected figure, Alan Greenspan, chairman of the Federal Reserve. Mr Greenspan has no control over America's foreign economic policy, but he has enormous credibility: a perfect 15th-century cardinal.

If we are indeed entering a world of Renaissance complexity, with many actors, public and private, overlapping jurisdictions, competing loyalties and dizzying change, where should the statesman look for wisdom? As it turns out, there does exist a highly intelligent guidebook seeking to preserve and enhance the power and autonomy of the state against its many challengers. Written in 1513, Niccolo Machiavelli's "The Prince" is available in most bookstores.

Can reform stick?

Michael Reid

SAO PAULO

It will be a difficult year for Latin America. There will be little or no economic growth; currencies will remain under pressure; foreign financing will remain scarce. Latin Americans have spent the past decade implementing painful free-market reforms, which were just starting to bear fruit. Many of them will feel, with some justification, that their countries are the innocent victims of flighty financial markets beyond their control. Some of them will start to doubt whether the reform effort was worthwhile. The question that will dominate Latin American political life in 1999 will thus be whether or not to retreat into the economic nationalism that was the region's response to a past world recession, that of the 1930s.

In general, the answer will be a qualified no. Latin Americans may have little enthusiasm for extending market reforms, but neither will many of them endorse radical adventures which threaten economic stability. The big exception could be Venezuela, perhaps because stability has not been achieved there. Its next president, due to take over in February after an election in December, might be Hugo Chavez, a populist nationalist and a former lieutenant-colonel who narrowly failed to take power by force in a bloody coup effort in 1992. He may yet be pipped by Henrique Salas Rohmer, a Yale-educated moderniser. And even if he wins Mr Chavez will probably step back from implementing the debt moratorium and siege economy he once threatened. But Venezuela is set for continuing instability, a headache for Washington given its strategic importance as an oil supplier.

At the other end of South America, voters are likely to opt for change, but of a less fundamentalist kind. Presidential elections in Argentina in October and in Chile in December 1999 could mark a swing to the moderate left. But both contests will be very closely fought. In Argentina, the opposition alliance, probably headed by Fernando de la Rua, the Radical Party

Michael Reid: Brazil/Mercosur correspondent for *The Economist*.

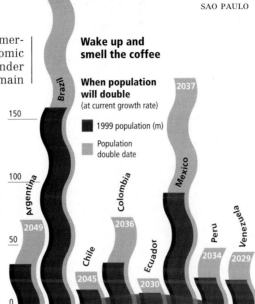

Wake up and smell the coffee

When population will double
(at current growth rate)

■ 1999 population (m)

■ Population double date

Women's share of labour force (%)
1970 ☐ ☐ 1999

GDP growth (%)
1997 ■ ☐ 1999

mayor of Buenos Aires, ought to beat the likely Peronist candidate, Eduardo Duhalde. In Chile, General Pinochet will inevitably cast a shadow but Ricardo Lagos, a market socialist, should still beat conservative and Christian Democrat opponents. But both men's chances of victory may be lessened if the economic outlook remains stormy. Confirmation

that discontent does not necessarily mean radicalism may come in elections in three of the region's smaller countries. In both El Salvador in March and Uruguay in November, left-wing parties which include former guerrillas may be defeated by conservatives. In Panama, if (a big if) the conservative opposition remains united, it should beat the ruling nationalists.

This underlying voter caution will reinforce the determination of policymakers in many countries to preserve the hard-won gains of reform, even if that requires tough measures. Growth will be sacrificed: taken as a whole, Latin America will be lucky to grow by 1-2%, down from around 2.5-3% in 1998 and 5.2% in 1997. Many governments will proclaim their commitment to free trade while quietly clamping down on imports. They will hope that after a fairly orderly pause, their countries will be poised to resume faster growth by the end of the year, with their democracies and their economic reforms intact.

But it could yet be much worse than that. Whether it is depends on two factors. The first is the world economy. Latin America will be hit hard by low prices for its exports of commodities (oil, minerals and grains) as the world economy slows. Commodity prices are unlikely to improve much until 2000. Worse still, a sharp slowdown in the United States economy will hit Latin America's exports of manufactures. But lower interest rates in the United States could cause investors to look more kindly on emerging markets once again. Even so, external financing will remain scarce and expensive for Latin America, with any thaw coming only towards the end of the year.

The second key to Latin America's year is Brazil, which accounts for 45% of the region's GDP. In 1999 Brazil will be the southern hemisphere's biggest question-mark. As he embarks on his second term in January, President Fernando Henrique Cardoso will have only a few months at most to implement the Draconian fiscal measures he was unable and unwilling to take in his first term. Failure to do so would make almost inevitable a disorderly devaluation of the currency, the *real*, and Mr Cardoso would struggle for the rest of his term. Success in bringing the fiscal deficit under control would still mean that Brazil will face a bleak 1999,

Mexico's moment of truth

There is a dismal pattern in the political economy of Mexico. Almost like clockwork, at the end of a president's six-year stint in office, crisis strikes. President Ernesto Zedillo's mission in 1999 is to lay the groundwork for an orderly transfer of power the following year and to avoid the financial crises that have blighted successive presidential transitions.

In Congress, where the opposition parties now have a majority in the lower house, the government will need to show a willingness to negotiate. The stalemate in the poor southern state of Chiapas, where the peasant uprising is moving into its fifth year, is unlikely to be broken without a serious search for

consensus. Concessions will also be necessary to win legislators' approval for financial reforms, including the formal assumption by the state of bad loans removed from banks during the 1995 crisis. This is controversial, because of evidence of abuses by wealthy bankers, but essential if banks are to fulfil their role of efficient financial intermediation.

Following Mr Zedillo's decision to abandon the tradition of handpicking the Partido Revolucionario Institucional's presidential candidate, the nomination will probably be decided towards the end of 1999 by primaries in which traditionalists will be pitted against modernisers.

Zedillo could do something right in 1999

---

with the economy in recession and the risk of bank failures. But such is the price of consolidating the country's still-recent victory over decades of inflation, and of the procrastination of Mr Cardoso's first term. It would allow Brazil to loosen its exchange-rate peg early in 1999, without risking a return to inflation, and the country's medium-term prospects would be bright.

This amounts to an enormous challenge of political leadership, since it requires marshalling broad support for abolishing perks and privileges embedded in the constitution. Brazilians are a pragmatic lot, and most of the country's politicians know that fiscal rectitude can no longer be postponed. Among those who will hope so are the next-door neighbours. Argentina's success in the 1990s has depended in part on its currency board, the arrangement under which the currency is pegged by law at parity to the dollar. Any collapse in Hong Kong's currency board would damage the credibility of Argentina's. Add to that a Brazilian devaluation, and the consequences would be dire: Argentina would probably adopt the dollar, and Mercosur (South America's leading trade block) would come under severe strain.

Peru will buck the regional trend, with growth accelerating as the country recovers from its battering by El Niño in 1998, but President Alberto Fujimori's manoeuvring for a third term in 2000 will cause political tension. For Colombia, 1999 may mark a turning point. It could see the setting up of organised peace talks involving President Andres Pastrana's government, left-wing guerrillas and right-wing paramilitaries. There are grounds for only the most

fragile optimism. More bloodshed is certain, as each side attempts to improve its negotiating position, and any talks will be complicated and long drawn-out. But the alternative is the steady breaking apart of the country, amid mounting violence and falling investment.

It will be a year in which Latin Americans have little appetite for new trade ventures. The year's main diplomatic jamboree, a European Union and Latin America summit (in Rio de Janeiro, on June 28th-29th) will be a disappointment. Though the EU may decide to

launch free-trade talks with Mercosur, neither side will want to move quickly. And later in the year, it is Cuba's turn to play host to the annual Ibero-American summit, an affair that brings together leaders from Latin America and Spain and Portugal. For Fidel Castro, this is an unprecedented chance to play host to a large international gathering, but some of his visitors will take the chance to make pointed calls for political freedom in Cuba. One day this last bastion of western dictatorship will fall but do not expect it in the forthcoming year.

Africa scrambles for Africa

Patrick Smith

Expect a more African Africa in 1999. The continent will look to its own resources as it tries to fend off the effects of global recession and patch up its turbulent regional alliances. There is little choice. America's bubble of interest in Africa will fade—as Europe's did long ago. And the bail-outs of Asia and Russia mean that the international agencies will be cutting back Africa's share of assistance in 1999.

Businesses in South Africa, Nigeria, Kenya and Egypt will continue to build up their continental portfolios, buoyed by Africa's doubling of GDP growth rates since the early 1990s. But plans for boosting intra-African trade are plagued by regional instability. The "African-Renaissance" axis running from Ethiopia and Eritrea in the north-east through

Rwanda, Uganda, and Congo to Angola in the south-west was blasted apart in 1998 by the civil war in the Democratic Republic of Congo. There are still hopes for diplomatic settlements in 1999 in the Ethiopia-Eritrean border war and Angola's civil war, but the interlocking conflicts around the Great Lakes region are less tractable. Expect no solutions in the coming year.

The beleaguered president of the Democratic Republic of Congo, Laurent Kabila, will continue to call on help from Angola, Zimbabwe, Sudan's National Islamic Front regime and Hutu extremist militias, while his opponents rely on Rwanda and Uganda. Without effective negotiations between the two sides, the de facto secession of rebel-held eastern Congo from the rest of the country will remain a reality. The 1999 nightmare is that Congo's war will spin out of control,

Patrick Smith: editor of *Africa Confidential*.

Watch out for simultaneous translation software, enabling two politicians, one speaking English and the other Arabic, to argue with each other fluently.

exacerbating conflicts on its borders.

There is much greater reason to be optimistic about Nigeria in 1999, if it sticks to its plan for free elections as proposed by General Abdulsalam Abubakar. After 15 years of military muddling, the general's suggestion of civil rule will raise the prospect of a Nigerian revival. Even moderate success in privatising Nigeria's oil industry and public utilities would produce a major economic upturn. Best placed to benefit from a faster-growing Nigeria are Ghana and Côte d'Ivoire, where years of tortuous reform are persuading bolder foreign investors to buy into their stockmarkets.

The 14 member countries of the CFA franc zone (formerly pegged to the French franc) will need to keep a wary eye on the launch of the euro in January. These countries hope that strong growth in Europe will boost demand for their exports and inward capital flows. But if the CFA franc becomes pegged to a "hard" euro, it would undermine competitiveness.

Currency worries and fiscal fights with the IMF will further weaken the governments of Kenya's president, Daniel arap Moi, and Zimbabwe's president, Robert Mugabe. Both are septuagenarians and paid-up members of the Big Man school of politics. They could hang on for another three years before the next elections. But many of the party faithful share the growing popular resentment of official corruption and economic decline. Either of these Big Men could take early and welcome retirement in 1999.

Africa's best news will be in Mozambique where the ruling Frelimo Party is holding elections, having negotiated some $5 billion-worth of foreign investment in steel and aluminium smelters, and a gas-export project to South Africa. The probable election winner, Frelimo's President Joaquim Chissano, will have to battle to keep inflation in single figures as GDP grows at around 15% a year.

In southern Africa's other successful economy, diamond-rich Botswana, politics will get trickier for the new president, Festus Mogae, who faces populist challenges from within and without the ruling party. Mr Mogae's diplomatic agility should see him through. Less certain is the fate of President Bakili Muluzi's government in Malawi's elections. Amid political confusion, the benefits from tough economic reforms have not filtered down, and many expect the late dictator Kamuzu Banda's Malawi Congress Party to make a comeback.

At the other end of Africa a trio of ballots will be overshadowed by the continuing rise of political Islam. Few expect the presidential election in Algeria to stop the seven-year war between the military and extreme Islamist militias. Having pushed out former President Lamine Zeroual, the military will demand a veto over the civil candidates. It

Mandela will step down

will, however, consider a deal that co-opts some of the Islamists.

In Tunisia's security state, nothing will be left to chance under the tight control of former policeman Ben Ali. There's no chance of Ben Ali losing power. A question-mark hangs over Morocco's ballot in the form of the much-delayed referendum over the future of Western Sahara.

King Hassan II, relying on his credentials as a pro-western stalwart against Islamism, has obstructed the vote for almost a decade. The stakes are rising: Western Sahara could revert to war against Rabat, with Algeria's backing, if the referendum is delayed again.

South Africa

Thabo Mbeki, president of the ruling African National Congress (ANC), will become president of South Africa in 1999. How will that change life in this fragile republic? The answer, in a nutshell, is not a whole lot.

The succession will merely formalise a process that has been under way for some time, with the 80-year-old Nelson Mandela serving as the country's senior elder statesman and Mr Mbeki running the show on a day-to-day basis. South Africa will be going to the polls in May or June 1999 in the country's second all-race election and the result is a foregone conclusion: the ANC will win hands down. Only the size of its majority will be in doubt. The real contest will be between the opposition parties, each one trying to establish itself as a legitimate political force capable of challenging the ANC in the years to come. Regardless of politics, crime and fear remain South Africa's real problems.

What happens after Chris Stals steps aside as governor of the South African Reserve Bank in mid-1999 is far less certain. The ANC has already named Tito Mboweni, a former labour minister, as his successor, which alarmed businessmen and sent the rand on another rollercoaster ride. Mr Mboweni's appointment is designed to head off pressure from the ANC's traditional allies—the organised trade union movement and the South African Communist Party—and to keep them off the streets, but the move raises serious concerns about the future independence of the bank and the stability of the currency.

Following the collapse of the rand in 1998, South Africa will be plagued by currency volatility for much of the year, with a distinct risk of further speculative attacks. Although the lower rand will benefit exporters, this will be more than offset by the impact of high real interest rates. Inflation will rise to an average of more than 8% in 1999, and real GDP growth of 2% will fall short of what South Africa needs.

KEY INDICATORS

	1997	1998	1999
GDP growth (%)	1.7	0.5	2.0
Inflation (%)	8.5	6.5	8.4
Commercial prime rate (%)	20.0	21.4	19.5
Exchange rate			
R per DM	2.66	3.26	3.85
R per $	4.60	5.80	6.70
Current account (% of GDP)	-1.5	-1.6	-1.9

E·I·U EIU COUNTRY ANALYSIS AND FORECASTING

BORDERLESS

Wherever people live, NYK delivers.

From the little house down the lane to a sprawling metropolis, if a place can be reached by sea, or road or rail, NYK reaches it.

As a total logistics megacarrier, NYK has created a distribution management system

that comprises almost every means of transport. For 110 years,

NYK has been delivering to people the world over, and we aim to be at it well into the next century.

NYK ALTAIR
PANAMA

NYK LINE
NIPPON YUSEN KAISHA

Western Europe

From January 1st 1999, the EU's single currency, the euro, will be launched (it will become the sole legal tender in participating countries by July 1st 2002) and monetary policy will be conducted by the European Central Bank (ECB) in Frankfurt. Expect the ECB to tighten monetary policy slowly as the EU's economic recovery proceeds. Market confidence in the euro will be strong.

AUSTRIA

GDP: $222.2bn
GDP per head: $27,347
Population: 8.1m
GDP growth: 3.4%. Inflation: 1.5%

• The left-right coalition government, composed of the Social Democratic Party and the conservative People's Party, is likely to remain in power following a federal election due no later than December 1999.

• The populist Freedom Party will suffer from the aftermath of a financial scandal that has undermined its claim to be untainted by the clientelism of Austrian politics.

• Having passed through the trough of the economic cycle, which was deepened by the fiscal constraints of the Maastricht criteria, the economy's prospects are excellent. Austrians can look forward to strong growth without attendant inflationary pressure.

To watch
Four former communist states seeking to join the EU (where people are free to move between countries) have borders with Austria. This has raised fears of a sharp increase in immigration.

BELGIUM

GDP: $259.8bn
GDP per head: $25,445
Population: 10.2m
GDP growth: 2.6%. Inflation: 1.4%

• All eyes will be on elections, set for June. The Liberals and the moderate nationalists will together receive the largest share of votes (more than 30%) both in Flanders (the Dutch-speaking region) and Wallonia (the French-

Budget balance
% of GDP

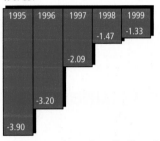

1995	1996	1997	1998	1999
-3.90	-3.20	-2.09	-1.47	-1.33

speaking region). But they will still need to find another partner to form a government.

• A reform of the police and judiciary should improve the transparency and efficiency of the justice system and help to soothe Belgians' disenchantment with the country's institutions.

DENMARK

GDP: $186.4bn
GDP per head: $35,073
Population: 5.3m
GDP growth: 2.3%. Inflation: 2.4%

• The Faroe Islands' push for more independence will present a challenge to the government in Copenhagen—not least because the Social Democrat-led coalition depends on support from one of the two Faroese members of parliament. Many Danes might be happy to see the heavily subsidised Faroes break away.

• Denmark is not among the founder members of EMU. Nevertheless, it will try to maintain exchange-rate stability vis-à-vis the new European currency. This will be formalised within a new exchange-rate mechanism, ERM-2, which will link the krone to the euro.

• The coalition re-elected in mid-1998 has spent its political capital in forcing through a fiscal austerity package designed to cool an overheating economy. Economic growth will therefore slow from rates of 3-4% in recent years to a more sustainable level.

FINLAND

GDP: $131.2bn
GDP per head: $25,364
Population: 5.2m
GDP growth: 3.4%. Inflation: 1.8%

• A general election is scheduled for March 1999. It will lead to a broad-

based coalition government, resembling the Social Democrat-led "rainbow" coalition in power at present. One of the most contentious election issues: the use of nuclear energy, on which the coalition parties are split.

• Although Finland has substantially distanced its economy from Russia since the Soviet break-up, it nonetheless remains more exposed than other EU countries to developments there (8% of its trade is with Russia). Finns will keep a nervous eye on their big neighbour.

• The only Nordic country to take part in the first wave of EMU, Finland will face a tricky adjustment as its monetary policy moves into the hands of the European Central Bank. Its economy is expected to grow faster than the EU average, so for Finland ECB monetary policy could be inappropriately loose.

To watch
Finland becomes president of the EU in the second half of 1999: the Finns will promote their idea of a "northern dimension" for the EU.

FRANCE

Government debt
% of GDP

1995	1996	1997	1998	1999
52.2	55.4	57.7	58.5	59.5

GDP: $1,622.7bn
GDP per head: $25,425
Population: 59.2m
GDP growth: 2.1%. Inflation: 1.2%

• For a while after France's victory in the World Cup, French politicians enjoyed a pleasant reverie induced by some of their highest opinion-poll ratings recorded. In 1999 they will return to earth. But disarray on the right should ensure that Lionel Jospin's Socialist government does not have to face a general election before 2000 at the earliest.

• Elections for the European Parliament in June may force some resolution of

All figures are 1999 forecasts unless otherwise indicated.

Inflation: year-on-year annual average.

Dollar GDPs calculated using 1999 forecasts for dollar exchange rates.

Source: except where indicated.

The Economist Intelligence Unit

the right's confused state, but they are more likely to indicate who is likely to benefit the most: the left or the far-right National Front.

• The introduction of the euro from January 1st 1999 will boost competition and investment, but France will have to maintain tight fiscal restraint, as its structural deficit is still too large.

GERMANY

Trade balance
% GDP

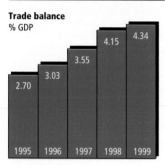

1995	1996	1997	1998	1999
2.70	3.03	3.55	4.15	4.34

GDP: $2,431.4bn
GDP per head: $27,418
Population: 82.5m
GDP growth: 1.8%. Inflation: 1.5%

• Gerhard Schröder's red-green coalition will have to take on the challenge of reforming the social-security system. The system has been under growing strain since unification and the high unemployment of recent years has underlined the case for reform.

• Germany will have the EU's presidency in the first half of 1999. The way it handles the role will be a test of the strength of its commitment to the EU's eastward enlargement, which could easily get bogged down in the absence of vigorous German leadership.

• The multiple crises that have afflicted Asia (especially Japan) and Russia will still be affecting German exports in 1999; as a result growth is not likely to strengthen in 1999. Many German banks, heavily exposed to Asia and Russia, will struggle to restore their balance sheets to health.

To watch
Preparations for moving the government and parliament to Berlin, heralding an eastward shift in Germany's centre of gravity.

GREECE

GDP: $124.0bn
GDP per head: $11,739
Population: 10.6m
GDP growth: 3.2%. Inflation: 4.0%

• Economic policy will be ever more focused on ensuring participation in EMU. The government wants to meet

the Maastricht criteria for membership by the end of 1999 to allow it to join EMU on January 1st 2001: ambitious (especially in view of Greece's stubbornly high inflation), but not impossible.

• The drive for EMU entry will mean tighter policy across the board. As Greeks feel the effects, this will not be popular.

• Privatisation of the bloated state sector will gather momentum, but it will still be held back by powerful opposition and be too slow to make a radical difference.

IRELAND

GDP: $83.2bn
GDP per head: $22,537
Population: 3.7m
GDP growth: 6.9%. Inflation: 3.4%

• The Northern Ireland peace process will overshadow every other issue in the Republic, as it will in time have a profound effect on all Ireland, north and south.

• Provisions for the establishment of north-south bodies to formulate policy on an all-Ireland basis in limited areas will require Irish ministers to reach agreement with their Northern Irish counterparts. This will provide opportunities for development of all-Ireland bodies, but will also contain risks that civil servants in the Republic are careless of unionist sensibilities.

• Maintenance of Ireland's successful de facto incomes policy, based on tripartite negotiations to ensure wage moderation and industrial peace, will be a top economic priority. Controlling inflation is essential for the competitiveness of an economy which exports the equivalent of 85% of GDP.

ITALY

GDP: $1,294.3bn
GDP per head: $21,685
Population: 57.7m
GDP growth: 1.6%. Inflation: 1.8%

• Massimo D'Alema's new coalition government is constitutionally guaranteed to survive until May 1999, but strains will be apparent before then. However, the administration should survive the important 2000 budget negotiations, before a new election is called in early 2000.

• Fearing instability on its doorstep and a further influx of refugees, Italy will do everything in its power to prevent Albania lurching from crisis to crisis.

• Lobbying will gather apace to promote an Italian as the next president

of the European Commission, a decision EU governments will take in the first half of 1999. Two former premiers, Giuliano Amato and Romano Prodi, are possible candidates.

Budget balance
% of GDP

1995	1996	1997	1998	1999
-7.70	-6.70	-2.70	-2.75	-2.29

THE NETHERLANDS

GDP: $396.7bn
GDP per head: $25,159
Population: 15.8m
GDP growth: 2.7%. Inflation: 1.9%

• Calls for a tougher stance on immigration policy will grow louder, with the Liberals (the second-largest party in parliament and in the government coalition) pushing for stricter limits on asylum-seekers.

• Growing Dutch unease about the country's large net contribution to the EU budget could lead to a less accommodating Dutch position in EU matters.

• Economic growth will slow, as the business cycle passes its peak. But it will be strong enough to keep the Netherlands' reputation as a star performer, for its combination of robust development and low unemployment.

NORWAY

GDP: $165.3bn
GDP per head: $37,339
Population: 4.4m
GDP growth: 3.0%. Inflation: 2.8%

• The Christian Democrat-led coalition, which came to office in September 1997, has proved to be surprisingly durable, but it is still fundamentally unstable and could be brought down over a number of economic issues. The Labour Party would be favourite to resume office.

• The 1999 budget includes measures to dampen the domestic economy. Despite weak oil prices the offshore hydrocarbon industry will continue to generate budget surpluses, which will be used to accumulate financial resources in the Petroleum Fund, Norway's insurance policy for the future.

• Having suspended its policy of

exchange-rate stabilisation during the financial turmoil of mid-1998, the central bank will once again pursue its objective of krona stability, especially with the euro.

PORTUGAL

GDP: $117.6bn
GDP per head: $11,846
Population: 9.9m
GDP growth: 3.3%. Inflation: 2.9%

• The Socialist Party is likely to retain power in the election due by October 1999.

• Portugal will be a founder member of the EU's single currency, but the maturity of its economic cycle may mean that monetary policy under the European Central Bank is looser than is suitable for Portuguese conditions. Inflation could also rise as a result of pre-election laxity in fiscal policy.

To watch
Portugal has only limited direct exposure to the economic crises in Asia, but it is vulnerable to negative sentiment surrounding emerging markets; prolonged turbulence in equity markets could lead to a general loss of consumer and business confidence.

SPAIN

Budget balance
% of GDP

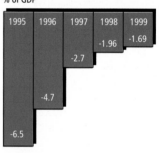

1995	1996	1997	1998	1999
-6.5	-4.7	-2.7	-1.96	-1.69

GDP: $592.1bn
GDP per head: $15,032
Population: 39.4m
GDP growth: 3.4%. Inflation: 2.5%

• The minority Popular Party government looks stable now that the Catalan nationalists of Convergence and Union have agreed to support it for the remainder of the current legislature (which will end in March 2000 at the latest).

• The challenge facing the prime minister, José Maria Aznar, is to ensure that his party, which is only marginally ahead of the Socialists in opinion polls, reaps the electoral dividends of a booming economy and falling unemployment.

• The economy should continue to grow vigorously in 1999, albeit on a moderating trend as the foreign balance's contribution to growth turns more strongly negative than in 1998.

To watch
Basque terrorism—or the lack of it. In announcing an indefinite ceasefire, are the Basque terrorists of ETA, like the IRA in Northern Ireland, serious about replacing bombs with the ballot box?

SWEDEN

GDP: $251.3bn
GDP per head: $28,312
Population: 8.9m
GDP growth: 2.9%. Inflation: 1.9%

• By returning the Social Democrats to office and doubling the strength of the Left Party, Swedes voted to strengthen their already formidable welfare state. Forget about any tax relief in 1999.

• The election also strengthened the position of the parties most opposed to EMU membership, which will thus stay off the Swedish agenda.

• Despite heavy welfare spending, Sweden will be able to maintain a budget surplus in 1999, helping to reduce its debt burden.

To watch
Legal manoeuvring over the touchy—and expensive—issue of the closure of nuclear power stations.

SWITZERLAND

GDP: $273.2bn
GDP per head: $37,891
Population: 7.2m
GDP growth: 1.8%. Inflation: 0.8%

• The government has made considerable efforts to improve its international image, which has taken a battering over allegations of Swiss co-operation with the Nazi government in Germany in 1933-45. But some of the damage will take years to repair.

• Switzerland's internal stability is legendary, so news of constitutional amendments could raise eyebrows. But the changes planned are minor. Some acceleration of federal decision-making is likely as a result.

• The Swiss central bank will pursue its recent policy of maintaining the Swiss franc's broad stability against European currencies and "shadowing" the euro, even if that policy is unofficial. In the longer term such an approach will lead to a greater convergence of Swiss interest rates with euro rates.

TURKEY

GDP: $207.5bn
GDP per head: $3,159
Population: 65.7m
GDP growth: 4.1%. Inflation: 64.7%

• Despite an agreement which should guarantee new elections in April 1999, pressure for delay from the generals may encourage the multi-party coalition under Mesut Yilmaz to hold off on the polls until 2000. With pro-Islamist sentiment still strong, there is little advantage for any secular party in pushing for elections soon.

• Turkey and Greece will snarl at each other across the Aegean, but barking rather than biting should remain the order of the day.

To watch
Efforts will be made to patch up relations with the EU, which have suffered (to the dismay of Americans worried about regional stability) through snubs over Turkey's application for EU membership and through Greek obstructionism over economic aid.

UNITED KINGDOM

Unemployment rate
%

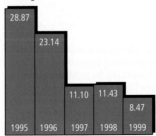

1995	1996	1997	1998	1999
8.2	7.5	5.6	5.6	6.2

GDP: $1,450.6bn
GDP per head: $23,478
Population: 59.3m
GDP growth: 0.8%. Inflation: 2.7%

• A tough year for the British economy. Growth will slow, particularly in the early months. Monetary policy will continue to ease, however, as inflationary pressures recede, while fiscal policy will become more expansionary when the government's new, three-year framework for public spending comes into force.

To watch
Will growing Scottish nationalism produce a serious push for full independence?

Eastern Europe

BALTIC REPUBLICS

GDP:	Estonia: $4.8bn
	Latvia: $6.7bn
	Lithuania: $9.6bn
GDP per head:	Estonia: $4,275
	Latvia: $2,729
	Lithuania: $2,605
Population:	Estonia: 1.5m
	Latvia: 2.4m
	Lithuania: 3.7m
GDP growth:	Estonia: 4.4%
	Latvia: 5.0%
	Lithuania: 3.0%
Inflation:	Estonia: 8.5%
	Latvia: 6.0%
	Lithuania: 8.0%

• Estonia is the only Baltic country admitted to the first round of EU enlargement talks. Sound fundamentals and a strong regulatory framework, coupled with the stability of the currency board, should cushion the impact of Russian contagion. However, the current-account deficit, already in excess of 10% of GDP, could widen further.

• In 1998, Latvia boasted high growth, low inflation and currency stability while the current-account deficit was manageable. The country reduced its trade ties with Russia following a political row over Latvia's large Russian minority. But the Russian market remains very important for some sectors and more than 10% of Latvian GDP depends on the transit trade of Russian goods. Latvian banks' exposure to Russia is also significant. The Russian crisis will therefore dampen GDP growth in 1999.

• Lithuania will be hit even harder. Before the rouble's collapse, one-fifth of its exports went to Russia, with another fifth going to other parts of the ex-Soviet Union. Lack of demand from the east will therefore affect the current-account deficit, which hovers at over 13% of GDP in 1998. Despite the currency board, the litas is prone to fears of a devaluation. GDP growth will come down in 1999 and inflation will pick up again.

Consumer prices
% change

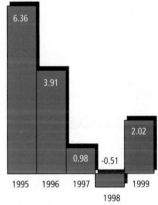

1995	1996	1997	1998	1999
28.87	23.14	11.10	11.43	8.47

BULGARIA

GDP: $13.0bn
GDP per head: $1,585
Population: 8.2m
GDP growth: 3.0%. Inflation: 8.5%

• Chaos in Russia should not drag the Bulgarian economy down with it. Bulgaria still buys 25% of its imports from the Russian Federation but now sells less than 10% of its exports there.

• There will be some damage to the current account, exacerbated by the lev, which has inevitably undergone some real appreciation. Foreign investors are also likely to be more cautious.

• Any threats to the prime minister, Ivan Kostov, will come from within. He has been criticised for an authoritarian style, and this could be a problem if growth does not pick up. But do not expect to see Mr Kostov running into serious political problems.

CZECH REPUBLIC

GDP
% real change

1995	1996	1997	1998	1999
6.36	3.91	0.98	-0.51	2.02

GDP: $56.6bn
GDP per head: $5,538
Population: 10.2m
GDP growth: 2.0%. Inflation: 7.0%

• The June 1998 general election failed to deliver political stability. The Social Democrats lack an overall majority and now preside over a minority government in alliance with the Civic Democratic Party. This may have temporarily filled a vacuum, but provides no basis for stable government. Fresh elections are likely.

• After a slight contraction of GDP in 1998, a recovery is likely in 1999. The central bank's reluctance to ease its tight monetary approach will keep growth modest.

• The Czech Republic seems likely to suffer only a marginal direct impact from the turmoil in Russia. Its access to international capital markets will be hit—making a tight fiscal policy and careful management of the balance-of-payments deficit essential.

To watch
Constitutional reform. Another weak government emerging from an election has increased pressure for electoral reform to modify the proportional system with some more direct elements.

HUNGARY

GDP: $51.9bn
GDP per head: $5,134
Population: 10.1m
GDP growth: 4.5%. Inflation: 13.7%

• The impact of the Russian crisis and a slowdown in EU growth will shave about one percentage point off Hungary's real GDP growth in 1999.

• The Budapest Stock Exchange was knocked flat by the financial turbulence in Russia. Recovery will be slow as confidence in the market will be undercut by the situation in Russia.

• Tensions are already apparent in the government coalition, with the concentration of power around the prime minister causing problems. These tensions will increase.

• The ruling Federation of Young Democrats-Hungarian Civic Party (Fidesz) will continue to indulge in populist and nationalist rhetoric, making Hungary's neighbours uneasy.

POLAND

GDP: $160.7bn
GDP per head: $4,149
Population: 38.7m
GDP growth: 5.6%. Inflation: 9.1%

• The centre-right coalition which is composed of Solidarity Electoral Action and the Freedom Union has been weakened by defections and has had to rely on the support of the Democratic Left Alliance. In 1999 expect to see further in-fighting and an increasingly embattled government.

• The impact of the Russian crisis has been limited and Poland is well set to survive in a healthier state than most of its neighbours. So successfully has Poland adapted its patterns of trade since 1991 that it is the possibility of slowing growth in the EU which presents the greatest threat to Polish economic health.

To watch
Threats to coalition cohesion. Further departures are likely and the emergence of the right-wing Patriotic Movement could provide a base for more defectors to head.

ROMANIA

GDP: $43.5bn
GDP per head: $4,149
Population: 22.5m
GDP growth: 3.0%. Inflation: 25.0%

• Romania's prospects were already grim before the Russian crisis, following its failure to secure a new lending agreement with the IMF.

• The effect of the post-Russia turmoil will be to compound Romania's domestic problems and further to undermine external confidence.

RUSSIA

Consumer prices
% change

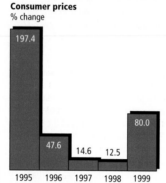

1995	197.4
1996	47.6
1997	14.6
1998	12.5
1999	80.0

GDP: $239.7bn
GDP per head: $2,466
Population: 146.6m
GDP growth: -7.0%. Inflation: 80.0%

• The reform process is over as far as 1999 is concerned: the year will see a gradual turning inward, with controls being re-established on trade, currency and prices, steps backwards in the eyes of the IMF, but inevitable in the circumstances.

• Yevgeny Primakov's cabinet has an unbalanced look about it—with moderate reformers back-to-back with old-style central planners—but the government's direction will be largely backward-looking. The government and the IMF will want to keep up some relationship, but commercial financing is out of reach for the foreseeable future.

• Boris Yeltsin's health is always a source of uncertainty, but in 1999 there are so many others that it seems less crucial than usual. Legislative elections are due in 1999, but expect the president to hang on until the presidential poll in 2000.

To watch
A headlong depreciation of the rouble could force the government to print money in even larger quantities—hyperinflation could then result, with serious consequences for political stability.

SLOVAKIA

GDP: $19.5bn
GDP per head: $3,613
Population: 5.4m
GDP growth: 0.8%. Inflation: 11.0%

• The new government faces massive economic problems, but will get a more sympathetic reception than its predecessor.

• There is one bright spot in an otherwise gloomy economic outlook for Slovakia: as a large energy importer from Russia, its balance of trade may actually benefit from the chaos in Russia's markets and low crude prices, as long as there is no major disruption to supplies.

• Growth will slow to, at best, a halt in 1999, as the koruna depreciates and unemployment rises.

UKRAINE

GDP: $45.6bn
GDP per head: $3,158
Population: 50.6m
GDP growth: -1.0%. Inflation: 25.0%

• The impact of the Russian crisis will dominate everything and Ukraine can argue plausibly to be the worst affected of all Russia's neighbours.

• The hryvnya is facing severe and ongoing depreciation, fuelling inflation, cutting real incomes and thus forcing the country back into recession.

• Russia's debt default will make it impossible for Ukraine to issue Eurobonds in 1998 or 1999, increasing its reliance on IMF funding. The IMF will want to support Ukraine through the crisis, but domestic political pressure against the economic reform programme may interrupt that process, after which the Fund may not be able to justify continuing support.

GDP
% Real change

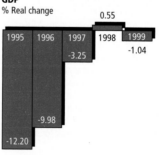

1995	-12.20
1996	-9.98
1997	-3.25
1998	0.55
1999	-1.04

Asia Pacific

AUSTRALIA

GDP: $368.6bn
GDP per head: $19,462
Population: 18.9m
GDP growth: 1.0%. Inflation: 1.5%

• Despite the electoral failure of Pauline Hanson's xenophobic One Nation group, the inconvenient issues which it has fed on—particularly, growing popular disillusion with central government—will not vanish.

• Having weathered the initial effects of the Asian crises in 1998, Australia will take the main hit in 1999. Exports to Asian states will fall further and low commodity prices will hurt the current account.

• Although growth is likely to slip in 1999, spending on the Olympic Games, which are scheduled for Sydney in 2000, will provide some relief.

CHINA

GDP
% real change

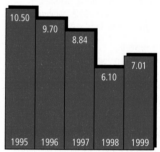

1995	10.50
1996	9.70
1997	8.84
1998	6.10
1999	7.01

GDP: $978.3bn
GDP per head: $779
Population: 1.25bn
GDP growth: 7.0%. Inflation: 6.0%

• Devaluation of the yuan is likely in 1999, but only if international financial markets stabilise, allowing the government to act without setting off another round of regional instability.

• Despite increased government spending on infrastructure, growth will slow—and with it the reform process.

• China will take a supportive, rather than confrontational, approach to most of its neighbours.

• Output is rising from state-owned companies but merely feeding stockpiles.

To watch
Provincial instability, especially in the north-west, as ethnic groups become restless.

HONG KONG

GDP: $159.6bn
GDP per head: $23,474
Population: 6.8m
GDP growth: -2.2%. Inflation: 3.5%

• The multiple regional crises will continue to take their toll on Hong Kong's economy and another contraction is in store for 1999, albeit a smaller one than that suffered in 1998.

• The Legislative Council will see more and more confrontations between pro-democracy deputies and the leadership. The government will come under more pressure as unemployment rises.

• Property prices will continue to fall, but wages will prove inflexible, putting Hong Kong's long-term competitive position at risk.

INDIA

GDP: $376.8bn
GDP per head: $382
Population: 986.2m
GDP growth: 5.7%. Inflation: 9.3%

• This being India, another election in 1999 is always a possibility; the ruling coalition is beset with serious disagreements. Congress may try to cobble together an alternative coalition, but is more likely to wait until it can launch a credible election bid to form a more stable government.

• India's fraught relationship with America is likely to ease through 1999. Executive waivers in Washington will dull the immediate effect of sanctions imposed after India's nuclear tests.

• After slowing in 1998, GDP growth will accelerate again in 1999. The industrial expansion will be sluggish, but agriculture will have a good year.

To watch
Pakistan. India's always difficult relationship with its northern neighbour needs to be carefully controlled, lest it go nuclear.

INDONESIA

GDP: $122.9bn
GDP per head: $590
Population: 208.2m
GDP growth: -2.3%. Inflation: 15.9%

• After 1998, anything will seem an improvement, but 1999 is not going to bring much relief for the beleaguered Indonesians. Unemployment is close to 20m and almost half the population slid into absolute poverty in 1998. Yet a further, albeit smaller, contraction is in store in 1999.

• Crucial legislative elections are scheduled for May. The opportunity to

vote in a real democratic poll is a novelty for most Indonesians and the results of that vote are likely to decide who will stand in the presidential election due at the end of the year.

• The current president, B.J. Habibie, has managed to distance himself from the ousted leader, Suharto, but will struggle to be a serious challenger in the presidential election. Both Amien Rais and Megawati Sukarnoputri are capable of forming powerful alliances.

To watch
Misery. Rising unemployment, falling real wages and inflation have led to much ruin and rioting. Deepening disorder could put elections in jeopardy.

JAPAN

GDP
% real change

Year	Value
1995	1.38
1996	4.09
1997	0.81
1998	-2.28
1999	0.24

GDP: $3,190.7bn
GDP per head: $25,129
Population: 127m
GDP growth: 0.2%. Inflation: -0.1%

• The political and bureaucratic system will remain in the doldrums, with the Liberal Democratic Party riven by factions and the administration struggling to cope with the myriad elements of Japan's economic crisis.

• Economic recovery will be slow, as a tottering financial infrastructure complicates the government's attempts at salvage.

• The prime minister, Keizo Obuchi, has a limited ambition: to survive until party elections in September when he could hand the baton over and retire. Even that may prove beyond him.

KAZAKHSTAN

GDP: $23.5bn
GDP per head: $1,415
Population: 16.6m
GDP growth: -2.5%. Inflation: 19.5%

• Russia's continuing importance to Kazakhstan has again been demonstrated by the immediate impact of the financial crisis there on the Kazakh economy. In 1999 the effects of the rouble devaluation will still be

percolating through, causing Kazakh GDP to shrink.

• The poor prospects for oil prices in 1999 seem to negate any chance of the economy staging a recovery. The tenge will continue to slide.

• President Nursultan Nazarbayev will do his best to distance himself from the government's economic failures, but with little success. As conditions worsen throughout the country he will have to rely ever more heavily on the security services to retain control.

MALAYSIA

GDP: $63.0bn
GDP per head: $2,772
Population: 22.7m
GDP growth: -2.1%. Inflation: 5.5%

• More than ever, Dr Mahathir dominates the ruling party, UMNO. But popular support for his former deputy, Anwar Ibrahim, and growing agitation over the economic crisis threaten to be an explosive mixture.

• Malaysia has chosen to ignore the IMF and take its own route out of the regional crisis with exchange controls, an expansionary fiscal policy and low interest rates to boost growth. But by mid-1999 this strategy will be close to collapse, and will lead to another U-turn.

To watch
Capital controls, as interventionist measures are likely to be modified or dismantled late in 1999. Only then—and provided structural problems in the financial sector are fixed—will Malaysia again attract new foreign direct investment.

NEW ZEALAND

Domestic demand
Growth %

Year	Value
1995	4.9
1996	4.8
1997	3.6
1998	1.3
1999	0.9

GDP: $52.4bn
GDP per head: $13,502
Population: 3.9m
GDP growth: 1.0%. Inflation: 1.5%

• The government is expected to limp on only until the budget debate begins

in February. An election is likely to follow.

• The government will hope that revenues from privatisation will help shore up its fiscal position. Possible targets for privatisation in the next year include several state assets that were previously deemed off-limits: TVNZ, New Zealand Post and electricity generators, ECNZ and Contact Energy. Opposition to such sales will be strong.

PAKISTAN

GDP: $61.4bn
GDP per head: $405
Population: 151.6m
GDP growth: 1.2%. Inflation: 11.5%

• Nawaz Sharif's Pakistan Muslim League government will stay in power, but policy inertia in the face of the balance-of-payments crisis will heighten its vulnerability to street protests.

• Despite help from the IMF and others, the risk of default on external debt remains a real one.

• Growth will be constrained by inadequate investment in agriculture and industry. Pakistan's narrow export base, low value-added production and deteriorating external environment will frustrate any sustained rise in exports.

To watch
Regional politics. Added to the Kashmiri flashpoint, Pakistan's support for the Taliban in Afghanistan will continue to prejudice relations with Iran.

PHILIPPINES

Government consumption
Growth %

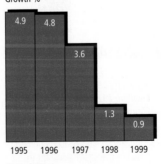

Year	Value
1995	5.4
1996	5.2
1997	3.6
1998	2.0
1999	1.8

GDP: $69.0bn
GDP per head: $899
Population: 76.8m
GDP growth: 2.3%. Inflation: 5.5%

• President Josef Estrada does not face direct challenges to his authority, but his economic plan will remain controversial. Many fear that his populist approach to politics will be mirrored in his economic policy.

• The effects of the regional currency

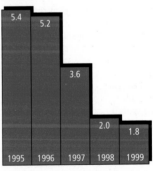

crises and the aftermath of the El Niño weather phenomenon have taken their toll. Growth will be disappointingly low.

• Investment projects will help the economy ease its way out of trouble.

SINGAPORE

GDP: $87.6bn
GDP per head: $27,181
Population: 3.2m
GDP growth: 1.4%. Inflation: 1.7%

• The ruling People's Action Party will not let up on dissent. Exercises in popular "consultation" will be spurious.

• "Asian values", much touted by the former prime minister, Lee Kuan Yew, are no longer in fashion. That will not prevent the government from trying to reinvent them.

• The authorities will try to restructure the banking system, but it will be hurt by developments in Malaysia.

To watch
Resentment about the positions and salaries of senior officialdom, which could become more open if the economic gloom deepens.

SOUTH KOREA

GDP: $287.0bn
GDP per head: $6,135
Population: 46.8m
GDP growth: -2.3%. Inflation: 5.7%

• The president, Kim Dae Jung, will struggle to impose reforms along the lines required by the IMF. Opposition will come from the leading *chaebol* (conglomerates) and from workers worried about rising unemployment.

• Despite a more liberal approach to foreign investment, the economy will shrink in the absence of corporate restructuring.

• North Korea's foolish and provocative behaviour could undermine Mr Kim's "sunshine" policy towards the north.

To watch
Relations with Japan. The two countries are supposed to co-host the 2002 football World Cup, but financial and other problems could threaten this collaboration.

TAIWAN

GDP: $264.7bn
GDP per head: $12,074
Population: 21.9m
GDP growth: 4.8%. Inflation: 2.9%

• Growth will be better than in most Asian countries, but slow by Taiwanese standards. Industry and the financial

sector are proving responsive to the regional upheaval.

• Taiwan will be under considerable pressure to reach some sort of accommodation with the mainland. Otherwise, it will become more isolated politically, which will hurt the economy.

• Graft in politics will remain a key issue for the public at large. Attention may also focus on military corruption.

THAILAND

GDP: $131.7bn
GDP per head: $2,135
Population: 61.7m
GDP growth: -0.1%. Inflation: 7.0%

• The coalition government led by the Democrat Party prime minister, Chuan Leekpai, is expected to call an election in mid-1999. The opposition New Aspiration Party will hope to gain from Thailand's economic woes.

• The economy will go on contracting in 1999, albeit less severely than in 1998. Restructuring will take time and incur serious economic and social costs. Widespread protests, strikes and labour disputes are probable.

• Commitment to the IMF-backed reforms could wane. But Malaysia's unhappy example will discourage the government from a change of course.

To watch
Yen weakness or Chinese devaluation could put heavy pressure on the baht.

GDP
% Real change

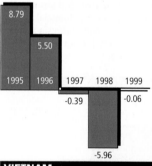

VIETNAM

GDP: $25.7bn
GDP per head: $324
Population: 79.5m
GDP growth: 5.0%. Inflation: 10.0%

• The new leadership of the party is theoretically committed to economic reform, but may prove reluctant to make the necessary hard choices.

• Progress on privatisation and banking reform will be slow.

• Inflows of foreign direct investment will lessen. Domestic industry faces severe problems. Growth will suffer.

North America

CANADA

GDP: $622.2bn
GDP per head: $20,250
Population: 30.9m
GDP growth: 1.9%. Inflation: 1.3%

• 1999 should see public disaffection with the government's economic performance force an election ahead of the required schedule, if growth slows so far as to threaten a real contraction. With commodity prices low and credit rates high, all the ingredients are there for a severe slowing of growth in 1999.

• A provincial election in Quebec is expected in the spring and will once again push the debate over the country's unity to the fore. This will be compounded by the recent Supreme Court decision on Quebec's constitutional right to secede.

UNITED STATES

Exchange rate
¥ : US $

1995	1996	1997	1998	1999
94	109	121	137	139

GDP: $8,848.4bn
GDP per head: $32,616
Population: 272.3m
GDP growth: 1.6%. Inflation: 2.4%

• The president's personal life will continue to intrude on his public one. However, a more Democratic Congress means that life will be less difficult for him. Impeachment will almost certainly be avoided, but the decision is essentially a political one.

• Fund-raising by candidates for the 2000 presidential elections will increasingly dominate the political scene. Al Gore should end 1999 in a strong position to secure the Democratic nomination.

• The economy will weaken in 1999. Crises in emerging markets will strangle export growth and hit corporate profits, while weaker equity prices will dent personal wealth and confidence, and hence consumption. The current account will deteriorate even further as the emerging world attempts to export its way out of recession.

Latin America

ARGENTINA

GDP: $223.9bn
GDP per head: $6,177
Population: 36.2m
GDP growth: 3.4%. Inflation: 2.3%

• Presidential and congressional elections are due in October. Economic worries, a desire for change and some popular disillusionment with corruption and cronyism in the Menem administration threaten the Peronists. But the opposition alliance has pledged to stick to liberal economic policies.

• The likely Peronist candidate is Eduardo Duhalde, the governor of Buenos Aires province, now that President Carlos Menem has decided not to seek to change the constitution in order to run for a third term.

To watch
The cost of maintaining the peso-dollar peg amid global financial turbulence will test Argentina's determination to avoid devaluation.

BRAZIL

Consumer prices
% change

1995	1996	1997	1998	1999
76.82	16.48	6.44	2.97	3.46

GDP: $789.4bn
GDP per head: $4820
Population: 163.8m
GDP growth: 2.8%. Inflation: 3.5%

• In his second term, President Fernando Henrique Cardoso must press for the rapid approval of structural reforms which have remained deadlocked in Congress for the past four years. The list of such reforms— social security, tax and federal-regional revenue-sharing arrangements—is daunting, as are the barriers to be overcome in Congress.

• Until these reforms are approved, the fate of the currency, the *real*, will keep the world on tenterhooks.

• The adverse external environment will damage growth. A recession is possible, as high interest rates depress private consumption and the government attempts to rein in public spending.

To watch
Revenues from privatisation. With the economic outlook so uncertain, will the planned sell-off of electricity assets and other utilities prove as lucrative as the telecoms sale in 1998?

CHILE

GDP: $82.6bn
GDP per head: $5,497
Population: 15.0m
GDP growth: 4.1%. Inflation: 4.8%

• Unless the centre-left Concertación coalition mishandles the internal primary for its presidential nomination, it will be well-placed to win a new six-year mandate at the December 1999 presidential election. This assumes that the Christian Democrats agree to support Ricardo Lagos, the leader of Concertación's socialist wing.

• Of all Latin American countries Chile is most exposed to Asia's economic troubles. Coupled with its dependence on the (deeply depressed) price of copper, this will guarantee another tough year in 1999, with possible further slippage of the exchange rate.

• However, Chilean economic prudence should keep domestic demand growth below GDP growth. This will gradually reduce the current-account deficit from an unsustainable 6.4% of GDP in 1998.

COLOMBIA

GDP: $102.6bn
GDP per head: $2,466
Population: 41.6m
GDP growth: 2.6%. Inflation: 17.9%

• The new president, Andrés Pastrana, sees an end to Colombia's long-running civil conflict as his political priority. This is likely to remain elusive.

• On the economic front, he can expect to make some progress towards establishing tighter control over the fiscal balances.

• The government's new band for the peso will be further challenged in 1999, as commodity prices (especially oil) continue to fall.

To watch
The peace process. Although both of the two leading guerrilla organisations seem eager to participate in peace talks, concessions are unlikely. Even in the event of progress, the government must try to incorporate the paramilitaries into the peace process.

MEXICO

GDP
% real change

1995: -6.22
1996: 5.16
1997: 7.01
1998: 4.31
1999: 4.17

GDP: $452.4bn
GDP per head: $4,559
Population: 99.2m
GDP growth: 4.2%. Inflation: 12.6%

• Leading figures in the Partido Revolucionario Institucional (PRI) will compete to be the party's candidate for president in the elections in 2000. For the first time, the PRI plans to pick its candidate through primary elections, probably by the end of 1999.

• The main PRI contenders are Manuel Bartlett, the hardline governor of Puebla, and Francisco Labastida, the interior minister. The finance minister, Jose Angel Gurria Treviño, will almost certainly run if the party stops barring candidates who have not held elective office.

• Mr Gurria will in any case have plenty to think about as he tries to steer Mexico's impressive economic recovery through the turbulence in world markets, with the oil price weak and demand no longer buoyant in Mexico's main market, the United States.

VENEZUELA

GDP: $111.0bn
GDP per head: $4,606
Population: 24.1m
GDP growth: 2.7%. Inflation: 40.1%

• Fiscal reform is the main target for the new government in 1999, but it will prove politically difficult. Vested interests will resist any attempt to reform the economy.

• The popular mood will support moves against corrupt senior officials, at least in the early, honeymoon period of the government that emerges from the election in December 1998.

To watch
Public-sector reform. Venezuela is in the world super-league of bloated bureaucracy. The new administration will have to address the issue of the highly inefficient state sector if it is to put Venezuela's fiscal accounts on an even keel.

Africa

NIGERIA

GDP: $30.6bn
GDP per head: $276
Population: 110.6m
GDP growth: 4.4%. Inflation: 20.0%

• Transfer to civilian rule has been postponed from October 1998 to June 1999. But Nigeria's history does not fill observers with confidence that the latest attempt will be any more successful in the medium term than previous efforts.

• The transition programme includes the obligatory commitment to economic reform designed to placate western bankers and politicians. But implementing any such programme will be extremely challenging, particularly with oil prices so low.

To watch
Southern, Yoruba anger over the detention and death of Chief Moshood Abiola could provide the basis for discontent if the transition process appears to be little more than a cover for a continuation of rule by a largely Muslim and Hausa elite.

Government debt
% of GDP

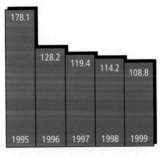

1995: 178.1
1996: 128.2
1997: 119.4
1998: 114.2
1999: 108.8

KENYA

GDP: $9.0bn
GDP per head: $295
Population: 30.6m
GDP growth: 1.9%. Inflation: 9.0%

• Although the bombing of the American embassy in August 1998 did induce a brief display of unity among party leaders, this is unlikely to translate into constructive longer-term political co-operation to address Kenya's serious problems.

• Prime among these, the issue of the succession remains a worry in President Daniel arup Moi's last term in office. Failure to nominate a vice-president, and thus his favoured successor, has fuelled divisions within the ruling party

and will continue to undermine political stability in 1999.

• There is little hope for recovery from Kenya's present economic crisis unless the government successfully brings its excessive spending under control. The budget set out plans for a balanced budget in the current financial year, but the public-sector wage bill and servicing domestic debt will remain major barriers to achieving this.

SOUTH AFRICA

GDP: $105.1bn
GDP per head: $2,616
Population: 40.2m
GDP growth: 2.0%. Inflation: 8.4%

• Currency instability will remain a constant problem as the rand continues to suffer from speculative attacks, but attention will focus in 1999 on the elections due in the second quarter of the year.

• State expenditure should be closely watched in early 1999 as the government gears up for the polls by seeking to ease discontent among different sections of society, in particular the trade unions.

To watch
Election turnout. The level of apathy surrounding South African elections may determine whether the African National Congress (ANC) can take sufficient votes to be able to usher in constitutional amendments. A high turnout will favour the ANC but its allies will view the consolidation of so much power in one party with concern.

Middle East

ALGERIA

GDP: $51.3bn
GDP per head: $1,657
Population: 30.9m
GDP growth: 4.0%. Inflation: 7.5%

• Unfortunately for ordinary Algerians, the government seems to have accepted the violent status quo, despite the death toll on civilians. There will be no movement towards finding a negotiated solution to the domestic conflict.

• The new consultation agreement with the IMF will mean that the government is under less pressure to follow the Fund's prescriptions. Reforms will continue, but large-scale privatisations involving redundancies are unlikely.

• Investment will remain concentrated in oil and gas. Security problems will continue to discourage investment elsewhere.

EGYPT

Government debt
% of GDP

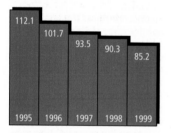

112.1	101.7	93.5	90.3	85.2
1995	1996	1997	1998	1999

GDP: $89.5bn
GDP per head: $1,386
Population: 64.5m
GDP growth: 5.1%. Inflation: 4.6%

• A monolithic regime backed by the security services faces no real challenge to its grip on power. But it will still indulge in mass arrests and detentions of suspected Islamist opponents as a method of maintaining that position.

• Economically, Egypt remains firmly in the IMF's good books and although in 1999 it will no longer receive direct financial support form the Fund, the government will continue its restructuring programme. Privatisation will speed up, starting with telecoms.

To watch
Islamist groups, which retain the ability to stage dramatic and damaging attacks on foreign interests. Despite improvement in security since the massacre in Luxor in November 1997, tourists remain vulnerable.

IRAN

Budget balance
% of GDP

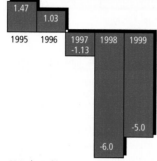

1995	1996	1997	1998	1999
1.47	1.03	-1.13	-6.0	-5.0

GDP: $85.7bn
GDP per head: $1,352
Population: 63.4m
GDP growth: 0.6%. Inflation: 25.0%

• International perceptions of the world's first Islamic republic will soften as President Mohammad Khatami seeks to improve Iran's external relations, even with the Great Satan, America. But opponents of the Iranian government within the American Congress will bar a complete abandonment of sanctions.

• At home, the power struggle between conservative clerics and more moderate reformers will intensify. Although each side will score some individual victories, the momentum is moving in the moderates' favour.

• Debt-service payments will, as ever, be the defining factor for economic policy. The government has its work cut out to meet its schedule. But new borrowing and drawing down reserves might see it through a tough year.

To watch
Relations with the Gulf states, improving thanks to the growing role of Saudi Arabia's Crown Prince Abdullah.

IRAQ

GDP: $5.7bn
GDP per head: $247
Population: 23.0m
GDP growth: 8.0%. Inflation: 105.0%

• Iraq's economic fate rests with the UN Security Council. Britain and America will oppose any relaxation of sanctions, but France, Russia and China will favour such action.

• Low oil prices will mean that Iraq will struggle to export crude up to its current UN-approved ceiling, but smuggling will ensure a sufficient flow of revenue to sustain the regime.

• Some European oil companies will drop their inhibitions about moving back into the country.

ISRAEL

GDP: $97.6bn
GDP per head: $16,138
Population: 6.1m
GDP growth: 2.3%. Inflation: 4.4%

• The peace process will remain prey to strains within Binyamin Netanyahu's administration. The prime minister's reliance on right-wing groups means that even movement already agreed with the Palestinians cannot be guaranteed to take place.

• The coalition will become even more unstable. Disputes over military deployment in the West Bank and over budget allocations will combine with distrust of the prime minister to make the government increasingly fragile. Its collapse and new elections are possible.

• Relations with America remain key and in the long term are not under threat, but Mr Netanyahu's approach to peace negotiations will continue to strain the government's relations with perhaps the most pro-Israeli Washington administration ever.

Growth in private consumption
%

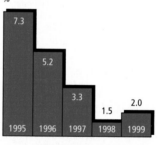

1995	1996	1997	1998	1999
7.3	5.2	3.3	1.5	2.0

JORDAN

GDP: $8.6bn
GDP per head: $1,439
Population: 6.0m
GDP growth: 1.9%. Inflation: 2.9%

• King Hussein's health following another cancer diagnosis is the main political uncertainty. Although the succession is clear, and the country's stability under a new monarch—the king's brother, Hassan—would be maintained, Jordan without Hussein would not be the same.

• The peace process, although sealed for Jordan by the 1994 treaty with Israel, is still an open question for most Jordanians, with wary eyes on the Israeli government and its approach to withdrawal from the West Bank.

To watch
The dinar, already under pressure because of poor economic results, will struggle further if the king's health deteriorates.

LEBANON

GDP: $18.6bn
GDP per head: $4,389
Population: 4.2m
GDP growth: 3.6%. Inflation: 4.7%

• The prime minister, Rafiq Hariri, now has the support of thousands of freely elected local councillors who owe their positions to his determination to introduce a measure of western-style democracy, rather than to their family names. More important, he remains the favoured choice of the Syrian government. His position seems fairly secure for the coming year.

• Confessional divisions will be as important as ever in 1999 and the government will have to juggle the different ambitions of Sunnis, Maronites, Shias and Druze. The Shias will be particularly challenging as the most numerous but also the poorest group, who bear the brunt of the ongoing confrontation over the Israeli-occupied area of the south.

• Syria remains the arbiter for Lebanese defence and foreign policy. Israel is unlikely to withdraw from the south until it receives firm security guarantees, which the Syrians are unlikely to give until Israel agrees to withdraw from Syria's Golan Heights. No chance of that under Israel's current government. This unstable border will haunt those on both sides of it.

SAUDI ARABIA

GDP: $149.2bn
GDP per head: $7,126
Population: 20.9m
GDP growth: 1.0%. Inflation: 4.0%

• As in Jordan, attention will be on regular bulletins of the king's state of health. This is extremely fragile and a rapid succession could take place at any time. The crown prince, Abdullah, is set to take over and the transfer of power should be peaceful, but a weak economy, rising unemployment and politically difficult fiscal reforms will prove a challenging combination for the Al-Saud clan.

• As the world's largest oil producer, the Saudi economy's path follows oil prices, and the collapse of the market in 1998 ensures a contraction. 1999 will prove tricky for government finances.

• The American military presence in the country remains controversial. Although the Saudis are not about to ask the Americans to leave, sentiment throughout the region towards the United States will probably require the government to indulge in some gentle criticism of America, particularly on Israel and the peace process.

General trends

G8 GDP
1999, $bn

USA	8,848
Japan	3,191
Germany	2,431
France	1,622
UK	1,451
Italy	1,294
Canada	622
Russia	240

Source: EIU

• The slowdown in world growth triggered by the Asian crisis will hurt all economies in 1999. World output will grow by only 1.7% in 1999. Developing countries will still tend to experience the highest growth. Sub-Saharan Africa will lead at 2.6%, but hard-hit Asia will trail—along with OECD countries—at 1.5%.

• There will be strong convergence between the sectors of telecommunications (fixed and mobile), information technology, news and entertainment media, and consumer goods. 1999 will see huge strides made towards a digital society. This may yet start to benefit poorer countries as the Internet becomes more accessible and semiconductor prices fall.

• For many manufacturers, the euro will bring increased price transparency and stability for products sold across the euro zone. There will be a narrowing of price differentials and the general direction of convergence will be downwards. This will encourage longer-term investment in more efficient manufacturing capacity.

Sources: Analysys, Banker, BP Statistical Review of World Energy, Barclays Economics Department, Business Week, Campaign, Computer Reseller News, Datamonitor, Dataquest, EIU, Financial Times, Flight International, Forrester Research, Gold Fields, Global Telecoms, Henderson Crosthwaite, IBM, IMF, Woking-based INTECO Corporation, International Data Corporation, IPA, J.P. Morgan, KPMG, Merrill Lynch, Mobile Communications International, OECD Economic Outlook, OECD Insurance Statistics, Oxford Economic Research Associates, Petroleum Economist, PNE, Reuters, Salomon Smith Barney, Sigma, Travel and Tourism Intelligence, VNU, Wired, WPP, Zenith Media.

Production

AEROSPACE

• Airbus and Boeing have promised to stop rattling sabres after a series of mutually crippling competitive bids which culminated in Airbus being awarded a BA contract with over-tight profit margins. The civil aviation titans say they will concentrate on increasing profitability rather than ferociously undercutting each other in a race to grab more market share.

• 1999 will see Airbus begin work on a new 100-seater aircraft, the A318, designed to rival Boeing's sluggish-selling 717, and due to enter service in 2002. Meanwhile Boeing is downsizing. It will reduce its workforce by 18,000 to 28,000 by the year's end.

• The Eurofighter moves into production 18 years after its conception, bringing business to 400 companies and securing 150,000 jobs. Britain has ordered 232 planes, and the first will be delivered to the Royal Air Force in 2002.

Top five aerospace companies
by sales, $bn

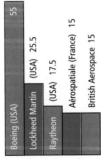

Company	$bn
Boeing (USA)	55
Lockheed Martin (USA)	25.5
Raytheon (USA)	17.5
Aérospatiale (France)	15
British Aerospace	15

Source: Aerospace magazine

• In the United States defence sector, Lockheed Martin and Boeing will compete fiercely over the contract for the Joint Strike Fighter, a $100 billion programme with initial orders estimated at over 3,000 aircraft.

To watch
The saga of Airbus Industrie's consolidation will drag on. Ministers expect the pan-European confederation to become a limited company by mid-1999. But the French are anxious about a merger between Germany's Dasa and British Aerospace, while BAe and Dasa are concerned that the French government has too large a stake in Aérospatiale. A compromise is needed soon.

AGRICULTURE

Top tea producers
1999, '000 tonnes

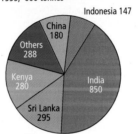

Producer	'000 tonnes
India	850
Sri Lanka	295
Others	288
Kenya	280
China	180
Indonesia	147

Source: EIU

• Barring production crises, there will be few price increases for cereals and animal feed over the next five years. As big consumers in the emerging world improve their storage capability and the opening of world trade leads to a rise in the number of producers, price volatility will diminish.

• Genetically engineered plants will be introduced over millions of hectares of farmland in the next few years. A new generation of virus-resistant engineered plants will appear.

• On January 1st 1999, the WTO arbitration on the EU's banana-import policy comes into effect. The EU will end its current licensing system with the African, Caribbean and Pacific countries. Expect further amendments to the new regulations as politicians in America and the EU voice their discontent.

• The EU will still not drop its nine-year-old ban on American and Canadian hormone-treated beef. It will seek a scientific fig-leaf for maintaining the ban.

• The reform of CAP will slowly gain momentum. Olive oil and tobacco are the first sectors to be reformed. Negotiations on changes to other important sectors—dairy, beef and cereals—will not be concluded until late 1999 when the WTO is set to launch a drive to free farm trade.

• World production of sugar will reach record highs of 128m tonnes. The surplus is expected to rise significantly in 1999 to 2.24m tonnes against 1.74m in 1998. India, South Africa and China will deliver record outputs.

• Although Brazil's coffee production will be 15% lower, coffee production overall will rise by 11% against a 1.2% rise in consumption. Prices of sugar and coffee will fall.

CARS

• The world has too many production lines churning out cars and trucks. Vehicle sales will drop by 8% to 45m, their lowest level in a decade. The industry has the capacity to produce 71m cars. Pressures on car makers to cut prices and costs, and to merge or close will increase.

• Environmental pressures will increasingly affect the European car industry, which has a lot of catching up to do. The development of new fuel-efficient engines to comply with the EU's latest limits on noxious chemicals (to be partly introduced in 2000) will cost the industry $60 billion. The new regulations will lead to big gains and big losses.

• The highest long-term growth in car sales will be in China, India, Thailand, Romania and Mexico. In Western Europe, sales will drop to less than 13m units. The Japanese share of that market will rise to 12% in the next two years, thanks to their massive cost-cutting programme and a lower yen. This will entail great difficulties for Fiat, Renault and PSA, all overly dependent on their home market. In the Eastern block, Lada will remain the strongest manufacturer despite increased competition.

• Consolidation among car producers and component manufacturers will gather pace. Japan and South Korea

World registrations of new passenger cars 1999, m (Total 35.6m)

Region	m
Western Europe	13.7
NAFTA	9.2
Japan	4.2
Pacific Rim	2.7
South America	2.0
Eastern & Central Europe	2.0
Others	1.3

Source: EIU

will be the first hit by this development. Fuji-Subaru, Isuzu, Suzuki and Daewoo are the likely targets.

• GM will remain the largest car maker overall, although its share of world car output is expected to fall to 13.5%. Ford/Mazda will still be second but will lose this place in the long term to Toyota. Volkswagen will remain fourth and Fiat fifth.

• The introduction of fuel cell cars on the market is not far off. Most of the world's big car companies will be launching dozens of prototype vehicles in 1999. Mercedes-Benz will build 40,000 fuel cell cars a year by 2004. Ford, Toyota and GM will be sticking to the same sort of timetable.

CHEMICALS

• The recession in Asia will knock down demand for chemicals by at least 1% a year until 2002. However, the major European chemical companies insist that their substantial investment plans for the Asian region, the Middle East and Venezuela will remain intact. Prices will be depressed well into 2000. Agrochemicals and engineering plastics will be little affected. Polyester and PVC will suffer more. Expect further mergers and acquisitions.

• Miniature chemical reactors will pave the way for the future. These reactors will cut today's monster chemical plants down to the size of a car, with huge financial and environmental gains.

COMPUTING

• Late in 1999 Microsoft will ship its long-awaited NT5 operating system, renamed Windows 2000, in a bid to shift Windows '95 and '98 customers onto the stable but expensive NT platform. But the world's dominant software company faces challenges, as "open source" Linux—a free UNIX-based operating system—gains credibility, and as the PC declines in favour of consumer-electronics devices such as set-top boxes. And if the US Justice Department wins its antitrust action, Bill Gates will have to take more care in brandishing his market power.

• Some of the froth is blowing off Silicon Valley's bubbling economy. Turmoil in Asia and a slowdown in some areas of IT spending in America will continue to take their toll on chip-makers and some software companies. As cost-control efforts start to bite, the overheated labour market (and demand for foreign workers on H-1B visas) will cool. But venture capital dollars will still flow into promising Internet and data networking start-ups, two robust areas of California's high-tech economy.

• Expect burgeoning sales of hand-held devices (palmtop computers and personal organisers) from 2m units shipped in 1997 to 8m by 2001. The market will fragment as devices get smaller, smarter and more specialised. Psion, the world's biggest manufacturer of hand-helds, will compete with Windows CE-based products and other small operating systems. Psion is buoyed by its new Symbian venture, which will seek to establish its operating system as the industry standard for convergence with mobile-phone technologies to give wireless Internet access.

• IBM's new SOI chip will give a further fillip to the integration of high-speed compact computing with wireless telephony. Expect the first SOI-equipped product to ship in the third quarter. It will almost certainly be an Apple Macintosh desktop computer with a processor speed in gigahertz.

• In 1999 DVD-ROM (digital versatile disk read-only memory) drives will be standard in many mid- to high-end PCs. Toshiba and other PC makers are working on recordable DVD-RAM (random access memory) drives. Hitachi is expected to launch a DVD-RAM camcorder, recording on to 5.2 Gb disks. Meanwhile Sony, Philips and Hewlett-Packard are pushing an incompatible rival, DVD-RW (rewritable). Analysts expect consumer confusion.

Top software companies
net income $m

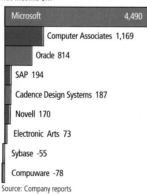

Company	$m
Microsoft	4,490
Computer Associates	1,169
Oracle	814
SAP	194
Cadence Design Systems	187
Novell	170
Electronic Arts	73
Sybase	-55
Compuware	-78

Source: Company reports

To Watch

Apple is on the up. Founder and "interim" CEO, Steve Jobs, has restored profitability. 150,000 iMacs were sold within a week of release. Sales of this flagship consumer-geared network-ready Internet terminal could top 1.5m by mid-year, rescuing the Macintosh from its creative industry ghetto. Expect the new generation OS-X operating system to ship in the third quarter of 1999.

CONSUMER ELECTRONICS

Internet screenphones worldwide sales
m

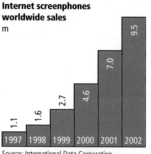

1997	1998	1999	2000	2001	2002
1.1	1.6	2.7	4.6	7.0	9.5

Source: International Data Corporation

• V Sync Technology of Japan will launch a smart fridge connected to the Internet via high-speed cable networks. An LCD screen is integrated into the fridge door, running all hours on Windows or Linux, and tripling up as a cable TV screen. With an expected price tag around $700 above the standard refrigerator mark, this 24-hour kitchen goggle-box and surf-terminal might be the order of the day for space-starved young urbanites.

To Watch
The onward march of digital video. DVD players sold in greater numbers (350,000 units) in America in their first nine months than VHS did in its first two years. The consumer phase of the European launch will be under way in 1999, but rival pay-per-view style DiVX still commands the loyalty of some key film distributors.

ENERGY

• Oil stockpiles will rise rapidly. The decline in South-East Asian demand for crude oil has been steeper than expected. On the supply side, the OPEC quota is likely to be ignored. Iraq and Libya will gradually increase their output as international restrictions are eased. Russia will try its best to increase oil production to buy its way out of its continuing financial crisis. A real price collapse to below $10 a barrel cannot be ruled out.

• Gas prices are also predicted to fall. Two consecutive mild winters and high inventory runs in North America and Europe will send prices to 10-year lows. Asia could well emerge as a net exporter of gas. A mild winter is likely to leave inventories high well into the first quarter of 1999.

• Vast resources will be devoted to building and expanding pipelines. Russia, which produces the bulk of the world's gas, is turning its attention away from Europe and looking at transporting gas to Asian markets, especially China.

• Keep watching the Caspian region. Oil exploration and development activity will gather apace in Kazakhstan and in offshore sectors of Azerbaijan. Gas prospects in Turkmenistan look equally good. Iran, too, is intent on rapidly developing its oil industry and becoming the main transit route for oil from the Caspian region as American sanctions ease.

• Though the Danish North Sea will boom, expect a general slowdown in the North Sea oil sector. Falling oil prices will force near-depleted fields to shut down. Norway will restrict foreign development licences to give its own firms a boost.

Electricity consumption
Kilowatt hours per head

Developing countries	814
North America	13,100
Eastern Europe and CIS	4,170
EU	6,300
Nordic countries	15,766

Source: UNDP

• The EU electricity market will be liberalised in February 1999. Consumers of over 40 billion kilowatt hours will be able to choose their suppliers. About 400 companies will be eligible at the outset.

• China's coal industry will go into rapid decline. China is to close some 22,000 coal mines by 2000. Hydro-electricity is set to take over.

PHARMACEUTICALS

• Although health-care reform in the West and in Japan will increase pressures on the industry to cut costs, profits are expected to remain buoyant this year. 1998 saw an impressive array of drug launches and a series of efforts to control manufacturing costs. In the long term, however, the margins of the major drug companies will come under increasing pressure from the widespread promotion of generic drugs.

• EU countries' efforts to harmonise legislation on approving drugs will cut the time taken for new drugs to reach the market. Within five years, America and Europe will have made preliminary steps toward simultaneous approval of new drugs.

• Pharmaceutical marketing is becoming ever more important. Sales forces will grow. New marketing strategies are being developed. Direct-to-consumer advertising and socio-economic studies are back in fashion.

• The worldwide cholesterol-lowering drugs market will double in size by 2002 to $16 billion-worth of sales.

Top five pharmaceutical companies sales, $bn

Company	Sales $bn
Merck and Co	23.6
Johnson & Johnson	22.6
Bristol-Meyers Squibb	16.7
Roche Holding	13.3
Glaxo Wellcome	12.9

Source: J.P. Morgan

Look out also for the migraine-drug market, where sales are expected to increase by 25% in the next year to $2.3 billion. Imitrex and Amerge by Glaxo-Wellcome will have 75% of this market. Growth in the anti-depression market will slow to 13%, down from 17% in 1998. Expect a growth rate of 38% for American diabetes drugs, an increase in sales volume of $1 billion. Watch out for Viagra, with an estimated $1.6 billion-worth of sales expected in 1999.

PRECIOUS METALS

• The gold price will range between $250 and $300 per oz. On the demand side, no recovery can be expected from the Asian markets. Gold will flow out of those countries. India's growth in demand for the yellow metal will be particularly sluggish. On the supply side, there will be continuing hedging by the gold companies. Expect further selling by the central banks, especially Russia's.

• Silver will fare better than gold. Despite the obsolescence of silver-halide photographic film, demand is expected to grow. Much silver has been taken out of circulation. Expect a price of approximately $5.60-5.70 per oz.

RAW MATERIALS

• Aluminium, copper and lead production will exceed consumption in 1999. The prices of these commodities are expected to fall by 4%. The closure of many loss-making plants will then push prices back up from mid-1999 onwards. The surplus of metals will be whittled away during the course of 2000 as world growth is expected to revert to pre-crisis rates. Russian stocks will become depleted as operations suffer from a lack of investment. By 2000, metals prices could well be 10% higher.

• The existing surplus of rubber will grow rapidly. Production in South-East

Asia will start gaining momentum in 1999 as the effect of El Niño begins to fade. A slowdown in car sales in the OECD and in Asia will weaken demand. Tyre manufacturers already have ample stockpiles of rubber. The decision by Thailand and Malaysia to withdraw from INRO in order to manipulate prices more efficiently is expected to have very little impact on prices.

Top rubber consumers 1999, '000 tonnes

Region	'000 tonnes
North America	1,250
China	1,171
EU	948
Japan	712
India	597.4

Source: EIU

TEXTILES

• The demand for cotton will recover in 1999 thanks to a 5% increase in consumption in India and Eastern Europe. This will coincide with a decline in cotton output from 19.35m tonnes to 19m tonnes because of flooding in China and heatwaves in America. Expect an increase of 6.5% in cotton prices this year, and 10% in wool.

• The Textile and Clothing Agreement, which will come into effect in January 2002, will liberalise a further 18% of the developed countries' imports of textiles and clothing. This will lead to a long-term rise in global demand.

• Regionalisation will play a more prominent role in the textile trade. Mexico will increase its exports to America in accordance with NAFTA, squeezing out Asian exports. The Asian countries which have devalued their currencies will not suffer. Textile producers from China, on the other hand, will suffer a lot more.

Top cotton producers 1998–99, m tonnes

Uzbekistan 1.2
Pakistan 1.6
Brazil 0.42
India 2.7
Others 5.48
US 3.6
China 4.0

Source: EIU

Services

ADVERTISING

• The industry expects growth toward the year's end, with an American presidential election in 2000, the coming Olympics in Sydney and the general millennial focus. Although international agencies have been burned by the Asian crisis (and a few by exposure to the Russian market), Singapore and Taiwan will be notable growth areas, as will Poland. Competition in global telecommunications will boost advertising revenues.

• Professional firms (in law, banking, consultancy, engineering) are showing an increasing interest in branding. The big five accountancy firms will lead the way. Ernst & Young is hiring DMB&B at $100m. Deloitte Touche Tohmatsu, PriceWaterhouseCoopers and Andersen Consulting are all investing similar sums in building branded global identities. Analysts are sceptical at the prospect of complex professional services being branded like commodities.

Where advertising will grow 1997–2000, %

Country	%
China	87
Portugal	50
Czech Rep	45
South Africa	26
Philippines	21
Belgium	20
Ireland	19
Chile	19
India	19
Greece	17

Source: Zenith Media

AIRLINES

• Global alliances will bring further consolidation to the industry, but the great potential for cost synergies has yet to be fully exploited. Earnings will remain high as long as these alliances remain antitrust exempt. But regulatory strictures (particularly in the form of EU aviation policy) will begin to creep in.

• Passenger traffic will grow at an average annual rate of 5.3% over the next ten years.

To watch
Low-cost carriers will exploit the no-frills segment of intra-Europe air travel, set to grow fourfold by 2002.

BANKING

• The banking industry will be under intense pressure throughout 1999. Bad debts in emerging markets, lower margins and new technologies will keep bankers alert to dangers. The share prices of banks will be slow to recover. Asian banks, which are partly responsible for the crisis, will be experiencing major internal restructuring and recapitalisation programmes. Japan and South Korea will be in the spotlight. Expect more privatisations, more mergers. Even China will be streamlining the operations of its "big four" state-owned banks.

• The arrival of a single currency will accelerate the mergers of financial institutions across Europe as national financial services markets fade. Consumers and companies in the more protected countries will benefit in the form of lower credit costs and higher returns on their investments. European banks will also have to face increasingly fierce competition from American powerhouses.

• Further deregulation will enable banks across the world to move into insurance, given its attractive growth prospects.

• IT will offer many new channels through which financial institutions are able to interact with customers. Customers and banks will be able to benefit from a vast wealth of information on each other. America and Asia will lead in this respect. This process of virtualisation will increase competition as customers will find it easier to defect.

HEALTH CARE

• Health-care reform in America and Europe will accelerate consolidation among health-care providers. The federal government will cut its Medicare bill between 1999 and 2002, pressuring hospitals and doctors to appoint more of the large and powerful bodies which purchase medical supplies for thousands of patients. In Europe, by the end of the next decade, the medical supplies required by millions of Europeans will be purchased by just a few thousand hospital and physician buying groups. Japan, too, is beginning to talk of health-care reform.

• Medical smartcards will burgeon in Europe. The cards will soon include medical records, administrative functions and drug prescriptions. Card systems will yield enormous savings, but will raise controversial questions about privacy.

• America's managed-care companies

are in for a rough ride. Competition will drive acquisitions and mergers in this sector. The 1,000 or so now operating will dwindle to no more than 100 by the next decade. Expect new state and federal government legislation advocating better customer service. The right to sue one's managed-care company is a future possibility.

INSURANCE

• Consolidation in the insurance sector will continue as insurance premiums stay low and insurers are flush with cash. Expect acquisitions of life-insurance companies to occur only within the same country because of international differences in social-security systems and tax legislation. This will remain true in Europe even after the introduction of the euro. However, expect a wave of cross-border consolidations of the non-life insurance companies.

• El Niño has not delivered the major disasters it has previously inflicted on the world. However, as its effects diminish over the course of 1999, expect more tropical cyclones in the Caribbean and on the East coast of America. Accident premiums there will rise.

• Asia and Latin America offer the most attractive growth markets in international insurance. Premium volume is expected to grow by 10% annually in those regions. The highest growth will be in China, approximately 15% in real terms. Development in these emerging markets will result from economic growth, rapid ageing of populations and reforms of the various social-security systems. Life-insurance markets will be the most important.

• Watch Allianz, ING, Generali and Prudential. These firms will pursue aggressive strategies of international acquisitions.

MEDIA

• Cinema attendance will level out in America, but extensive multiplexing (except in the already developed markets of France, Germany and Britain) will boost European audiences by 60m to 967m, a rise of 140m from 1997 levels.

• There will be a sharp rise in the use of the Internet as an entertainment and news medium. Digital interactivity and TV set-top Web access will blur the lines in domestic media technology.

• Internet music sales will soar, from $87m in 1998 to $225m in 1999. In association with American record companies, IBM will launch a digital music distribution system, currently

Technology uptake
years from inception to 50m users

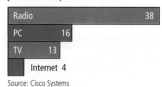

Source: Cisco Systems

codenamed the Madison Project. Consumers will be able to download their requests from Web to hard disk.

To watch
Digital TV takes off in Europe, offering interactive services, high picture quality, near video-on-demand movies and pay-per-view sport. America will be held back by disagreements between networks and cable operators over high-definition TV.

RETAIL

Internet commerce growth
USA sales, $bn

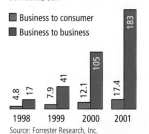

Source: Forrester Research, Inc.

• The advent of the euro will affect supply chains in Europe which have evolved to serve mainly national markets. As currency barriers come down, prices will converge rapidly, bringing new demands on retailers and forcing them to overhaul fragmented supply and distribution systems.

• The biggest change in retail will be the projected growth of "electronic commerce" on the Web, which will be one of the principal engines of economic growth over the next ten years. Total online shopping revenues for air travel, book, music and software sales in Germany, France and Britain will reach $3.3 billion in the next five years, up from 1997's $68m. The American market is expected to reach $37.5 billion by 2002. 20% of new and used vehicles will be bought using the Internet within the next two years.

• Spending on e-commerce software will grow at an average annual rate of 41% over the next four years to $285m. But more must be invested in software for inventory databases, customer records and Web publishing to exploit e-commerce fully.

• China's consumer-goods market will soar when it revamps its

unsophisticated distribution structure. Supermarkets and convenience stores will account for 25% of all consumer goods retailed in China by 2002.

To watch
E-commerce will lead to innovative online retail practices. Priceline.com's patented "name your own price" system of buyer-driven transactions is a sign of things to come.

TELECOMMUNICATIONS

• The growth of Internet telephony will slash international calling costs. The market is expected to hit $2.5 billion by 2004, up from $49m today. Expect Ericsson to enter the fray in 1999. The telecoms giant has been talking to major customers with a view to selling them technology that transmits telephone calls over the Net.

• High-speed Internet access will be taken up by 16m American households by 2002. The high usage of broadband connections will create opportunities for service and content providers. Cable companies will be the leading providers of broadband services, taking around 80% of the market by 2002. Such cable subscriptions will rise dramatically from 350,000 now to over 2m by the end of 1999, driven by falling prices and increasing consumer awareness.

• Psion's new Symbian joint venture (with Ericsson, Nokia and Motorola) will yield "smart" phones, capable of Internet connection, and with basic computing based on Psion's EPOC operating system.

• Work begins on the TAT-14 fibre-optic cable link between Europe and America. The $1.5 billion project is a joint initiative backed by 11 carriers including AT&T, British Telecom, Cable and Wireless, Deutsche Telekom and France Télécom. The cable, scheduled for completion by the end of 2000, will be able to carry 7.7m calls

Top cellular subscribers
subscribers per 100 people

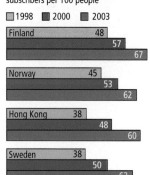

Source: Strategis Group

simultaneously. 80% of this traffic will be allocated to fast Internet access.

• The West European cellular market will grow rapidly. Italy leads, with an annual growth rate of 89% for 1998 and a projected 31.3m users (19.8% of European subscribers) by 2002. Britain is currently in second place, but Germany will gain a greater market share by 2002, with 26.4m customers against Britain's 21.9m.

TOURISM

Top tourist attractions in Europe
number of visitors ('000)

Source: www.euromonitor.com

• The global tourism market will remain flat through 1999. Economic uncertainties will keep tourists closer to home. Europeans will increasingly travel within Europe, Asians within Asia. Americans will travel abroad less in the shadow of threats from extreme Islamist movements. Latin America and the Caribbean will gain from this, thanks to their proximity to the US and their relative stability. The collapse of the rouble will hurt tourism in Eastern Europe. But the tourism industry will make a bid for recovery early in the next decade. It could grow at twice the rate of GDP and create 100m new jobs across the world by 2010.

• Online travel sales are predicted to increase by 68% in 1999 to $3.2 billion, following a 130% rise in 1998. They are forecast to increase tenfold over the next 8 years. However, traditional distribution and retailing agency operations will flourish alongside the new technology.

• Popular new destinations will include the communist countries, which are gradually opening up to mass tourism. Cuba, Vietnam, China and maybe even Mongolia will experience double-digit growth in the years to come. Southern Africa will also be developing its huge potential as a multicentre tourist destination. Zimbabwe will receive 2m tourists. Bombs and violence permitting, Tanzania is hoping to increase visitor arrivals to 500,000 a year by 2000. For the adventurous, Mozambique and Namibia are following suit.

They wouldn't have survived their migration
if they couldn't have stopped at their feeding grounds;

they couldn't have stopped if construction
on a nearby power plant had scared them away;

the construction wouldn't have waited
if not for the engineers of ABB.

Last year in South Humber Bank, UK, one of the wonders of technology
collided with one of the wonders of nature and something wonderful happened.
Nature survived.
The largest combined cycle power plant in Europe was under construction.
Unfortunately, it was on a site adjacent to a feeding ground for migratory birds.
Fortunately, the company doing the construction was ABB. You see, ABB is one company
that's not only committed to the business of electric power generation, it's also committed
to the preservation of the environment.
And it's a commitment that stretches from ABB's senior management
all the way through to its subcontractors on the construction site.
Which is why during the months between September and March,
construction on the plant, which might have alarmed the migrating birds and
prevented them from feeding, was abruptly stopped.
The power plant, which is representative of modern power plant technology
(highly efficient with minimal impact on the surrounding environment), was finished
only after the birds had completed their annual migration through the area.
A fact that made English environmentalists very happy.
Not to mention the birds.

INGENUITY AT WORK

.WORK THE
WEB

ONE OF THOSE SITUATIONS WHEN YOUR BOSS REALLY GETS TO YOU.

8.45am, Hotel Lazio. The sales rep is on his fourth cup of coffee. His boss is now an hour late for their pre-brief and his most important client meeting to date is in 45 minutes. His vision of the chairman handing him 'Sales Rep of the Year' disappears as he checks his watch for the umpteenth time. His (e-mail)[1] notification sounds on his laptop. **8.46am**, one new message. The boss is delayed in traffic. From here on it's up to him, he opens the attachment and keenly tweaks his presentation (incorporating the key points that he needs into his pitch)[2] **9.15am**, he uses his remaining time to connect to the company intranet via the Web and (review the shipping status and get the latest prices)[3] **9.30am**, he makes his presentation, on time. **11.00am**, his biggest order ever is in the bag. He goes back into the company intranet and (calculates the commission he'll receive from the order)[4] But his mind is elsewhere – a shiny red F50 pulls into the hotel car park. He makes a mental note to log-on later that day to check the company car policy.

HAVE A (PRODUCTIVE)[5] DAY WITH LOTUS.

[1]Lotus Notes. [2]Lotus Domino Replication. [3]Lotus Mobile Messaging.
[4]Lotus eSuite spreadsheet applet. [5]www.lotus.com

An IBM Company

Screen test

Bill Gates   SEATTLE

For almost as long as it has existed, the television business has been trying to transform inactive couch potatoes into interactive programme participants. Back in the early 1950s, American children's TV shows toyed with interactivity, offering crude cellophane screen overlays on which young viewers could sketch their own scenes. Television is now on the brink of a new interactive era. This time it will fulfil its promise.

Television has seen amazing progress in its half-century of prime-time—a period in which the number of TV sets worldwide has soared to around 1.4 billion. Colour TV, VCRS, stereo sound, cable and satellite have transformed the way we watch the box. Yet its underlying technology has hardly changed. Most transmissions still use the same old analog technology that broadcast America's first TV shows in the 1940s. Programmes are displayed on the same old-fashioned cathode-ray tubes. And a modern TV set still has no way of telling who, if anyone, is watching the programmes and advertisements flickering across its screen. Magazine publishers know more about their readers.

All this is about to change, as terrestrial broadcasters, cable companies and satellite operators begin moving to a new digital-TV standard. 1999 will see the start of a broad roll-out of digital infrastructure and transmissions in both the United States and Europe. By the end of the year, broadcasters and cable companies will offer digital TV in the top 30 markets in the United States, and trials are already under way in several European countries.

Digital TV, in turn, makes possible

Bill Gates: chairman and chief executive of Microsoft Corporation.

other significant technological advances. It makes the lifelike images of high-definition television (HDTV) a reality. It means that all the shows you watch will start out as bits—the same kind of ones and zeros that are processed by your computer, making the two truly compatible technologically. And thanks to universal software and Internet standards, a new generation of intelligent TV will blend the entertainment of television with the interactivity of the World Wide Web.

Other factors are also working in

favour of intelligent TV. To transmit instantaneously all those bits into and out of the TV in your home or office, you'll need a high-bandwidth connection. Usefully, the global supply of bandwidth is starting to explode. Cable-TV operators, telecoms companies and numerous new players are building vast new fibre-optic networks that will, in time, link almost every home and office in the United States and elsewhere. Constellations of satellites will within a few years start offering broadband two-way transmissions around the world. And thanks to technologies such as ISDN and

ADSL, even the ageing twisted-copper telephone line now packs more bandwidth than Alexander Graham Bell could ever have dreamed of.

Sharp pictures, better sound, instantaneous interactivity and seamless integration between TV and the Web will all be for nothing if the programming does not meet viewers' expectations.

Here, the intelligent-TV industry has learned a lot from its earlier unsuccessful interactive trials, and from what works best on the Web. That is why the pilot programming which is now being enhanced for this coming generation of intelligent TV will offer viewers much more than another way to order in pizza.

For example, while watching your favourite football team, you will be able to click on the remote control and call up a menu on your TV screen, much like the ones computer users are familiar with. It will wrap round two sides of a slightly shrunken picture, so you will still be able to watch the game. But at the same time you will also be able to do lots of other things. For example, you could call up details from a related Web site about players; watch replays and get scores from other games; order merchandise related to the game; or simply read the general news headlines.

Or perhaps you will be watching a favourite sitcom, and want a reminder of last week's plot, or a biography of one of the characters, or to buy a sweater just like the one you've seen on the screen. And during the commercial break, you may go on another online shopping spree, thanks to the prompting of an interactive advertisement. Then your children might want to watch an educational programme, and again they'll be able to download information, do online research to help with their homework, and ask questions interactively.

Many TV shows these days are deficit-financed, and rely on broad syndication to make a profit. Interactivity offers new revenue streams—for example, from commissions on online merchandise sales, which are likely to become one of the biggest sources of electronic commerce. Intelligent TV also allows programme makers to add value to re-runs. Thanks to universal Internet and software standards, it will be possible to add interactive content to existing programmes at very low cost. That will attract additional viewers and, as a result, extra advertising dollars.

Three generations of adults grew up expecting TV to be a passive, one-way experience, but today's viewers are increasingly living a Web lifestyle. They expect their entertainment to be interactive, two-way and customised to meet their needs—which is why more than 400,000 people already use Microsoft's WebTV. Some research shows that those children who have a computer at home watch less conventional TV—they prefer interactivity, they want to be in control.

But for intelligent TV to succeed, it will also have to be easy to use—the biggest market, at least initially, may be for what some observers have called "lazy interactive TV". So the interface must be really simple—nothing more complicated than today's remote control. And eventually the television, like computers, will use a more natural interface. It will respond to voice commands and incorporate an "intelligent assistant" that will learn your likes and dislikes, and help you find programmes.

The TV will also become one of the main interfaces for your home's local network, controlling everything from lighting and heating to the security system. A lot of what you can now do on a computer in your office—such as e-mail—you will also be able to do via TV from the comfort of your couch. Flat-screen technology will make it possible for an unobtrusive wall-mounted TV screen to be built into every room. Within a decade intelligent TV will be as familiar as the Web is today.

THE WORLD IN 1999 Usually the health of the economy dictates asset prices. In 1999, expect asset prices to determine the economy. Unhealthy.

Indecent exposure

Edward Carr

"It's only when the tide goes out", Warren Buffett once remarked, "that you learn who's been swimming naked." In 1999 there will be a lot of bare bottoms. Even without the inevitable ebb of financial turmoil from the markets into the real economy, this year was going to be an uncomfortable one for managers. As it is, reputations will suffer, the fashionable commitment to shareholder value

Not much fun when the tide goes out

will be tested, and grand schemes for re-organising the corporate landscape will come to seem merely grandiose.

Most conspicuously, 1999 will damage managers as a class. Just think what a wonderful few years it has been, despite the longer hours and the travel. Executives started the decade, in America at least, cast as villains bent on downsizing and re-engineering their companies into oblivion. However, emboldened by a superb run of profits, bosses had by the mid-1990s begun to stalk the corporate savannah in search of deals. As the number and value of their mergers and acquisitions broke new records, so the starched shirts in the boardroom took on a certain bravura. Favourable coverage of business found its way into publications, such as the *New Yorker*, with a keen eye for intellectual fashion. Chief-executives set out to burnish their reputations. Michael Eisner, of Disney, and

Edward Carr: business editor, *The Economist*.

Richard Branson, of Virgin, published autobiographies ("wrote" would be too strong a word for it) that are not appeals to a way of doing business, or memoirs safely revealed in retirement, but self-promotion. Managers have even been paid like film-stars. Wage-packets padded with tens of millions of dollars of share options are more often met with admiration than outrage.

By the end of 1999 this will seem like a golden age. Part of the forthcoming discomfort is of the managers' own making. It was they, after all, who stuffed annual reports full of promises when ideas ran short during the 1990s. Back then it sounded decisive and visionary to pledge to "raise return on capital to 15% by 2000", or "complete the transformation from widget-basher to a widget-services group for the new millennium". In 1999 managers will begin to appreciate how many of these ambitions cannot be realised in time. Where pledges are not quietly dropped, expect excuses.

And, to be fair, excuses are to hand. The performance of world stockmarkets has greatly exacerbated the problems that managers would have in any case faced in trying to keep profts growing. From 1992-97 the profits of companies in America's S&P500 rose by a total of 135%, almost four times more than the increase in their sales. Much of the extra margin came from lower costs (especially lower labour costs), lower interest rates and a favourable tax regime. According to a survey by Bain & Co, a management consultancy, nine out of ten American managers now say they want to increase profits by increasing revenues. Hence a shift from management tools such as re-engineering and total quality management, which concentrate on costs, to strategy, benchmarking, and mission and vision statements, which are designed to outmanoeuvre competitors and motivate employees.

This shift towards increasing revenues now looks nigh-on impossible. For many firms, the extra sales were supposed to come from foreign markets. The poor share-price performance of multinational companies such as Coca-Cola demonstrates how forlorn those prospects are. And firms such as Procter & Gamble have more or less admitted that they will not be able to increase sales through price rises at home.

Part of the solution will be to shed

We believe the most important element in business is imagination.

Cap Gemini is the largest European IT services and business consultancy company.

Imagination, trust and partnership are fundamental elements of our culture. They are the core values that define how we work, and are central to everything we do.

Ideas know no boundaries. By working together, nothing is impossible.

Ideas People Technology

THE TOYOTA HYBRID SYSTEM: A BREATH OF FRESH AIR FOR THE ENVIRONMENT.

*E*very day on the roads of Japan, thousands of **Toyota Prius** motorcars are proving that "environmentally friendly" can be a practical reality. Under the hood of the Toyota Prius is our new **Toyota Hybrid System (THS)**, a revolutionary combination of electric motor and gasoline engine technologies. With THS, the Toyota Prius achieves 28km/l* fuel efficiency, twice that of a conventional car, and emits only half the CO2. For you as a driver this means a potential 50% cut in your gasoline bill. The Prius also reduces carbon monoxide, hydrocarbons, and nitrogen oxides to 90% below Japanese regulatory standards. The Toyota Prius is the world's first mass-produced hybrid vehicle. We are now preparing for introduction to North American and European markets by the year 2000, by optimizing THS performance to local conditions. The Toyota Hybrid System is one of many advanced solutions we are developing for 21st century motoring. Because at Toyota we realize that to be the best car company now means being the cleanest car company.

*Japanese 10/15 mode testing, which emulates mainly city driving conditions.
Chestnut tiger butterflies, like the Asagi-madara (Parantica sita) shown above, migrate thousands of kilometers, demonstrating a natural fuel efficiency that is an inspiration to Toyota engineers.

——— Visit our website at http://www.toyota.co.jp/Lighthouse/ ———

TOYOTA

How bad will it get?

Pam Woodall

Economies that account for more than one-third of global output enter 1999 either already in recession or seriously stuttering. World output has grown by under 2% in 1998, down from an average rate of 4% in the previous four years. But the outlook for the next twelve months is grimmer: the world economy will grow by only 1-1.5%—its slowest rate since the early 1980s. By past standards that would count as a recession.

In the previous three world "recessions"—in 1975, 1982 and 1991—global output never actually declined, but expanded by an average of 1.5%. Most rich developed economies suffered a fall in GDP, but the developing world continued to grow. This time, by contrast, it is the developing world that could drag the rich economies into recession. The above forecasts imply that 1998 and 1999 could be the weakest two consecutive years for the world economy since the 1930s. And even this assumes that America merely suffers a sharp slowdown. If America dived into a full-blown recession, then the outlook for the world economy would be grim indeed.

The economic casualty list gets longer by the day. Japan and most of the rest of East Asia are suffering a slump; Russia has defaulted on its debt and its economy is imploding. High interest rates and budget cuts will push Brazil into recession in 1999. Last, but not least, there are growing fears that the huge losses made by banks and hedge funds will cause a credit crunch that could push the developed world in the same direction.

When the devaluation of the Thai baht in July 1997 triggered the East Asian crisis, nobody expected that the global consequences could be so serious. After all, most economies' trade with East Asia is small compared with the total size of their economies. However, there have been other more powerful channels of contagion. One is commodity prices. East Asia is a big importer of raw materials, and so the region's slump has depressed the prices of oil and other raw materials. This has hurt commodity producers such as Russia, Latin America and Canada. Another, even more important route through which Asian flu has spread is

Pam Woodall: economics editor, *The Economist*.

investor confidence. Bruised by big losses in Asia and Russia, investors and lenders lost their appetite for risky assets of any sort—not only emerging markets, but equities and corporate bonds in rich countries, too. This has raised the cost of capital.

More dominoes may yet fall in the emerging world—China, for instance, remains worrying—but the fate of the world economy really hangs on America and Western Europe, which together account for two-fifths of world output. Both grew by a healthy 3% or so in 1998, but they will not remain immune. A credit crunch and a slump in exports to emerging economies could add to the forces that will cause a sharp slowdown in America in 1999. Over the

Who's in the soup
Share of world GDP (%)

United States 20.4
European Union 19.8
Other advanced economies 4
Latin America 8.8
Ex-Soviet block 4.8
Other developing economies 8
Other Asian economies 26.5
Japan 7.7

Source: IMF

past couple of years, easy credit and surging share prices have driven borrowing and spending by American firms and households to unsustainable levels. Even without the fallout from Asia, America's financial bubble would eventually have burst.

In contrast, the 11 economies which will adopt the single European currency on January 1st look less vulnerable. Western Europe is less dependent on exports to emerging economies, and it has not seen the same frothy—and hence unsustainable—sort of growth as in the United States. The biggest worry

is that the new European Central Bank, eager to build up its anti-inflationary credibility, will try to be tougher than the Bundesbank and be slow to cut interest rates if necessary.

To judge how severe the global slowdown will be in 1999, keep your eye on four crucial factors. First, will Japan's $500 billion package to bail out its sick banking sector—and thus revive its economy—work? Second, is an end to the East Asian crisis in sight? Falling interest rates and rising export volumes could mean that these troubled economies will start to turn up in the second half of 1999, but their massive debt burdens will constrain growth. Third, will Wall Street crash? If share prices drop by 30-40% from their peak, this would severely depress spending in the United States. And fourth, how quickly will central banks cut interest rates if growth does slow sharply?

The world faces its most serious financial crisis since the 1930s. Indeed, there are disturbing parallels between now and the eve of the Great Depression, such as overvalued share prices, falling commodity prices and excess industrial capacity. But there are also some big differences: countries are no longer on the gold standard, which limited their ability to ease monetary policy as output slumped; public spending is today a much higher share of GDP, which automatically helps to stabilise demand; and, most important of all, policymakers have hopefully learned their history lessons.

The Great Depression was largely the result of some huge policy mistakes. In the 1930s, America's Fed failed to act as lender of last resort, so widespread bank failures caused a severe contraction of the money supply. Governments also raised taxes during the slump to try to balance their budgets. Today policymakers have a better understanding of how economies work and how monetary and fiscal policy can be used to prevent depression.

If Japan fails to implement fully its bank bail-out package; if central banks fail to cut interest rates as bank lending dries up and stockmarkets crash; if austere governments resist any widening of their budget deficits as demand slumps; if economies retreat behind protectionist barriers; if all these things happen, then the world might indeed face a global depression. But one would hope that policymakers could not be that incompetent.

The trouble with closing your business at night

is that 3 billion potential customers just woke up.

Now, thanks to e-business, customers can look, choose, order and pay while you sleep. Whether they're brand new customers, existing customers or even your business partners, e-business can connect you safely and securely, 24 hours

e-business

a day, anywhere in the world. Imagine. Tonight when you go to bed you could be counting sales instead of sheep. That's IBM's e-commerce solution based on Net.Commerce. And like all our e-business offerings, it's just a click away.

www.ibm.com/e-business

Solutions for a small planet

risk by entering into alliances rather than making acquisitions or investing in large new businesses. Alliances have, in any case, been increasing in recent years. According to John Harbison and Peter Pekar, consultants at Booz Allen & Hamilton, the proportion of revenue of the thousand largest firms in America that has come from alliances has more than doubled since 1990 to 21% and is still growing.

But there will also be renewed emphasis on restructuring. In Europe that will be no bad thing. The continent's business people have begun to sort through divisions of large national firms in order to construct groups with focus and a continental scale, but there is still much to do. Americans with money and expertise are keen to be involved. And not only the investment banks: raiders such as Asher Edelman have, for instance, been chivvying France's Taittinger empire to restructure its rag bag of hotels and other luxury goods businesses. In America, by contrast, many people are still crowing over the downfall of "Chainsaw" Al Dunlap, the consummate cost-cutter. A return to cutting there will be less well received: there are fewer obvious opportunities to cut, and labour markets are tight.

It is not just managers' public image that will suffer. Many managers embraced the creed of shareholder value and share options just as the remarkable rise in the stockmarket got underway—rather like pagans converting to Christianity the moment the lions had been withdrawn from the games. Now that the beasts are back in the ring, age-old conflicts between managers and shareholders will begin to deepen. There will, for example, be a tussle over the share options that many managers have come to regard as their right. The obvious way to make options valuable again is to lower their prices—which, according to West-Ward Pay Strategies, a consultancy based near San Francisco, is already common among high-tech firms that have suffered sharp declines in their share prices. But blue-chip companies are in a dilemma: not to reprice options will prompt numerous defections; on the other hand, repricing will invite the fury of investors, many of whom feel, understandably, that they have already borne their share of pain.

Most managers are experienced cost-cutters. They will put their heads down and try and get their last, biggest merger to work. But don't rule out flamboyance. This is 1999 and millennarianism will reach its zenith. Management theory has never been known for its reserve.

A joint enterprise

Linking arms

Charles Grant

Expect a big shake-out in the European defence industry in 1999—and the first pan-European mega-merger. The restructuring will affect many of the 1m people employed by the EU's defence industries. It will also—in a high-tech industry which many governments regard as "strategic"—have big implications for European foreign policy.

In the second half of the 1990s, as budgets shrank, the American defence industry underwent rapid restructuring. Four giant companies—Lockheed Martin, Boeing, Raytheon and Northrop Grumman—now dominate the American market. In the EU, by contrast, there was much talk of pan-European mergers, but little action.

Change is coming. America's trust busters recently blocked Lockheed Martin's planned acquisition of Northrop Grumman. Lockheed Martin, with defence sales of $18.5 billion (and total sales of $28 billion) had got big enough, they decided, without digesting Northrop Grumman's $9 billion business. While Northrop's future remains uncertain, it is now clear that the big four will not be allowed to merge among themselves. There are no more mega-deals left to be done in the United States.

All eyes, therefore, will be on Europe. Such rationalisation as there has been in Europe has tended to be among firms of the same nationality; thus France's Thomson-CSF took over the defence-electronics businesses of Dassault and Alcatel. Cross-border mergers have been few

Charles Grant: director of the Centre for European Reform, a London-based think-tank.

and far between, and confined to specific areas, such as that between the missiles businesses of British Aerospace (BAe) and a French company, Lagardère.

But there are signs of a more vigorous cross-border restructuring emerging. BAe has bought 30% of Sweden's Saab. Britain's GEC has announced a series of defence-electronics joint ventures with Italy's Alenia. And the British, German and French governments are engaged seriously in talks on the creation of a "European Aerospace and Defence Company" (EADC) that would unite their military aerospace industries.

Although pan-European consolidation will gather pace in 1999, there will be no EADC. Instead there will be a British-German grouping, built around BAe and Dasa, and a state-dominated French grouping, based on Aérospatiale. The French are likely to remain apart for three reasons.

The first is that Lionel Jospin's government is unlikely to privatise its defence companies quickly enough to satisfy the British and the Germans. In 1997 it sold more than half of Thomson-CSF's capital. In 1998, in an attempt to stave off a merger of BAe and Germany's Dasa, it announced plans to sell 48% of Aérospatiale's shares. But BAe and Dasa are still reluctant to work with an

 The American defence budget will rise by 10% to $280bn. Britain's will fall by 2.3%. The gap between allies grows.

Aérospatiale in which the state holds a big stake. Would it really be run on commercial lines, so that, for example, surplus labour could be shed when necessary?

The second reason is the lack of common programmes among the three countries. Since BAE and Dasa are the dominant partners in the Eurofighter project, there is an evident industrial logic to their merger. France decided to develop the Dassault Rafale, a comparable aircraft, on its own.

Nor, in the foreseeable future, are there likely to be common programmes around which the three military aerospace industries could coalesce. Britain will need a replacement for its Tornado bombers after 2010, as will Germany, but France will not need a new bomber at that time because the Rafale serves as a bomber as well as an interceptor. Britain will face a choice between developing a new bomber, probably based on the Eurofighter, and perhaps in collaboration with the Germans; or buying the Joint Strike Fighter (JSF), an American aircraft still under development. Given that the JSF will probably cost less than a new aircraft, it is more likely that Britain will plump for the former.

The third reason why the French military aerospace industry is likely to be left behind is that many senior figures in the defence establishment remain viscerally anti-American. They prefer pan-European restructuring as a means of creating European companies that are strong enough to compete against their American peers. However, John Weston, boss of BAE, Europe's largest defence company (with defence sales of $10 billion), favours restructuring in the EU so that European firms are large enough to form alliances with the Americans from a position of near-equality. Many in the British and German defence establishments share that view.

Lockheed Martin will be looking round Europe in 1999 for companies with which it could exchange equity. The logic for an American firm such as Lockheed is evident: since it cannot grow further at home it has to expand abroad, through local partners. Meanwhile European firms, at least in Britain and Germany, hope that a transatlantic alliance will offer access to American technologies and markets. Both Britain's GEC and BAE have expressed an interest in parts of Northrop Grumman. In the long run, therefore, the competition is less likely to be between European and American defence firms than between rival teams of transatlantic partners. And it will be a better industry for it.

A car crash waiting to happen

Graeme Maxton

Expect to see a major consolidation of the world's vehicle industry in 1999—and for several good reasons. Global sales fell in 1998 (by around 6%), though few took much notice. The markets of Europe were booming, reaching record new levels. The North American economy remained buoyant for most of the year and vehicle sales there were healthy. And even if Japan was in recession, Toyota and Honda were making record profits thanks to the drop in the value of the yen. So what if sales were

All dressed up and nowhere to go

plummeting in South East Asia and South Korea? So what if the markets in South America were jittery? These places offer small volumes for the world's car and truck makers. More than three-quarters of all new vehicles are still sold in the United States, Europe and Japan. Even more are produced there.

This was the calm before the storm, a storm that will break in the year ahead. 1999 will be the second year of

Graeme Maxton: associate editor, Economist Intelligence Unit.

decline—and a third and fourth will follow it. The American and European vehicle markets have passed their cyclical peaks. Japanese demand is weak as consumers remain cautious amid the economic gloom. Sales in the rest of Asia will not recover for some time. Overall, world vehicle sales will drop by another 8%, perhaps more, to their lowest level for a decade. Even the most successful manufacturers face a year or more without any growth.

This is bad news. But what is worse is that this is happening just as the world's production lines are increasing to meet a demand that will not materialise. Factories must close. And so must many companies. Stand by for a spate of mergers and takeovers in 1999 such as have characterised the banking and telecoms industries in 1998. With factories able to churn out more than 71m cars and trucks a year, overcapacity will be around 30%.

The world's most successful car makers have plenty of cash but nowhere to invest it. Who wants to build new factories when demand is declining and there are too many already? Who wants to invest in the emerging markets any more? This leads inexorably to the conclusion that one problem might solve the other. That the largest, most successful and most financially healthy car makers will use their cash to absorb the weaker ones. They could increase their share of a market while it is in decline. They could get rid of some of that excess capacity. They could make investments in the emerging markets while costs are extremely low and wait until the inevitable recovery begins.

So who might come out on top and where will the battles be fought? The biggest firms are pretty safe. For years, the world's vehicle industry has been led by just a few dominant companies. General Motors, Ford, Toyota and Volkswa-

In the nation where highways are part of history, we've got

ghway that's making history.

CABLE & WIRELESS

Celebrated in print, on film and even in song,

highways are part of America's culture.

This year we acquired one of the biggest

SuperHighways in the USA.

We now own and operate one of the

world's premier Internet networks with the

ability to offer our customers not just the

latest in communications, but the future of

communications.

It's for innovations like this that we created

Cable & Wireless Global Businesses.

A genuine response to our customers' needs,

it means we can deliver the world-wide reach

they demand and guarantee network reliability.

Cable & Wireless is one of the world's largest

carriers of international traffic.

We want to lead the world in integrated

communications.

If anyone can do it Cable & Wireless can.

And will.

For the Global Calling Card
that lets you call the World, call us.
FreeCall **0500 100 505.**

www.cablewireless.com

Our global customer service centres people can communicate in
But what did you expect from a truly world-wide communication.

...host any language in the world.

...mpany?

CABLE & WIRELESS

We have Customer Service Centres

located around the world. Which means that

wherever in the world our customers

are and whatever their problem might be,

we make sure that they'll be able to speak to

someone in their own language.

It's for reasons like this that we created

Cable & Wireless Global Businesses.

A genuine response to our customers' needs,

it means we can deliver the world-wide reach

they demand and guarantee network reliability.

Cable & Wireless is one of the world's largest

carriers of international traffic.

We want to lead the world in integrated

communications.

If anyone can do it Cable & Wireless can.

And will.

For the Global Calling Card

that lets you call the World, call us.

FreeCall **0500 100 505.**

www.cablewireless.com

gen have been the top four for a decade. In 1998 they were joined by Daimler-Chrysler which, with an output of almost 4m vehicles, is very much in the first tier.

The second tier is much more vulnerable. It consists of Fiat, Nissan, PSA, Honda, Renault and Mitsubishi—each of which built between 1.7m and 3m vehicles in 1998 and has for years fought a close battle to get nearer the top. There will be changes here. But even more vulnerable are the other 19 or so independent car and truck makers which come behind them. Many of these are in trouble. Yet they contain some big names—

from both a global and national perspective. Companies like BMW, Suzuki and Isuzu in the big markets and Proton, Daewoo and Maruti from the emerging ones. Companies that may lack the scale and resources to withstand a serious downturn.

So expect a rash of takeovers. These will be presented as the strong buying the weak, as the free market at work. That may be so. But it can be viewed another way: as the throwing of good money after bad, as the wealthy buying assets that they would never have built themselves.

cost at least double in 1999.

One of the most striking aspects of the Year 2000 problem is the uncertainty that surrounds it. Nobody knows for sure how widespread it is likely to be. Only fairly recently have companies realised that the problem is not confined to elderly mainframes. Many newer computer systems use software first developed in the days when it would have been expensive to store those extra two digits, and are therefore vulnerable.

An effect of such uncertainty is that it is difficult to be sure how far companies and government bodies still have to go to make their operations millennium-safe. The necessary information is bound to come mainly from information technology departments, and has to be taken on trust. But IT departments are not well-known for completing projects on time.

What is clear is that many companies and even more governments have begun work late, and are finding it harder and more expensive than they expected. As 1999 progresses, two kinds of bug stories will appear with increasing frequency: the story of organisations that are running behind, and the story of millennium-bug problems that crop up before the end of the year. These will create a growing mood of uncertainty and alarm which will affect the behaviour of the public and of financial markets. Individuals will change their behaviour: for instance, they will take business trips and holidays during 1999, rather than risk a flight in 2000. So will companies: for instance, they will build stocks to see them through if a key supplier cannot deliver for a few weeks.

The Year 2000 has begun

Frances Cairncross

The Year 2000 problem, otherwise known as the millennium bug, will dominate news stories—and business life—throughout 1999. And with good reason. Fixing computers to be able to read the date 2000 is already the single most expensive correction to a mistake ever made: and yet no one can predict whether enough will have been done in a particular country or company to stave off chaos. Here are some predictions:

● In most companies increasingly nervous boards of directors will want to be Year 2000 compliant by the first quarter of 1999, not the last. Companies that have not fixed the problem by, say, June 1999, will see some heavy dumping of shares on the stockmarket.

● Among the worst prepared will be some key public enterprises. Some big computer systems that keep the welfare state rolling (and the taxman gathering) will be in trouble. Watch the politicians struggling to own up to the problem late in 1999.

● It will become clear that there are a number of things that cannot become Year 2000 compliant on time or at a reasonable cost. Many of these will not be crucial to a company's operations. Most companies will aim to fix first the systems that can cause most trouble. Sometimes, though, they will misjudge it, and find too late that a vital piece of software is bug-ridden.

● Although most big institutions in most OECD countries will fix the problem adequately, a number of important similar institutions in emerging markets will not make it. So, will a bank in America, say,

be a willing counterparty to a bank in Ecuador, during the second half of 1999?

● Two events will provide a foretaste of what lies ahead. First, the launch of the euro at the start of 1999 will give people a glimpse of the problems that can arise when lots of computer software has to be altered. Second, as many programs manage services that run on the basis of

DOES 2000 MEAN ANYTHING TO YOU?

a full year (insurance policies, say), some will crash or fail when they enter the final year to 2000, early in 1999. Many, indeed, have already begun causing problems.

● Many companies, particularly those like banks that use huge, central programs, will find that the Year 2000 problem is a wonderful opportunity to clean out millions of lines of redundant computer code. As a result, their systems will be quicker and cleaner. The cost of writing new software codes will climb throughout the year. What two years ago cost about 50 cents a line to write, will

a key supplier cannot deliver for a few weeks.

However, one of the few certainties about the millennium problem is that it is an expected disaster. Unlike earthquakes or aeroplane crashes, it is an utterly predictable event. As a result, all but the most foolish companies and governments will make some preparation; and, as hysteria mounts in the press through 1999, their efforts will increase. They will also be spurred by the threat of legal action, and the difficulty of obtaining insurance.

Moreover, most companies and gov-

Frances Cairncross: author of "The Death of Distance: How the Communications Revolution will Change Our Lives"; public policy editor, *The Economist*.

ernments will apply their main efforts to the activities that matter most: the ones that could, if they went wrong, pose a threat to safety or to the solvency of the business. So aeroplanes are not likely to fall out of the sky (but they may be delayed); big banks are not likely to fail (but they may lose a customer's records); nuclear power plants will probably not blow up (but they may break down).

When the new century dawns, many of the problems caused by the millennium bug will turn out to be irritating but manageable. People will find ways to work around them. After a few months, most of the glitches—and especially the serious and damaging ones—will have been fixed. Does that mean the hysteria

about the bug will have been no more than fuss? No. For one thing, it is hard to imagine that there will not be a few serious incidents—perhaps in Russia which has been distracted from tackling the bug—which may have consequences elsewhere in the world.

More important may be the shift of economic activity back into 1999, leaving a void in the first months of 2000. Air traffic will plummet; destocking will replace stockbuilding; the financial markets will fall quiet, as many companies will have arranged to bring trades back into the autumn. The economic downturn, which may pause in 1999, will pick up with a vengeance as the world is gripped by post-millennium blues.

Britain will have a million foreigners living in it. In London, some 10% of workers will be from abroad.

relative pay is rising all the time. Better qualifications have helped too: in developed countries, as many women as men now enter higher education. In America, women's hourly pay rates over the past 20 years have risen from two-thirds to four-fifths of men's, and are still moving upwards. Young professionals with sought-after skills—say in information technology, accountancy or consulting—are already enjoying a unisex rate of pay.

All that is fine as far as it goes, but it does not yet go far enough. At the very top of the corporate tree, female fat-cats remain remarkably elusive. According to Catalyst, a New York-based think-tank, only 3% of the most senior jobs (chairman, chief executive or similar) in Fortune 500 companies are currently held by women. Expect a marked increase in 1999. Already, over 400 of the Fortune 500 companies have at least one woman on the board.

Among high-fliers in rich countries, many more women than men remain unmarried, and an even larger proportion childless. Even women with more workaday jobs are cutting back on babies. Except in America (where immigrants push up the birth rate), hardly any of the developed countries will produce enough offspring in 1999 to maintain their populations. Forecasters expect that in the next decade or two the share of women in rich countries who choose to have no children at all will rise, to perhaps one in four.

Executive, thy name is woman

Barbara Beck

If you are a misogynist, tough luck. Since women make up slightly more than half the world's population, it has never been possible to avoid them altogether. But at least there was a time when most of them were safely tucked away in their homes or were confined to the factory floor or the lower reaches of corporate life. Each year, however, their advance continues remorselessly. Now they account for half the labour force of most rich countries. And they are coming to get you higher and higher up the corporate ladder. They may even pinch your job in 1999, if you are a high-flying man about to join the senior management of your firm. Next year there will be more women nearer the top of the corporate world than ever before.

Women's conquest of the workplace has been remarkably rapid. Fifty years ago, only a third of working-age women in America—and an even smaller proportion in many European countries—had jobs outside the home. It was a way of bridging the gap between the end of school and the start of marriage or arrival of the first child. Now in some rich countries, particularly in America

and Scandinavia, the number of women in paid jobs is getting close to that of men. Elsewhere in Europe, particularly in the south, they have been slower to catch up, but numbers everywhere are rising. Single or married, childless or mothers, women have discovered the joys of a working life—and the reassurance of having their own pay packets.

True, on average those pay packets are still more modest than men's, but watch them getting fatter. Women's pay used to be scandalously lower than men's, even for the same work, but thanks to equal-pay and equal-opportunities legislation in many countries their

But who says that the best jobs come only in large, unwieldy lumps that require 80-hour weeks and lots of travel? Employees are prepared to pull out all the stops when they are needed, but they also want more time and flexibility for themselves, be it to look after children, to care for an elderly relative, to study for a further qualification, to work for a local charity, or just to lead a more balanced life. And increasingly, it is men as well as women who are asking for such deals. There is more to life than a spreadsheet.

Barbara Beck: surveys editor, *The Economist*.

Working women as % of total labour force ☐ 1960 ☐ 1999

Births per woman ☐ 1960 ☐ 1999

	USA	Japan	Sweden	France	Germany	Britain	Netherlands	Spain	Italy
Working women 1960	25.5	36.4	25.5	28.1	35.3	28.7	15.8	14.4	21.2
Working women 1999	46.5	43.6	51.5	39.8	41.3	43.3	37.4	32.2	33.4
Births 1960	3.6	2.0	2.2	2.7	2.4	2.7	3.1	2.9	2.4
Births 1999	2.1	1.4	1.7	1.7	1.3	1.7	1.5	1.2	1.2

Source: International Labour Office, World Bank

It's all coming together

C. Michael Armstrong, chairman and CEO of AT&T, stakes out where the big changes and chances are in communications.

As it does every four years, the global telecommunications industry will descend on Geneva next October for the world gathering it calls "Telecom".

Telecom '99 will be a solid week of speeches and seminars, deliberations and deals. Corporate chief executives will sit on panels with telecoms ministers during the day and talk with each other into the evening.

It will all look familiar, but the telecom industry is very different from what it was four years ago when the delegates last assembled. And it will be almost unrecognisable by Telecom 2003.

The big story of the past four years was how the twin forces of technology and competition changed the communications industry within individual countries.

Now technology and competition will redefine communications between countries. They will slip the constraints of national borders to make the very concept of "place" irrelevant.

That, in essence, is what multinational businesses have long wanted: seamless communications services that operate the same way in New York, New Delhi and New Zealand. Multimedia capabilities that make it possible to hold virtual meetings wherever an executive finds herself. Toll-free calling that crosses borders.

As an industry, we've been able to deliver only some of those services to the largest multinational companies, and even then the level of quality varied sharply from country to country. But now the communications industry is poised to bring such services to individuals as well.

Why the change? Customers demand it and technology enables it. The only thing more powerful than an idea whose time has come is a market that embraces that idea.

Use of global communications by the world's largest companies is growing by 19% a year. Use by small and medium-sized companies is growing even faster—about 25%. And consumer demand for international voice and data services is increasing by 20% a year. In fact, traffic between countries is increasing almost twice as fast as traffic within the countries themselves. Overall,

what is now a $40 billion market will grow to $200 billion in a few years.

Communications companies are racing to make the Internet a reliable business tool. They are using wireless technology to extend advanced services to under-developed nations. They are increasing networking intelligence to give their customers greater control over communications, making them reachable whenever and wherever they want, on their own terms.

Some time in 1999, data will

"Some time in 1999, data will overtake voice traffic on the world's networks."

overtake voice traffic on the majority of the world's communications networks. In fact, global communications traffic is rapidly becoming global data transfer. Technology's ability to digitise and transmit every form of information, combined with the ubiquity of the Internet, is redefining what the industry delivers to customers.

A number of giant mergers within the industry, with a market capital of some $194 billion, are up for regulatory approval in 1999. These reflect the fact that technology could remove the boundaries between markets: wired and wireless services, local and long distance, cable television and telephone, information and entertainment. Technology could bring these services together and so the market is bringing together companies that want to make customers an expanded offer.

In the United States, some of us believe that advanced, two-way services can be delivered through the broadband capacity of cable television networks, modified for communications use. So the boundary between cable television and a phone service will become increasingly

blurred. Some results will be dramatically visible in 1999.

In selected communities in the United States families will soon be able to participate in a preview of cable-based communications, news, information and entertainment services. They will, for example, be able to sort through still images from every CNN broadcast over the past 24 hours, click on one and instantly get a rebroadcast of the story.

Over time cable, upgraded for two-way service, offers greater promise, such as multiple phone lines activated at will by the customer. By Telecom 2003, such services—the product of competition and technology—will be commonplace in much of the United States.

The ability of the industry to transmit more and more information will generate exponential growth over the coming years. Cable ships will be laying a fibre-optic cable across the Pacific with the capacity to carry the equivalent of 8m calls, compared with a capacity of 40,000 calls on the first transoceanic fibre cable installed just 11 years ago.

The wireless revolution will continue full-bore in 1999. Falling prices driven by new competition and the strong appeal of new digital wireless services should more than fuel the annual growth rate of almost 30%, more than three times the rate for wired phones.

For the past 20 years, telecoms competition has been largely a phenomenon of the English-speaking world, beginning with the $70 billion United States long-distance market and spreading to the United Kingdom, Canada, Australia and New Zealand.

But now 72 countries representing over 90% of the world's telecoms traffic have committed to the WTO agreement liberalising trade in telecoms services. Too much of the world's communications services industry still operates in an environment of government regulation and quasi-monopoly. The arcane system of international settlement rates still allows some countries to charge grossly inflated prices for completing international calls.

So regulators have the crucial job of nurturing competition. If industry consolidation is inevitable, let regulators measure it against the yardstick of increasing customer choice.

Panasonic GD70. Because sometimes you can't have your hands free.

When you're tied up, you can't always reach the phone. That's why the GD70 is completely hands-free.

Its advanced microphone is incredibly sensitive. Just switch on the powerful internal speaker, and you can speak across the world without using your hands.

Add the latest Dual Band technology for even greater foreign coverage... large, easy-to-read displays... easy access to a host of advanced features... a silent vibration-alert – and you can see why the GD70 is the choice of high flyers all over the world.

For more information on the complete range of Panasonic Mobile Phones call **UK 0500 40 40 41.**

Panasonic
Mobile Phones

GSM | DUAL BAND 900/1800 MHz

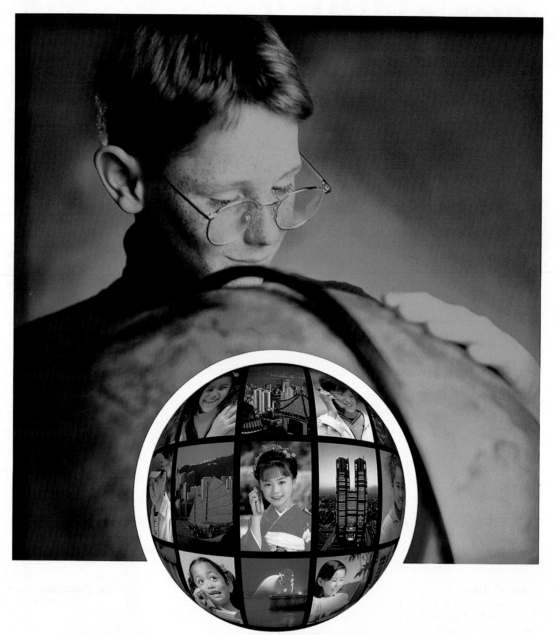

We connect.

Nobody knows Asia like we do. Especially when it comes to connecting people and businesses between nations. As Japan's leading telecom provider for over 100 years, we've been giving people the means to connect globally. Today, Arcstar Global Communications Services unite Asia, Europe and the U.S. via high-speed infocommunication highways. Our Global Systems Integration Service provides failsafe solutions for end-to-end corporate connections around the planet. Now, communicating with Asia is a simple matter of connecting with the right partner.

Arcstar

NTT
NIPPON TELEGRAPH AND TELEPHONE CORPORATION

Vulnerable giants

Jim Chalmers

No industry will change faster in 1999 than telecommunications. This is because there are plenty of technical breakthroughs in the pipeline that will become reality, regardless of recession, and because the spate of mergers between telephone dinosaurs in 1998 makes sense only if there is a huge restructuring in 1999. So this giant industry will have to behave with unusual dexterity. There may be less growth in the year ahead, but there will be more change. In an overdue shift in strategy, new skills as opposed to increased scale will be the drivers of future corporate deals.

In globalisation terms, there is already a "worldwide" telecoms network; unfortunately it is often unreliable or too expensive. It simply fails to connect a sizeable proportion of the world's population. So 1999 will see attempts to meld established networks, built on conventional telecoms systems, with new technologies, so that everyone, everywhere can eventually send or receive anything, anywhere.

Mergers, which have so far been based on geographical synergy, will suddenly become skills-based. Old-timers will seek to acquire competence in areas such as the Internet or new radio or satellite services. The resulting cultural clash between new and old will determine the long-term success of these collaborations and thus the shareholder value embedded in such deals.

An overriding issue surrounding attempts at industry consolidation will be how they "play" on the stockmarket. The high-tech sector looks inflated—even after the market turmoil of 1998—and many expect it to blow up with a bang in 1999. That in turn will damage the interests of those companies seeking access to capital to finance their expansion. The other restraint is politics. Expect regulation, rather than market forces, to be the real issue that batters the industry in 1999. Alarm bells are already ringing over the apparent failure of pro-competition initiatives in the United States and the European Union—as well as those further afield under the auspices of the World Trade Organisation. 1999 will see a re-examination of the rules of the game.

In the United States, the hiatus of an election year may forestall a rewriting of the lacklustre 1996 Telecom Act, although restless legislators could contrive to substantially alter its impact by blocking anti-competitive mergers or forcing through pro-competitive measures. In Europe, the Commission has scheduled a review of the market-opening measures which were put into force on January 1st 1998. Expect a battle over whether the individual member states or the EU authorities in Brussels assume ultimate responsibility for fostering more effective competition; if you live in Europe and you want better and cheaper services, hope that it is the latter that holds sway.

If regional and global telecoms regulation is thrown back into the vortex of lobbying, policy-making and legislation, then the prospects for real gains for consumers during 1999 look bleak. Yet that picture may change if new technologies succeed where laws and directives have failed.

Internet Protocol (IP) telephony—sending voice telephone calls over the ultra-cheap backbone of the Internet—should become fully established in 1999. Advanced mobile data and e-mail services, which direct new information and messaging services to the handsets of the growing army of cellular-phone users, will also have their commercial debut during the year. New services based on competing low-earth-orbiting satellite networks will be poised to remove blackspots and bottlenecks in truly global service provision, beginning in 1999.

Ironically, the advent of such services will have a significant impact only if these new tools are placed in the hands of old industry dinosaurs. The telephone companies alone have the scale—and the financial muscle—to take innovative technologies and employ them across broad swathes of the marketplace. The new markets which have been opened, on paper at least, by liberalisation will be assaulted by old, not new, companies. Telecoms, unlike computer hardware or software, is not a first-generation business.

One explanation for the low-key impact of deregulation so far has been the inability of would-be competitors to construct a solid business case on the back of existing technologies; conversely, to leave new technologies in the hands of small start-up players is to confine them to niche status.

These technologies could revolutionise service and costs in the industry—although incumbents will attempt to turn this into a "controlled evolution" rather than a full-scale storming of their citadels. Yet 1999 will be the year in which it becomes clear that they cannot hold back the forces of change.

Recognising this, the big companies will move from forming pacts with their peers to investing in the technology pioneers. Any company dealing in the world of the Internet, especially in IP telephony, will attract a premium price.

In a world where the telecoms and computing sectors are converging with each other and with the providers of the information content which they transport and receive, nobody knows where the industry's true value will lie in the future. The result is a long—but vague—shopping list for the major players in search of 21st-century competence. But the lingering presence of their 19th-century management boards may be a problem here.

Not all will pass the test or understand the need to improvise and change. Having just emerged blinking from the dark decades of the monopoly era, these companies are now being forced to think about—and re-think—their businesses as never before. Still revelling in the apparent industrial "legitimacy" conferred by the introduction of competition, technology will in 1999 force these companies to confront the reality which that entails. If your survival depended on it, you would probably choose not to depend on them.

HALLO, THIS IS YOUR SEXY DINOSAUR CALLING

Jim Chalmers: editor of *Public Network Europe.*

Sporting heroines

Second perhaps only to the boardroom, women have found the greatest difficulty in breaking into the world of sport. That will change in 1999. Women's tennis will, for the first time, prove more popular than men's—and will get more television airtime to prove it. So watch out for the still-teen sensations Martina Hingis (Switzerland), Venus and Serena Williams (USA), Anna Kournikova (Russia) and Mirjana Lucic (Croatia). They represent the new age of female superstars. After tennis, golf. The Korean rookie, Se Ri Pak, winner of the US Open at her first attempt, will invigorate the women's game in much the same way Tiger Woods has the men's. In athletics, the American sprinter Marion Jones should break world records in the short sprints or long jump at the World Championship in Seville (August 20th-29th). As memories fade of all those butch drug-filled communist women of the past decade, expect a new generation of brilliant, television friendly, female superstars to emerge, pushing men off one of their last pedestals of superiority.

Unfair advantage to Kournikova

The Internet leaves infancy

David Weir

LOS ANGELES

Somewhere along the way, that once-spirited debate over whether the World Wide Web would ever live up to its original hype just petered out. Maybe everyone on both sides got too busy creating new business plans to continue the argument. Or, maybe, lifting a phrase from that oddball American billionaire turned politician, Ross Perot, it is a simple matter of "case closed".

In any event, it is axiomatic by now that the value of a network increases exponentially as its number of users grows, so the potential wealth inherent in the Internet, though still expanding rapidly, will remain unrealised until many more people—and businesses—around the globe get wired.

Towards that end, 1999 will be a year when ever smaller and faster silicon chips sneak into virtually everything we use, whether for fun or profit. The subversive element in our lives that used to be called the "digital revolution" will leave the desktop computer behind.

Soon we will be able to do nearly everything we did on personal computers on powerful devices held in one hand. Those who argue that the Internet will merge with television are probably wrong; the Internet will merge with telephones instead.

The turning point will come as an ever-more functional network is accessible via handheld devices. Previously, with the exception of the Nokia 9000, most Personal Digital Assistants amounted to offline personal organisers that synchronised with data on the network only when plugged into a modem. The next generation of handheld devices, however, all integrate voice, fax and Internet in the same handsets. The alliance between Ericsson, Nokia, Motorola and Psion to push for their own operating system threatens Microsoft's quest to dominate the handheld market as it dominates conventional PCs.

1999 will be a year of landmarks for network connectivity in general. AOL, for example, can boast of one million people connected at any one time—seeing off

any lingering doubts about whether or not networked communities are here to stay. The number of online users in the United States, according to Jupiter Communications, will pass the 75m mark or over a third of the population (34m households). The rate of growth of the consumer Internet economy in Europe and Asia, meanwhile, is faster. Having started more slowly than America, Europe is now exploding. Led by Japan, Asia snaps at Europe's heels with 8.7m households online.

Commerce on the Net will reach a milestone soon with online shopping revenues touching $10 billion as the number of individuals making those purchases doubles annually. Consumer fears about credit-card fraud and privacy are giving way to a much greater need—convenience. The sun never sets on e-commerce empires, which will grow rapidly in 1999.

This is part of a larger shift—the emergence of what an American writer, David Brin, calls "the transparent society", with the erasure of old-fashioned personal privacy in any practical sense of the term. The active role played by the Internet in the sensational sex scandal of the American president is seen in hindsight as merely symbolic—nobody, starting with the top person in society, has any real defence against anybody else knowing whatever it might be they want to know about him.

The new markets created by globalisation and converging technologies unleash a vast demand for all types of creative services. No aspect of human culture or behaviour is too minute to attract a following. (Whether this represents an advance of civilisation is quite another question.) The entrepreneurial niche economies now recognised as characteristic of the last years of the millennium are fuelling yet another spurt of uneven global growth, even as the increasingly irrelevant nation states struggle to capture and control the benefits they provide. Anyone with access to the Internet and something to sell can drum up a worldwide market.

Higher bandwidth environments emerging here and there, primarily through the fat pipes offered by cable-modem delivery, provide a case in point. Initial user research confirms that surfers do exactly the same things they were already doing online—only more so. They consume more news, conduct more financial transactions (many more), process more e-mail, write more articles and reports, make more deals, visit more websites, and generate many more sales.

David Weir: vice-president of *Salon* magazine.

Tektronix®

AFTER DEVOTING
15 YEARS TO COLOUR,
WE'RE PROUD TO
INTRODUCE OUR SMALLEST
ACCOMPLISHMENT YET.

£1,395* FOR A NETWORK COLOUR PRINTER.

How can something which gives you so much, cost so little? All our experience of colour has gone into the new Tektronix Phaser® 740 line of printers. It's the first family of workgroup printers to deliver amazing photo quality colour at an equally amazing price. They give you up to 1200dpi** on everything from letters to spreadsheets and presentations. Plus they do everything else you've dreamed an office printer should do.

For a bigger picture of our smallest accomplishment visit us at www.tektronix.com/colouratwork/eng

Database marketing firm: unfortunately for some, power spikes never affect their direct mailing lists

Supermarket: made a killing in the 1997 brownout, now the only one in the neighbourhood

Delivery service: never misses a deadline, despite the best efforts of the weather

Football: live on TV every week, lightning or not

Internet Service Provider: stays up all year round, while others have their ups and downs

"It´s always easy to spot the companies with our UPSs"

Just look for these telltale signs:

a) they keep doing business when others can't,

b) they rarely, if ever, think about power protection,

c) they probably think that "UPS" has something to do with overnight delivery.

If, on the other hand, they can recite their UPS manual verbatim, then they are probably customers of one of those other UPS companies.

Because we at Exide Electronics believe that our customers have far more important things to think about, such as doing business.

We have developed the widest range of UPSs around, so you can keep doing business, regardless of what the power company or Mother Nature has to say about it.

And all in such a way, that you'll never have to think about power again. Well, at least not about the electrical kind anyway.

Now you know why some get ahead, and some don't.

Exide Electronics
221 Dover Road, Slough • Berkshire, England SL1 4RS
Tel. +44 1753 608 700 • Fax +44 1753 608 995
E-mail: info@exideups.com
http://www.europe.exide.com

Powerware – Uninterruptible Power Systems to protect your computers

♂**BTR**
A member of the BTR Group

POWERWARE
An Exide Electronics Company

Gizmos you've gotta get

Nicholas Valéry   TOKYO

What are the latest gizmos that well-heeled executives, media celebrities, net-savvy teenagers and technophiles everywhere will be sporting in 1999—filling the rest of us with awe and envy?

Following on from its success in Japan, expect to see more palm-sized digital video disk (DVD) players being toted by jet-setters tired of the fuzzy picture, tinny sound and heavy editing of in-flight movies. These portable devices, which play optical discs that look like a CD but store vastly more data, come with flip-up screens which have the new 16x9 proportions of the modern cinema (instead of television's dreary old 4x3). Better still, they provide pin-sharp pictures and digital sound even clearer than a CD.

Over the past year, the major studios have re-issued thousands of titles from their film libraries in the DVD format as the video industry prepares to ditch the venerable VHS cassette and prepare for the new era of digital television. The rush into portable DVD has been led by Panasonic. The price will come down from today's $1,000 as manufacturers churn out export models.

Global travellers will also be among the first to flaunt the iridium satellite telephone that is being introduced widely by Motorola. The hand-held Iridium phone can operate anywhere in the world—even in places where there are no telephone lines or cellular services—thanks to a constellation of 66 low-orbit satellites that now blanket the earth.

When a user is within range of a conventional telephone or cellular system, the Iridium phone handles incoming and outgoing calls by hooking itself up to the local terrestrial service. But in the middle of the jungle, desert, ocean or simply on a lonely road far from civilisation, the Iridium phone communicates with the rest of the world via the network of satellites overhead. Not cheap: handsets start around $3,000 and calls $5 a minute.

The recent phenomenon among college students of roll-your-own digital-music albums from tracks downloaded from the Internet has spurred a number of manufacturers to start marketing portable MP3 players. Computer-literate teenagers have taken the Motion Picture Expert Group's audio compression technique known as MPEG-1 Level 3 (or MP3 for short), developed for high-definition

Nicholas Valéry: bureau chief in Tokyo for *The Economist.*

television, and used it to scrunch CD tracks to a sixteenth their size without any loss of quality. This allows them to swap CD-quality songs over the Internet in minutes instead of the hours needed for downloading a typical four-minute track of uncompressed music. For copyright reasons, the process is largely illegal—though a number of music publishers (Goodnoise, MusicMatch and MP3.com) have begun distributing their wares in MP3 format.

Until recently, MP3 tracks had to be kept on a hard-drive and played back

Mum's on the phone

through the computer's audio system. Now downloaded songs can be stored in a little portable gizmo and carried around all day. The MP3 player of choice is the Rio PMP300 from Diamond Multimedia Systems. For $199, digital music addicts get a Walkman-like device that uses microchips to store up to 64 minutes of crystal-clear music and runs for 12 hours on two AA batteries. A similar product called MPman, from Saehan Electronics, costs $299.

Another little gadget that will be flying off the shelves is a portable GPS (global positioning satellites) receiver from Magellan called the Pioneer. Hand-held devices that use America's GPS to tell you your position on the earth's surface to within a few tens of metres have been around since the Gulf war. Yachtsmen, explorers and mountaineers have will-

ingly plonked down the $1,000 or more for the reassurance they provide. Tiny GPS receivers also feature in the $1,500 dashboard navigation systems that have become all the rage among car buffs over the past year or two. Hertz rents cars fitted with Magellan's PathMaster system for an additional $6 a day.

By getting the price below $100, Magellan has taken a piece of scientific apparatus and turned it into an executive toy. The Pioneer also happens to be hugely useful as well as fun—the mark of all great gadgets. The Pocket-sized Pioneer, with an actual recommended price of $139, has a water-proof rubber case, unbreakable antenna and runs for 24 hours on two AA batteries.

Much the same price but even more useful are the new generation of tapeless recorders that are no bigger than a credit card. Till recently, tapeless recorders—which store sound on microchips instead of magnetic tape—have been limited memo-takers, capable of recording no more than a minute or two's conversation. What has turned these novelties into full-blooded audio recorders is the arrival of the $120 Panasonic RR-DR60, capable of storing an hour's worth of conversation at a time. With its built-in screen, up to 99 audio files can be sorted and replayed at the press of a button.

THE WORLD IN 1999

China will decide whether to open up to more foreign trade or see its 13-year-old bid to join the World Trade Organisation fail. No pain, no gain.

The virtual firm

Michael Dell, CEO of Dell Computers, believes that management, ever more reliant on information, will soon migrate to the ether.

The information appliance. The network computer. The set box. The PDA. The Internet-enabled TV. These are the devices that many people predict will spell doom for the future of the personal computer. I do not agree.

There will be a use for some of these dedicated devices, but they cannot replace the performance or utility of the PC. Users have come to rely on the unparalleled flexibility, power and interactivity of the PC. And the business applications of the future, with their rich data and graphical content, will demand it.

Across the world, there is a huge untapped demand for PCs. In North America, there will be nearly two people per PC within the next two years. The forecast for Europe is nearly five people per PC. But in the highly populated emerging markets such as Asia and the Pacific Rim, there will be 41 people per PC. And governments in these new world economies are publicly committed to the rapid deployment of technology in order to compete.

Computer costs will continue to decrease, making higher levels of performance more cost-effective than before. The cost for raw processing power, or cost per MIPS, will have decreased from more than $10 in 1993 to under 40 cents in 1999. It is projected to be less than 20 cents by the end of this decade.

The simultaneous availability of bandwidth—that is, the ability to move more data at increasingly lower costs—will make it possible to manipulate ever larger amounts of data. By 2000, the explosion in fibre-optic cable is expected to raise the total transatlantic capacity almost tenfold.

But no development has greater potential to accelerate the growth of the PC industry than the Internet. I am not referring to online commerce, or the use of the Internet as a sales channel, even though industry analysts estimate that online commerce in the United States and Europe alone will exceed $270 billion by 2001.

In the buzz surrounding electronic commerce, what is overlooked is the potential of the Internet as a business-organisation system. The linkage of personal computers with network servers will change the very nature of our corporations. In fact, most companies with a network infrastructure already have the key building blocks to make this possible.

An Internet-based system can revolutionise business processes in a way that blurs traditional boundaries between supplier and manufacturer, and manufacturer and customer. This will eliminate paper-based functions, flatten organisation hierarchies, and shrink

"Physical infrastructures are becoming obsolete."

time and distance to a degree not possible before.

At the foundation of this change is a shift away from the things we have learned to value in the business and economic models of the 20th-century.
● The value of inventory is being replaced by the value of information.
● Physical assets are being traded for intellectual assets.
● Closed business systems are giving way to collaborative relationships.

This is the shift from vertical to virtual integration. If you look back at the emergence of any industry—and this is certainly true of the information industry—you will find that most companies integrated vertically in order to gain scale and provide maximum value to their customers.

The Internet makes it possible to bring customers and suppliers inside your business; to share openly critical business information and applications; to create true information partnerships. These partnerships, formed around information assets, will transform traditional notions of economic value.

Take one example that has a dramatic effect on transaction cost: the cost of inventory. In the late 1980s and early 1990s, we used to measure component inventory in weeks.

We now measure inventory in days. In the near future we will be clocking it in hours. By using the Internet to link production data from our suppliers' factory floors directly into the workflow of our own factories, the time is not far off when we will have real-time delivery of components. This will mean that every time a component is used, it will be automatically and immediately replaced. In the computer industry, where component costs typically decline an average of 1% a week, the economic value of real-time inventory is enormous.

Inventory velocity is just one of dozens of changes enabled by the Internet that boost the efficiency and speed of information sharing. Another is procurement. Although this sounds mundane, paper-based procurement is costly and cumbersome.

By using secure websites, customers are able to bring procurement online. One company estimated that the cost-savings in the first six months of such a programme were $2m; another reduced its purchasing staff from 15 people in different locations, to four people in one central location.

The Internet will redefine economic value throughout the supply chain. It will change how profits are made and lost in a number of industries.

A manufacturer will no longer be able to afford to treat a supplier like a vendor from whom every last ounce of cost-saving must be wrung. Nor can a customer be treated simply as a market for products and services at the best possible price.

Instead, both suppliers and customers will come to be treated as information partners, jointly looking for ways to improve efficiency across the entire spectrum of the value chain, not just in their respective businesses.

The companies that fully capitalise on the promise of the Internet will be those that realise investments in physical infrastructures are becoming obsolete. The productivity of their capital will be significantly improved over traditional systems because they will have replaced physical assets with information assets—and competition with collaboration.

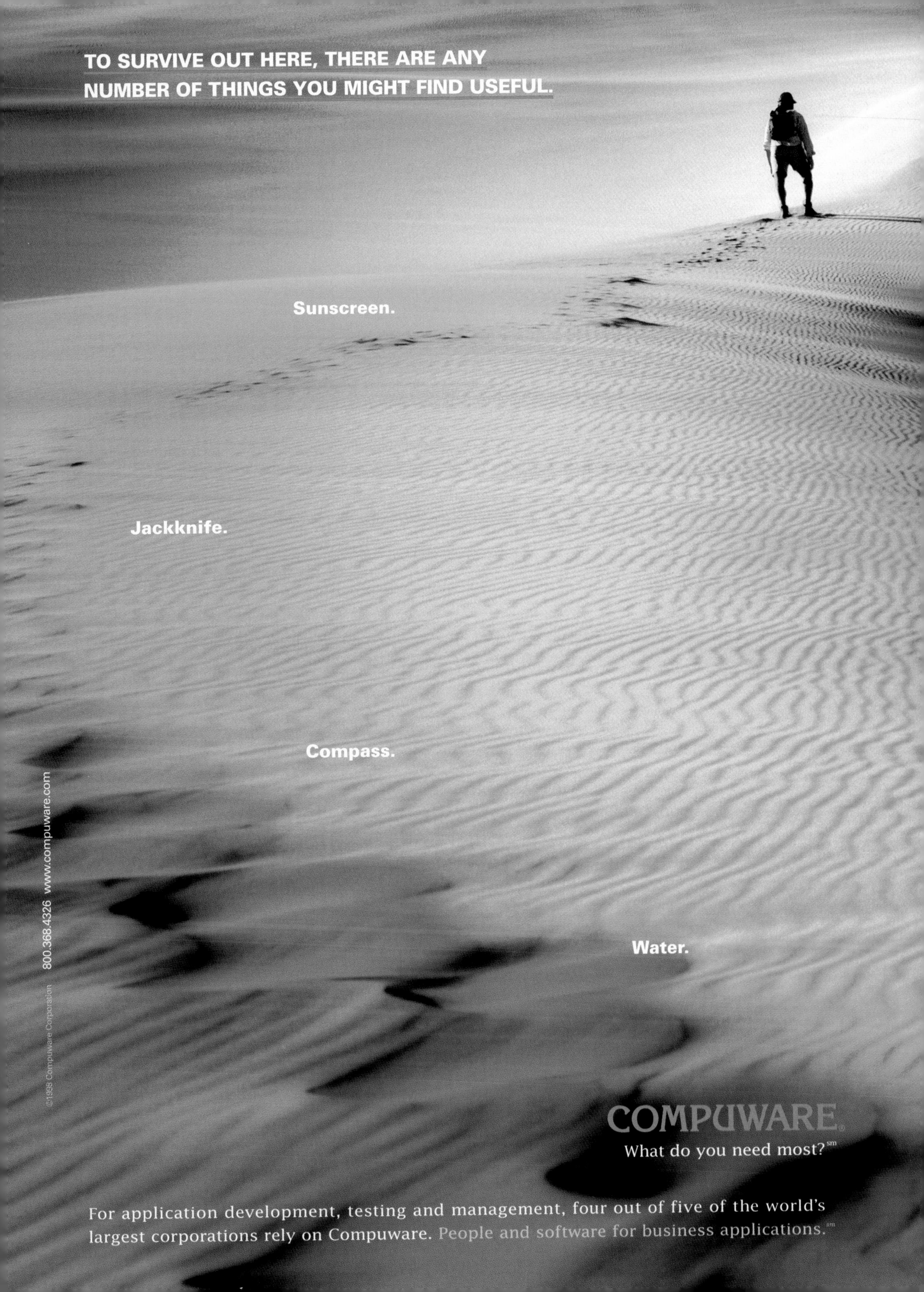

TO SURVIVE OUT HERE, THERE ARE ANY NUMBER OF THINGS YOU MIGHT FIND USEFUL.
Sunscreen.
Jackknife.
Compass.
Water.
COMPUWARE®
What do you need most?℠
For application development, testing and management, four out of five of the world's largest corporations rely on Compuware. People and software for business applications.℠
©1998 Compuware Corporation 800.368.4326 www.compuware.com

Who gives you the full picture?

At Dresdner Kleinwort Benson, we know how important it is to bring an in-depth understanding to our clients' business in order to manage risk and make the most of opportunities. This is why we maintain a long term relationship approach and employ leading industry experts who are able to apply their specialist knowledge to create global strategic insights. Combined with the balance sheet strength of the Dresdner Bank Group and our international placement power, this sector expertise provides clients with innovative solutions around the world.

For further information, contact Frankfurt on Tel: +49 69 263 16189 or London on Tel: +44 171 475 6016.

www.dresdnerkb.com

Get rich slow

Hamish McRae

It will be the year when the markets have to put it all back together again. There was always a significant possibility that the markets would lose their nerve during the course of 1998. They did. So priority one is the recovery of nerve after that truly bumpy second half. This return of confidence won't come quickly and it won't come evenly. There will be corners of the forest which will remain dark and deserted. There will however be other areas where decent returns will be achieved, provided (and this is a big proviso) that investors have the confidence to look through a global slowdown to the solid growth beyond.

Priority two is education. It is back to school. Markets have to learn, or rather re-learn, some very basic lessons, for example about the pricing of risk or about the appropriate valuation of assets in a zero inflation world. Is it a zero inflation world? Yes, it is. Or at least that is the most sensible assumption to make.

Priority three is to listen. Professional investors have to look to their customers' wants. They will probably find that we are moving towards a time when customers feel the preservation of wealth becomes a more important objective than beating the index on a quarterly basis. Customers want judgment and wisdom.

How the various markets perform during 1999 will depend on how investors, and particularly professional investors, rise to these challenges. There will be wonderful investment opportunities at a time like this. To say that would usually be a call for bravery, but this is a time not for the brave but rather for the wise and the patient.

Start with equities: in North America and Western Europe the markets will ask the tough question: "What is value?" They will conclude that the most primitive of valuations, the prospective price/earnings (P/E) ratio is the most useful. They will look at the historical range of P/E ratios for the various markets,

Hamish McRae: author of "The World in 2020" and associate editor of the *Independent*.

The good old days are gone

apply their best cut for earnings and feel comfortable only when the P/E ratios are also comfortably within their long-term range. By late 1998 a fair part of the adjustment in equities had been made, but looking forward the prime concern remained the prospect of earnings in 1999. If a slowdown in growth does seriously hit profits then some further rewriting will be necessary. Expect sentiment to remain weak during the first half of 1999 until corporate profitability is clearer. If it turns out that the best companies can make good profits in tough times, then expect a gradual recovery in confidence to take place during the second half of the year. If company profits continue to falter, confidence will take much longer to return.

In Japan, by contrast, confidence will depend less on the private sector and more on the public. A substantial reconstruction of the financial system will have to be made during the course of 1999 and work had started at the end of 1998. But confidence will remain fragile until it is clear that the Japanese economy's long pull out of recession is secure. There is

good news on the horizon, but more bad news meanwhile.

In all three main economic zones there are further complications as a result of currency concerns. In the United States the great question for the dollar is whether current accounts still matter. At some stage America will have to move towards a current-account balance, though the timing and the mechanism are unclear. The balance of probability is that the dollar will remain reasonably strong through 1999, despite these concerns, though maybe giving up some ground against the fledgling euro.

For Europe, a new currency, a new European Central Bank and a "one-size-fits-all" set of interest rates will take the region into unknown territory. Given the different points of the economic cycle in the various European countries, the interest rate within the euro area will inevitably be wrong for some parts. The tension will mount through 1999; although a collapse of the euro is possible, it is unlikely. Political determination will triumph over economic tension. But whatever the tensions in the early years of the next century, we will catch a glimpse of Europe's future. Will the euro be strong? Yes it will. Will Europe feel comfortable with a strong euro? No it won't.

In Japan the yen will have a crunch role in determining the pace of economic recovery. Rationally, the yen is fairly valued at about ¥120 to the dollar. But it needs to be unfairly valued given the collapse of the other currencies in the east Asian region. Expect a further decline, but maybe a glimpse of recovery before the year is out.

The really big financial issue in 1999, more important than the immediate twists and turns of the markets, will be how the world adjusts to deflation. There is no folk memory of an era when prices of goods and services are as likely to fall as to rise, though this was normal for the previous century. Indeed, the 20th-century experience of runaway inflation has

been unprecedented in European history. If normality is stable prices, then bonds become attractive long-term assets, not just bolt-holes when equities look weak. Equities have to earn their keep by paying decent dividends. Interest rates remain low and may move lower. Objectives like value and security become more important than quarterly increments to wealth. The game will be played long.

We will, during the last year of this century, catch a glimpse of the investment tone that will govern the markets through the first part of the next. Of course the economic cycle will continue, tamed maybe by competent central banks. And, yes, there will be future speculative bubbles. What will be new will be the long-term shift in investment attitudes. "Get rich quick" gives way to "Stay rich". Or for the newcomers, maybe "Get rich slow."

The City of London will have a nervous year. Will it capture the euro's heart? This is Frankfurt's moment of opportunity.

need to stay at home to minimise risk. Quite the reverse. They will run higher risks in having all their eggs in one national basket than in spreading their assets across the euro zone. As a result, capital is on the move. Of course, the free flow of funds is still being held up by idiosyncrasies in national rules on investment, taxation, corporate governance and so forth. But these are not set in stone. As capital increasingly travels across borders, the institutional framework will be forced to adapt. This is already visible in moves to establish pan-European stock exchanges, indices and takeover rules.

What is true for portfolio investors is also true for banks. Hitherto, most banks have lent most of their money at home— with the exception of lending to the very biggest corporate customers. Again, currency mismatching is the main explanation. Dutch banks, for example, did not have access to cheap peseta deposits in the way that their Spanish counterparts did. But from January, a euro deposited in Amsterdam can be lent in Barcelona without running any currency risk.

The freer flow of portfolio and bank finance throughout Europe will unleash competition. The providers of capital will no longer be confined within national boundaries but will hunt out the best returns across euroland. As a result, companies will have to

Capitalism's Trojan horse

Hugo Dixon

The process of European union is rich in ironies. But few more so than that the single currency will accelerate the replacement of the continent's stakeholder model of capitalism with one giving pre-eminence to shareholder value. Remember that monetary union was spurred on by a French socialist, Jacques Delors. And it is being seen in by centre-left politicians—Gerhard Schröder, Lionel Jospin and Massimo D'Alema—with the social democrat Tony Blair watching from the touchlines. And yet shareholder value, with its stress on how companies should be run in order to enhance their owners' wealth, is a philosophy more associated with the free-market right than the centre-left.

Part of the explanation is, of course, that these modern social democrats have embraced many of the nostrums of an enterprise economy. But EMU is also having unintended consequences. Monetary union was conceived largely as a macro project—which would require common interest rates and help drive forward the goal of political union. But there will also be micro effects. Most immediately, the single currency constitutes a giant leap towards creating a single capital market. Europe's capital markets are still astonishingly fragmented. Of the big markets, the most outward looking is Britain—and

even there less than 20% of its financial assets are invested abroad. In Germany, France and Italy, the figures are all around 5%.

There is, of course, a reason for this isolation: currency frontiers. In the old world of multiple currencies, investors ran a foreign exchange risk whenever they put their money abroad. Investment regulations often made it hard for insurance companies and pension funds to invest in foreign currencies. It is hardly surprising that the bulk of portfolio capital was trapped at home.

But from January 1999, all this changes. European investors will no longer

Hugo Dixon: Head of Lex at the *Financial Times*.

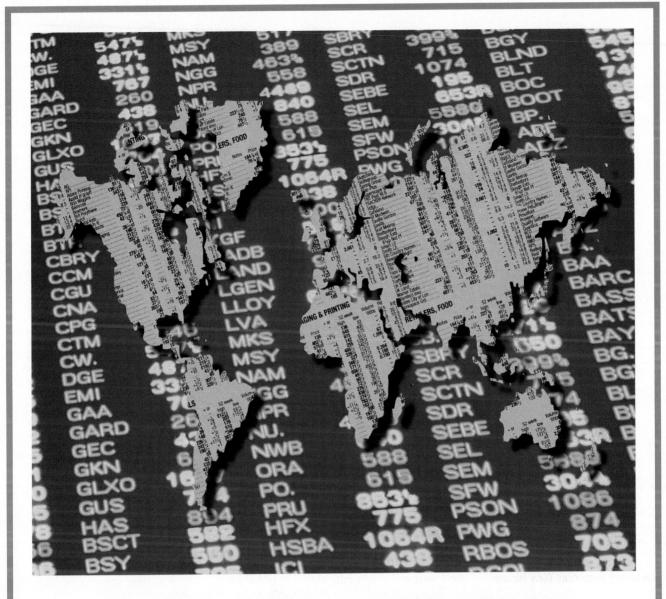

London – the world's choice

The companies on our market represent over 60 countries from around the world. By listing in London these companies have been able to reach a substantial and diverse institutional investor base and to raise additional funds in the world's most heavily traded international market.

To find out what opportunities a listing on the London Stock Exchange could provide for your company, call us now on +44 171 797 1242.

London **STOCK EXCHANGE**

www.londonstockex.co.uk. London Stock Exchange, Old Broad Street, London EC2N 1HP United Kingdom Fax +44 171 410 6861

iNTelLigent
telecommunications

data
voice
vision
internet

Effective solutions supporting your voice, data, vision and Internet requirements, delivered over NTL's future-proof network, will pave the way for your successful transition forward into the next Millennium.

Recognised as the best in the industry for customer service and service delivery*, choose NTL as your telecommunications supplier with confidence.

call today
0800 052 0800

NTL
Telecommunications

e-mail: business@ntl.com http://BusTel.ntl.com
*Source: Morgan Stanley Dean Witter Research, NOP. March 1998

sing for their supper. No longer will they be able to rely on trapped domestic capital being channelled their way. For the most successful, access to a large capital market will be a boon. But the poor performers will feel the heat. As the competition to attract funds moves up a gear, companies throughout Europe will be increasingly driven to advancing shareholder value.

But what about the softening in global economic conditions and the fading bullishness of investors? Wasn't shareholder value a phenomenon of the bull market? And so won't there now be a reversion to the old stakeholder mentality?

Not so fast. Shareholder value may have been a child of the long bull market but it now has an identity of its own. Moreover, in a bear market, companies could find themselves under even more pressure to advance shareholders' interests. After all, they will need to compete all the more vigorously to attract a limited pot of funding. The same goes for the real economy. If the demand for goods deteriorates, companies will have to work harder to win and retain business. The restructuring evident in Europe over the past two years will, if anything, be stepped up.

Of course, a change in investor appetite will change the way in which Europe's single capital market develops. Continental investors' nascent love affair with shares may take some time to revive. And the embryonic corporate junk-bond market may take longer to develop. Greater risk aversion among investors will also change the way in which shareholder value manifests itself. Gearing up balance sheets via share buybacks—the most popular way of demonstrating a commitment to investors during the bull market—will no longer seem such a sensible idea when liquidity is drying up. Hoarding cash as a cushion against bankruptcy, or in the hope of snapping up bargains as other companies face difficulties, could become the new orthodoxy. In the land of the illiquid, those with cash will be kings.

Though the form shareholder value takes may vary, the single currency will drive forward its adoption whatever the macroeconomic circumstances. The process of change it unleashes may be uncomfortable. But the spur it gives to corporate performance will, in time, do much to advance European prosperity.

Time to adjust our views

Sandy Weill

Capital markets do not pay much attention to a change of year, or a change of century for that matter. They react to trends and events.

The most fundamental trend in the past seven years has been the almost universal embrace of the capitalist model by countries around the world after the collapse of communism. Countries in every continent have set about privatising industries that were formerly operated as government monopolies. Furthermore, the example of Chile has led a movement toward transforming under-funded public pension funds into private funds along the 401-k model in the United States.

These movements energised capital markets and buoyed a heady optimism. There seemed to be no down. But then came a phenomenon that Alan Greenspan, chairman of the Federal Reserve, called a "vicious cycle."

The previously smooth road to capitalism took a sudden turn. This is testing the will of a number of political leaders who had previously expressed a fervent commitment to free-market principles as a means of growth for their countries and a signal for attracting foreign investment. Throughout 1999, it will become apparent that there is a distinct shortage of the skills necessary for effectively moving control from the public sector to the private sector.

Another defining trend is globalisation or, as we at Citigroup call it, "globality." In capital markets terms, this has meant the linkage of events in

Sandy I. Weill: Chairman and co-chief executive of Citigroup.

one part of the world to places far distant.

Fortunately, Latin America, which is feeling the pressure of distant events, has an advantage in having been through these problems before. It has learnt a great deal from the debt problems that debilitated the region in the 1980s. Many Latin American governments have first-hand experience with the high costs to society of trying to avoid market solutions to economic problems.

While the governments of emerging countries are being tested by recent events, so are financial institutions. With hindsight, it is clear that financial leverage has been too prevalent—and too widely tolerated by investors, lenders and counterparts. That tolerance already has undergone definite adjustment, but it will take much of 1999 for over-leveraging to be unwound.

Capital strength will be a decided advantage in the volatile, difficult markets of the coming 18 months or so. Our recognition of that fact was one of the driving considerations in merging Citicorp and Travelers Group, creating a diversified financial services company with $44 billion in equity.

There are two events on the calendar that will cause changes in the world's capital market, both anticipated but profound: one, European monetary union at the start of 1999 and the other, at the end of the year, when many computer systems are not made ready for handling the 2000 date. We will see an adjustment of trading patterns with

the onset of the euro and we will probably see caution about settlement as we approach the end of the year.

Harder to anticipate is how governments and multilateral institutions will respond to the challenges to world economic order. There has been a notable lack of decisive, imaginative leadership. Certainly the need is obvious. In countries like Japan and Germany, new teams are confronted by long-standing problems. In Russia, leaders need to determine how to tackle serious problems with limited resources. In the United States, a president who shows real understanding of the issues and who has assembled a solid economic team faces a hugely uncertain year. The multilateral institutions themselves will be increasingly criticised for not adjusting to the changing circumstances.

The common goal of 1999 should be the achievement of stable growth in free markets. This is still the most efficient means of allocating capital and focusing the productive energies of people around the world.

The Audi S8 quattro has a powerful 340bhp engine, radical aluminium space frame, permanen

For more informatio

our wheel drive and tiptronic transmission. No wonder it's light years ahead of its rivals.

call 0345 699777.

Audi

Vorsprung durch Technik

The euro's place in the sun

Stefan Collignon   PARIS

De Gaulle once called it an "exorbitant privilege" for the United States to have an international currency which allows near-painless financing of its external deficit. Since then, the monetary system has altered beyond recognition but the dominant role of the dollar still permits the accumulation of a huge external American debt. The advent of the euro will change all this, and with it the balance of the international monetary system. The creation of the euro will be the most important development of the system since Bretton Woods. It will mark a turning point comparable to the change when the dollar succeeded sterling during the inter-war years.

Normally, great currencies have been associated with great powers. The pound was the dominant currency of the 19th century because Britain's monetary policy, tied to gold, had a long history of stability. The British empire had become the greatest of its time. However, the pound suffered from the first world war and lost its reputation as a reliable reserve currency. Britain's power faded just at the time when the dollar appeared on the horizon. After the second world war, the size of America's financial markets and the stability of the dollar's value laid the ground for the dominant role of the currency. With the dollar anchored to gold, the era of Bretton Woods became a golden age for the world economy: strong non-inflationary growth, low unemployment, stable financial markets with fixed exchange-rates prevailed. The system broke down partly because it was so successful in creating and accumulating wealth and in opening previously isolated economies, partly because the American government was using the inflation tax to pay for the Vietnam war. In 1971 the dollar left gold and other currencies left the dollar.

This breakdown of the Bretton Woods system took the leadership of the monetary system away from governments and gave it to free world markets. Since then, external and internal insta-

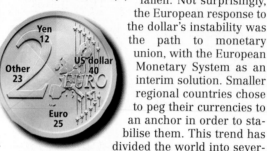

Cutting the currency pie

International private assets (%)

Yen 12
US dollar 40
Other 23
Euro 25

Official reserves (%)

Euro 20
US dollar 60
Other 14
Yen 6

bility has significantly increased and growth has fallen. Not surprisingly, the European response to the dollar's instability was the path to monetary union, with the European Monetary System as an interim solution. Smaller regional countries chose to peg their currencies to an anchor in order to stabilise them. This trend has divided the world into several currency blocks in which the blocks float against each other. However, exchange rates between key currencies like the dollar, D-mark and yen have become highly volatile.

How EMU will change the international landscape depends mainly on two questions. First, will the euro challenge the dollar as an international currency? Second, is EMU likely to make the international monetary system more or less stable?

There is little doubt that the euro will qualify in short order as a strong international currency. Markets take the stability and strength of a currency's domestic economy as a prerequisite to its use internationally. The euro is born into an economy as large as the United States, and so will be widely used in international financial markets as well as in commercial transactions. Furthermore, both currencies are fairly independent of external constraints: the degree of international exposure is approximately 10% for the United States and for the euro's domestic economies. Thus, both economies can manage their policies without being thrown off course by external shocks.

Will the new euro ever reach full parity with the dollar in the breadth and liquidity of its capital markets? The American securities market is still

roughly twice as large as the combined European markets. That will start to change in 1999. A large and liquid European financial market will emerge: the liquidity and diversity of its various debt instruments will be much larger than the present combined national debts. Moreover, technological progress will enhance the impact of the euro while improving financial-market efficiency. This will deepen Europe's financial markets and make the evolution of a euro-dominated bond market more independent of developments in New York. Wall Street and the Federal Reserve will still be the undoubted leaders of world monetary policy over the next five years. But over the next ten? Consider some of the changes in store. Commodity producers, for example, might shift their invoicing to the euro once it is perceived as a good and widely used currency.

Once confidence in the policies of the new European Central Bank is established, significant diversification from the dollar to the euro will take place. It is reasonable to predict a portfolio balance with the dollar and the euro each attaining 40% of world financial markets and 20% for all other currencies.

One lesson we should learn from the inter-war period is that exchange-rate stability is necessary for economic growth in the world economy. If neglect by policymakers causes excessive exchange-rate movements it will hamper world trade and productive investment. It will also undermine political stability in Europe and abroad. The creation of a large and relatively closed euro-zone makes exchange rates less dependent on internal policy objectives (such as reducing unemployment), but more volatile in respect to external objectives like the current account. Hence, convergence of economic policies will become crucial for the evolution of the world economy. As the euro grows up, so will it bring about a greater convergence between the dollar's domestic market and the EU.

In a post-EMU international monetary system it should become easier to co-ordinate monetary, but not necessarily economic, policies between the currency blocks. The G7 could become the G3—a prediction not for 1999 but for the near future.

How assets are held

EU 11 (%)

Government bonds 18
Private bonds 15
Equities 10
Bank assets 57

USA (%)

Equities 30
Private bonds 19
Government bonds 29
Bank assets 22

Source: Association for the Monetary Union of Europe

Dr Stefan Collignon: Association for the Monetary Union of Europe.

HOW MUCH WILL THE EURO COST YOUR COMPANY?

FIND OUT AT OUR EXPENSE.

Whatever the effects of the Euro on your business, it always pays to be prepared. But it won't cost you anything.

That's because, as one of the world's leading providers of packaged international business management solutions, we think it's our job to give you the facts, as well as the solutions.

And that's why we developed Euro Manager, a unique software tool to help you navigate the legal and financial complexities of Euro compliance, free of charge.

It takes an inventory of your processes. It calculates the implications for your systems. It documents the results. And it's just one more example of our determination to find out what you need and deliver it.

For your free copy (CD or web download) and more information about Exact Globe for Windows - our portfolio of Euro compliant products and services, call +44 (o) 1784 894577 or visit our web site at www.exactinternational.com. You need to know.

Exact
SOFTWARE

BETTER INSIGHT.
BETTER DECISIONS.
BETTER BUSINESS.

Money to be made on Wall Street

Matthew Bishop   NEW YORK

Wall Streeters are unusually pessimistic about the coming year. But many of them are in for a pleasant surprise. Whereas 1998 started well, only to turn bad with a vengeance, 1999 is likely to develop from unpromising beginnings into a vintage year, at least for the best banks and securities houses.

Wall Street—and other major financial centres—is still reeling at the suddenness of 1998's downturn. The most devastated were partners at Goldman Sachs. In August they were looking forward to picking up a truck-load of money from the investment bank's initial public offering in the autumn; a month later, the flotation was postponed indefinitely. But the turmoil in financial markets hurt everybody to some degree. Bonuses were down sharply, hard-boiled eggs compared with the golden ones of the preceding few years. The share price of many financial companies fell by half to two-thirds between July and September, crushing the value of equity-linked pay for many workers.

But, above all, two things underpin the pessimism. The year-old market difficulties abroad have finally arrived in America—which had seemed immune to them. Worse still, the downturn has hit Wall Street on several fronts all at once. In other recent bad years, there was one main source of trouble—the stockmarket in 1987, real-estate loans in 1991, and bond prices in 1994. But in 1998, the Dow plunged from July's all-time high, and prices tumbled even more sharply for other risky assets, ranging from emerging-market debt to mortgage-backed securities to junk bonds.

Even so, none of this is likely to last long. In the early 1990s, Citibank came within a whisker of going bust, and several other banks were barely any better off. But today, thanks to several years of record-breaking profits during the 1990s, most of the bigger Wall Street firms remain in reasonable financial health despite their recent knocks. Once confidence starts returning to the markets, they are well-placed to take advantage of the opportunities.

And what superb opportunities they will be. In the autumn of 1998, the prices of many securities fell to levels that, by

Matthew Bishop: New York correspondent, *The Economist*.

historic standards, look to be once-in-a-lifetime bargains. For instance, the yield on double-B rated US corporate bonds was nearly 700 basis points more than Treasuries—a spread last seen in recession, when companies were defaulting in droves. The gap between the price of a 30-year Treasury bond and a similar Treasury issued a year earlier rose to

There's opportunity in Greenspan's gloom

levels never seen before, which made no economic sense.

Prices fell to these absurd levels for reasons that look temporary and technical, not fundamental. Many investors had to reduce their risk-taking because trading losses had hurt their balance sheets. They sold heavily. In general, there was a reluctance to trade in risky assets. This was partly for balance-sheet reasons and partly because the near failure of Long-Term Capital Management, a hedge fund, made would-be buyers nervous that they could be on the wrong end of a big, forced sale of the fund's huge portfolio. Yet once these fears subside, and once risk-management models give the green light to resume risk-taking, it would be astonishing if Wall Street firms do not invest heavily in assets that, judged on their fundamentals, are available at give-away prices.

True, there may be exceptions to this happy trend. Emerging-market debt

prices may recover much more slowly than Treasuries and other developed-country fixed-income securities. More visibly, American shares may not resume their bull market. Yet even this will not hurt Wall Street as much as might be supposed, given the prominence of the stockmarket in the public eye. Investment firms do much of their trading in other sorts of assets. They do not necessarily need the stockmarket to go up to make a profit; they just need to be good judges of which direction it will go.

As for underwriting and advisory work, it needs only a period of calm and stability in the markets to kick-start the waves of mergers and initial public offerings and securitisations that stalled during the market downturn. The volumes could be large, as there is now a large backlog of deals.

This new business will be more profitable than before, because firms will be leaner. When things are going well, nobody wants to spoil the fun by doing nasty things like downsizing. But when the going gets tough, there is no more ruthless—or less loyal—employer than a Wall Street investment firm. Downturns are an opportunity to both cut and upgrade the workforce, axing the worst performers and poaching star performers from firms hit harder by the difficult market conditions. In 1999 this will be done with even greater zeal. Top management in most Wall Street firms own more shares and options than ever. The simplest way to boost a damaged share price is to swing the axe hard and often.

Like everything on Wall Street, the spoils of recovery will not be shared out equally. The bigger firms will bounce higher than their smaller rivals. Wall Street has long had too much capacity—but because times were so good, firms that should have died survived.

American firms will do better than their foreign rivals. The downturn comes at the worst possible time for the big European banks, which are already struggling to make an impact on Wall Street. Now it will become clear which of them are serious in their global ambitions. It will be no surprise if some choose to concentrate their fire on Europe—where they hope to benefit from the launch of the single currency—leaving the rich pickings to be had elsewhere to their American rivals.

THE WORLD IN 1999   **Dealing markets everywhere will retreat from "open call". Human traders are quaint, electronic ones efficient.**

Why markets will fall

Andrew Smithers

Expect a major world recession to start towards the end of 1999. It will be set off by the end of the Wall Street bubble. As share prices fall American households will seek to save more, not only because they will have less money for their retirement but because they will have smaller incomes. Employee stock options have been adding 1% or more of GDP to household incomes and a similar amount has been generated by mergers and acquisitions,which were running at 20% of GDP in the first half of 1998. This was double the rate of the previous year, which was itself a record. The M&A bubble will collapse with the market.

As the stockmarket falls, personal savings will rise. This is not really surprising, given they fell to only 0.2% of disposable incomes in June 1998. This compares with an average of around 6% over the past 20 years and 15% in Japan. As savings rise so consumption falls and as the trade deficit will continue to expand rapidly, corporate investment and profits will decline sharply. This will lead to a vicious circle, with poor profits causing the stockmarket to fall and the falling stockmarket leading, via higher savings, to even lower profits.

The psychology of American investors today is very like that of Japanese investors during their bubble. In the late 1980s investors were convinced that Japan had the strongest economy in the world based on the best technology and the best management techniques. Other countries were seeking to learn both. Investors have the same faith today about America as they had about Japan in the 1980s. The key difference was that Japanese management believed in long-term planning and never sacking anyone, while the current American fashion is a ruthless approach to hiring and firing. This difference will mean that the end of the American bubble will have a much faster impact on the

world economy than occurred when the Japanese bubble burst.

The American stockmarket is hugely over-priced. This can be shown from the "q" ratio. This is the comparison between the value the stockmarket places on corporations and the amount it would cost to replace all their assets at today's prices. The theoretical validity of this measure was first demonstrated by a Nobel Laureate, James Tobin, in 1969. At that time there was, however, no data available to test it. Since then, however, the data have been collected and two Cambridge economists, Donald Robert-

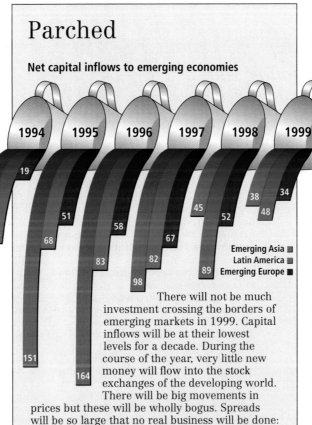

Parched

Net capital inflows to emerging economies

1994 · 1995 · 1996 · 1997 · 1998 · 1999

19

38 · 34
45 · 52 · 48
51 · 58 · 67
68 · 82
83 · 89
64 · 98
151
119 · 164

Emerging Asia ■
Latin America ■
Emerging Europe ■

There will not be much investment crossing the borders of emerging markets in 1999. Capital inflows will be at their lowest levels for a decade. During the course of the year, very little new money will flow into the stock exchanges of the developing world. There will be big movements in prices but these will be wholly bogus. Spreads will be so large that no real business will be done: there will be no liquidity. Such capital investment as there will be will come either from "vulture" funds, which seek to pick up assets at distressed prices, or from world financial institutions, such as the World Bank or the European Bank for Reconstruction and Development. These institutions will have lines of capital to buy in loans or equities at heavily discounted prices. The big multinationals, led by America, will also invest, not through equity stakes but by buying factories and brands wholesale: the risks are high but the rewards are potentially large.

son and Stephen Wright, have confirmed that the theory stands up by rigorous statistical testing of the data. This is exciting, as the sequence of a theory being postulated and then found robust under testing is more usual in the physical sciences than in economics. It is also worrying, as the data show the market in June 1998 was well over twice its equilibrium level and has about a 75% chance of falling over the next year.

It was the insight of Maynard Keynes that recessions are caused by the wish to save being greater then the wish to invest. As both have to match up in the event, this disequilibrium has to be resolved and its resolution leads to recession. This prevents companies and individuals from realising the saving they hoped to make. A Keynesian view suggests that the world economy is in very poor shape to withstand a Wall Street crash. Japan saves around 30-35% of its GDP and cannot profitably invest anything like this in its slow-growing economy. Furthermore, this slow growth is no short-term cyclical aberration, but is the economy's likely long-term path. Japan's working population is falling and very slow growth is likely while this continues. The country's intentions to save will thus be hugely in excess of any likely investment for many years to come. Meanwhile, the rest of Asia is suffering from a cyclical savings surplus of such severity that a rapid recovery is improbable. "Euroland" has a steady savings surplus shown by its persistent current-account surplus, so only the profligacy of the English-speaking peoples has provided the balance to absorb the excess savings of the rest of the world.

Wall Street's rush to the stratosphere has thus been the major driving force behind the world economy. This could not be more unfortunate, as all the past bubbles have been followed by major and often prolonged recessions. The problem is that recessions set off by asset price falls do not respond readily to falling interest rates. This should cause no surprise. As stockmarkets fall, the cost of equity capital rises sharply and banks become less willing to lend. The overall cost of capital rises, therefore, even if interest rates fall sharply.

Andrew Smithers: chairman of Smithers & Co. Ltd. London.

Equities all the way

Richard A. Grasso, chairman of the New York Stock Exchange, sets out to conquer the world.

The crisis in emerging markets of the past two years will make 1999 a critical time for global equity markets, both in terms of their role in the world economy and their structure.

Throughout much of the 1990s globalisation was gaining momentum. Cross-border equity trading more than tripled in the first seven years of the decade, and the value of privatisations grew sixfold. The crisis of the late 1990s slowed the trend. But globalisation is not dead yet; the forces behind it are simply too powerful.

In developed markets, raising equity capital has historically been a crucial factor in generating a nation's wealth. In emerging markets, equity capital will play a key role in the very survival and recovery of these economies.

Equity provides the economic goods that emerging markets need most. It balances the burdens of debt, provides the stability of long-term investment, offers cost-efficient access to capital, democratises participation in economic growth and lends the transparency of widespread ownership.

Of course, it is not a panacea. As the current crisis abates—and I will offer no predictions on exactly when, since recovery will take place at varying rates around the world—equity investment will rebound. It will search for economies operating under sound principles and enterprises offering the promise of value and growth. Equity markets will return to the business of raising capital.

For the securities industry, the crisis threw a new degree of complexity into the process of planning for the future. Following a long bull market, share prices fell sharply and the flow of new offerings slowed, while trading volumes soared amid increased volatility.

Do not take the trading-volume numbers as a sure indicator of things to come. If you were to use New York Stock Exchange (NYSE) trading volume as a proxy for equity-market conditions, the experience of 1987 is indeed a sobering example.

In September 1987, if we had projected the five-year trend in average daily trading volume to 1990, we would

"Trade in equities will follow the sun, across borders, time zones, oceans."

have anticipated trading 360m shares a day. But the market broke in October, inverting the growth curve. In 1990, we traded only 157m shares a day.

Based on the trend at the start of 1998, continuation of the previous five years' volume growth would produce one billion shares a day in 2001. But if the turn in the market we experienced in the summer of 1998 produces another post-1987 scenario, then we would see volume of only 515m shares a day in 2001—a starkly different picture not only for the securities industry but for companies seeking to raise capital in that environment.

There is another historical indicator to consider as well. At the beginning of this decade, the NYSE turnover rate (the volume of shares traded as a percentage of shares listed) was about 50%. In 1998, it has been 75%. And at the beginning of the century, as the revolutions in transport and mass production were getting into full stride, the NYSE turnover rate was above 200%. If today's accelerating transition to an information economy were to have the same effect, trading volumes would nearly triple.

Despite the variables, equity markets must plan for growth, and that means building the technological capacity to provide access to the market when it is needed most: when markets are moving rapidly. For the NYSE, that means keeping capacity five times ahead of average activity. By the end of 1999, we will have expanded capacity to five billion shares a day from 1998's three billion.

Here are some other developments:
● Within the next several years, many equities will trade around the clock, following the sun, as do major commodities such as gold and oil. Fuelled in part by the euro, capital will flow seamlessly across borders, time zones and oceans.
● Markets will intensify their efforts over the next few years to develop cross-border alliances to facilitate this trading, or to develop technology that will supplant their geography.
● The argument of how equity markets should develop will break out of its simplistic terms, in which order-driven systems are seen as competing with their quote-driven counterparts. Instead, markets will work to answer the essential questions: Who is the customer? What value is provided to that customer? How are customers' changing needs met? No single market model can address all the needs of all types of customers and stocks.
● The losses incurred by the securities industry in 1998 will renew the focus on cutting costs, and this will lead to further market consolidation. During the next few years, there will be new impetus to reduce redundancy, resulting in fewer markets. The surviving markets will be better equipped to compete in the new global environment.
● As stocks increasingly trade in multiple markets, those markets will compete to some extent with one another for a share of the order flow, but the international activity will also increase the size of the pie, instead of merely dividing it up.
● In the second or third quarter of 2000, America's equity markets and securities industry will switch to trading in decimal prices instead of fractions of a dollar. This will align the United States with the practices of most markets around the world and make pricing more understandable for investors.
● Within the next couple of years, the NYSE will begin trading non-American stocks, as well as American depositary receipts. This will give international asset managers more flexibility in trading these shares when the home market is not available.
● More companies with substantial share-ownership in multiple markets will consider following the lead of DaimlerChrysler in developing a single security that will trade worldwide.

Who'll play pension poker?

Leo Schulz

Over the past ten years an estimated 80% of London's pension-fund business has devolved into the hands of four managers: Mercury Asset Management, Phillips & Drew, Schroders and Gartmore. In 1999 the break-up will begin. And by the time of the next bull market these names will be but shadows of their former selves.

Success has brought rewards to the giants. The Big Four run about $1 trillion, implying annual income in the region of $7 billion. But this happy oligopoly will crumble for three reasons. One is performance, or the lack of it. The second is the changing nature of pension provision. The third is the onslaught of global competition.

Scarcely a beauty parade will go by in the next 12 months without one of the Big Four being fired. At the last survey by Combined Actuarial Performance Services, for the year to June 1998, the performance of each of the four was in the bottom quartile. Over the past three years, the four's average annual return is 14.3%. That is 3.6 percentage points under the median of 66 funds, and a roaring five percentage points below the upper quartile.

Pension liabilities are long-term and markets fall as well as rise. No one seriously expects constant outperformance. But three years of poor returns can matter. For Zeneca, a pharmaceuticals company which has reduced the proportion of its $3 billion pension fund placed with the Big Four, underperformance of five points a year implies a loyalty cost of $100m a year. In Zeneca's case, that is equivalent to 10% of pre-tax profits.

There is no simple explanation for what has happened, and therefore no simple solution. One analysis is to blame the strategy. Phillips & Drew, for example, market themselves as "value" investors. They buy stocks which they perceive as undervalued and hope to gain as the company increases profitability by restructuring, possibly through takeover.

But the market spent much of 1998 going the other way, tossing aside value stocks and scrambling for "growth", companies whose stocks are fully valued but which operate in a growing market. A classic value stock, one with a

Leo Schulz: writes on legal and investment issues.

strong brand in a sector ripe for consolidation is a British builder, Tarmac. Since 1995 its stock has fallen 15.5%. Over the same period, Glaxo Wellcome, the leading growth stock, has risen 170%.

At Schroders the story is different. Their view of the market has been overconfident. They have favoured small aggressive companies, assets that ought to outperform in a bull market. But the bull market of the past three years was an odd one, with a distinct preference for defensiveness. And it has come to a juddering halt. At the end of 1997 the Schroders pooled pension fund had 2% of its money in North America, where equities rose 38%, and 2.5% in the tiny Pacific ex-Japan markets, where equities fell 32%. Its preference for mid-capitalisation stocks was just as treacherous. In the year to June 1998, Britain's FTSE Mid-250 rose 26.5%, compared with a rise of 57.2% in the large-cap FTSE 100.

Everyone gets strategy wrong sometime. Schroders's preference for emerging markets was once what put them on top. Should the pound fall against the D-mark, Phillips & Drew's engineering exporters will look surprisingly interesting. If the strategy is not to blame, it must be the product.

What is wrong, in this view, is the "balanced mandate". This is where a company pension fund hands over its entire pot to one fund manager, who is then responsible for spreading the money across a range of markets and asset classes. Fund managers have been ingenious at devising ways—"processes"—to combine creativity and daring

THE WORLD IN 1999

In April, Britain's Individual Savings Accounts replace Personal Equity Plans as the official low-tax off-the-shelf investment product. Sales could reach £127 billion by the end of 1999.

with discipline and prudence. But it rarely works. One or two personalities will usually dominate, and even if they do not, a single firm running multiple, and presumably incompatible strategies, is in practice unlikely to be successful.

The answer, according to the consultant actuaries who have helped to create the current oligopoly, is specialised management. The pot should be handed out to managers class by class, one for British equities, one for overseas equities, one for fixed income, one high risk, one low. This "core/satellite" structure has the coincidental effect of putting a lot more money the way of consultant actuaries, but it is less popular with the fund managers, though they might also increase their total fees, who see it as a loss of power. If they, with their expertise and their focus, make allocation mistakes, what will happen when fund trustees, guided only by the flattery of their paid advisers, begin to make the decisions for themselves?

Stephan Breban, a partner at Watson Wyatt, cheerfully admits to the higher fees: "But if it is more cost effective it does not matter. The point is that it is an opportunity to make an exact match between a fund's assets to its liabilities."

The discomfort of the Big Four might be a little less painful for them were it not for the barbarians gathering at the gate, a gate that will be breached in 1999. One such tribe is Britain's traditional life assurers, several of which have pursued a double strategy of merging their assurance businesses and spinning off their investment management. These now include Standard Life, a prime brand among Britain's independent financial advisers, Royal & SunAlliance and Friend's Provident. The mega-merger of Commercial Union and General Ac-

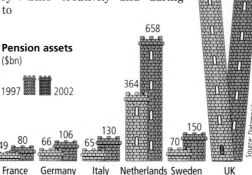

Pension assets
($bn)

1997 ▦ ▦ 2002

France 49 80
Germany 66 106
Italy 65 130
Netherlands 364 658
Sweden 70 150
UK 1432 2988

Source: Datamonitor

cident will form an entity with assets worth $170 billion.

Besides ambition and some pretty reasonable performance numbers, what these firms have—what almost defines them—is the thing for which until now they have been despised: retail networks. The Big Four have made their fortune on "institutional" business, managing company pension schemes. But the world is changing, and the expectations and responsibilities attached to pensions are changing faster than anything. The state no longer can, or wishes to, provide, and jobs now carry fewer and fewer non-cash benefits. The future is self-provision, which is retail. What the life companies can do and what the Big Four cannot do is to collect hundreds of thousands of small contributions.

The Americans, as so often, are ahead of the game. In a series of stunning mergers they have developed combinations of centralised, technically powerful, Wall Street fund managers and sprawling, Main Street retail chains. Morgan Stanley Dean Witter is perhaps the prime example. Salomon Smith Barney has gone even further, merging through its parent, Travelers, with Citicorp, and at the same time setting up an alliance in Japan with Nikko. What these would-be global brands are finding is that the average saver is deeply unnationalistic when it comes to above-average returns.

The attack has begun. Zurich Insurance has taken over the financial-services divisions of British American Tobacco, including one American and two British insurers and a centralised London fund manager. Merrill Lynch already owns Mercury, which it markets Europe-wide. Financial-sector mergers spurred by EMU are expected to bring fresh European players to London's lucrative and open market, following in the footsteps of UBS, which owns Phillips & Drew (but which might like to sell it), and Deutsche Bank, which owns Deutsche Morgan Grenfell, the closest competition to the Big Four. Meanwhile, the two names reputedly making the deepest inroads into the space left by the Big Four will be more familiar in the Midwest than in the Midlands—J.P. Morgan and Fidelity.

THE WORLD IN 1999 **Pressure will be on Austrian banks to start returning Nazi gold to Jewish holocaust survivors. Their 50-year delay will cost them dear: Swiss banks paid out $1.25 billion.**

Hong Kong's many troubles

But will it keep off the rain?

Hong Kong's economic traumas will persist in 1999. Output will shrivel, after shrinking 5% in 1998, so living standards will sink lower. Unemployment, formerly deemed high at 3%, will surpass 7% as companies go bust—or lay off workers to survive. Those in work, many burdened by mortgage payments on properties whose value has halved, can expect pay cuts in the year ahead.

Will the link between the Hong Kong and the American dollar last the year? Possibly. But the devastation wrought on the economy by high interest rates will eventually prompt the authorities to consider alternatives. An apt moment to replace the link would be in late 1999, if China, fretful of a narrowing current-account surplus, devalues the yuan.

Although fully part of China since 1997, Hong Kong has proved more economically vulnerable than the motherland, since it is an international financial centre, a small, open economy with the only fixed currency link in Asia for speculators to tilt at. The Special Administrative Region's government will be haunted in 1999 by its powerlessness to defend Hong Kong against external shocks and also by its own frequent mistakes.

If the world can avoid recession, the feeble beginnings of economic recovery in Hong Kong may show in late 1999 as interest rates edge down and exports pick up. But a return to stable and rapid growth is not yet on the cards. The territory no longer manufactures much and its exports are slowing, but it has yet to find a new role. While the government has so far resisted calls to re-industrialise, the former policy of "positive non-interventionism" has been compromised by moves to shore up property prices and massive government purchases in the stock and futures markets during 1998.

Tung Chee-hwa's "executive-led" government will have to decide whether to keep its arms folded and wait for the global troubles to pass or, instead, roll its sleeves up and prime the pump of domestic demand with even more publicly funded infrastructure projects than it is already promising.

What will the government do with the huge shareholding of private Hong Kong companies that it now owns? The equities will be put in a sheltered trust to provide future pensions. But the temptation to use these nationalised stakes to intervene in the running of the companies themselves will be too strong for China's politicians to resist. Expect meddling—and with it a powerful sign that Hong Kong's entrepreneurial magic is evaporating.

This gloomy view is likely to be reinforced in 1999 as talk of corruption and corporate theft speed through China. Hong Kong cannot remain immune. But without the strictest adherence to the rule of law and the rules of accountancy and corporate governance, Hong Kong's companies will suddenly look poor places for shareholders to put their money.

Hong Kong's great appeal is that, at its best, it mixes unfettered Asia entrepreneurism with Anglo-American corporate practice. It risks losing both elements irretrievably in 1999.

Are you a machine of many parts?

Alun Anderson

What will future historians remember about the impact of science during the last decade of the 20th century? They will not be much concerned with many of the marvels that currently preoccupy us, such as the miraculous increase in the power of home computers and the unexpected growth of the Internet. Nor will they dwell much on global warming, the loss of biodiversity and other examples of our penchant for destruction. Instead, the end of the 20th century will be recognised as the time when, for better or worse, science began to bring about a fundamental shift in our perception of ourselves.

It will be the third time that science has forced us to re-evaluate who we are. The first time, of course, was the revolution that began with Copernicus in 1543 and continued with Kepler, Galileo and Newton. Despite the Church's opposition, we came to realise that the Earth does not lie at the centre of the universe. Instead we gradually found we live on a small planet on the edge of a minor galaxy, circling one star in a universe that contains billions of others. Our unique position in the universe was gone for ever.

A few centuries later we were moved even further from stage centre. The Darwinian revolution removed us from our position as a unique creation of God. Instead we discovered we were just another part of the animal kingdom proud to have "a miserable ape for a grandfather", as Thomas Huxley put it in 1860. We now know just how close to the apes we are—over 90% of our genes are the same as those of the chimpanzee.

Increasing knowledge of our own genetics is one of the driving forces in the third great conceptual shift that will soon take place. Others are the growing knowledge of the way our minds work,

Alun Anderson: editor of the *New Scientist*.

our new ability to use knowledge of the nervous system to design drugs that affect specific states of mind and the creation of sophisticated scanners which enable us to see what is happening inside our brains. In the third revolution we are taking our own selves to pieces and finding the parts which make up the machine that is us.

Much of the new knowledge from genetics, molecular biology and the neurosciences is esoteric. But its cultural impact is already running ahead of the science. People begin to see themselves not as wholes with a moral centre but the result of the combined action of parts for which they have little responsibility.

"It's Nobody's Fault" is the title of a popular American book on "difficult" children. Many difficult children, the book explains, are not actually difficult but are suffering from Attention Deficit Disorder (ADD). There is nothing wrong with them or the way they have been brought up. Rather, the part of the brain which controls attention is short of a

particular neurotransmitter.

ADD is currently the world's fastest growing psychological problem. In the United States, a survey showed that 1.5m children between the ages of five and eighteen were being treated with a drug, Ritalin, for the disorder. Since then the number taking the drug is believed to have doubled.

You might, as many people do, question the way in which the disorder has been diagnosed on such a staggering scale. But that is not the point. The cultural shift is that people are not responsible for their disorders, only for obtaining treatment for the parts of them that have gone wrong.

The more we know about the parts of ourselves, the more cures for our defects

THE WORLD IN 1999 Led by America, 14 countries join forces in the largest ever joint technology venture: the building of the international space station.

will appear. Prozac is one example. The bestselling "Listening to Prozac" claimed the drug "can transform pessimists into optimists, turn loners into extroverts". And Prozac, the book explained, "was not so much discovered as planfully created, through the efforts of a large pharmaceutical firm...the likely result of this form of research is not medicines that correct particular illnesses but medicines that affect clusters of functions in the human brain."

Even when a treatment is not to hand, the notion that we are made of "clusters of functions" remains strong. Genetic analysis supports this view. A gene linked to alcoholism has been located and a Gallup poll has revealed that the great majority of Americans consider alcoholism to be a disease. There are claims of genes too for obesity, homosexuality and even for laziness.

Some claims about genes may be silly. Or you may think that the current conceptual shift is just a re-run of old arguments about the relative roles of nature and nurture. Instead, take one drug, Viagra, as an example of the new way of thinking about ourselves. If you suffer from impotence, it might have a variety of physiological causes. Or you might just be anxious about sexual performance. But Viagra does not make such fine distinctions: it acts at the level of the chemical reactions that control the blood flow needed to maintain an erection.

Once we can dissect ourselves into parts and know how the parts work, it really does not matter what was the initial cause of the problem. If you own a car and the brakes wear out quickly, it is not important whether you've been driving the car too hard or you bought cheap brake shoes to begin with. You just need to change the brakes.

The more direct means we have of changing who we are, through changing the parts that we are composed of, the harder becomes the question of who was the person who made the decision to change, before becoming someone else. This will be the real issue for the 21st century: who are we, if we are the sum of our parts and science has given us the power to change those parts?

THE WORLD IN 1999
Expect more lifestyle drugs. Too fat? Reductil tells the brain, rather than the stomach, not to eat. Feeling shy? Take Seroxat to become an outgoing, bubbly person. New in 1999? A margarine that measurably reduces cholesterol.

Thanks for the memory

Steve Connor

The final year of the century will mark an important milestone in the understanding of the human brain. It is the year when several independent lines of inquiry will converge towards a truly unified programme of research into what has been described as the most complex structure in the known universe. The end result will be a revelation about the innermost nature of the human psyche.

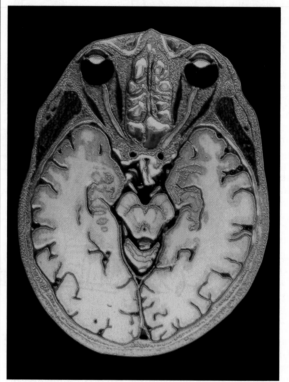

Now, where was I ?

René Descartes, a 17th-century philosopher, set the ball rolling when he summed up his own consciousness with the phrase, "I think, therefore I am." Since then, the study of what goes on in our heads has had a chequered history, dominated by the early 20th-century schools of psychology and the largely discredited approaches of Sigmund Freud and Carl Jung. But over recent years, especially during the 1990s (the "Decade of the Brain"), the study of the brain has undergone something of a sea change.

Any discussion of the human brain has to start with some facts about its phenomenal intricacy. It weighs between one and two kilograms (although size

Steve Connor: science editor for *The Independent* in London.

bears no relation to intelligence) and is composed of about a hundred billion nerve cells, or neurons. Each of these electrically excitable cells is connected with up to 10,000 others through a series of junctions, called synapses. Each synapse can call upon dozens of chemical messengers, called neurotransmitters, to pass a nerve impulse from one cell to another. If you started counting all the connections in just the cortex of the brain (the outer layer that is highly developed in humans), it would take you 32m years, counting at a rate of one synapse a second. Another way of looking at your brain is to look at the sky on a clear night—you have more connections between your ears than there are stars visible with the best telescopes.

In 1999 memory, one of the least-understood yet critically important functions of the brain, will be an important area of research. How is it that we can remember things from our childhood yet forget where we left the car keys? Why can we remember things from years ago when, during that time, all the neurotransmitters in the brain will have been replaced several times over? Is it inevitable for our memories to deteriorate as we get older? And if we lose our memory, we lose our identity. More people will experience severe memory loss as an ageing population suffers increasingly from the brain decay associated with senile dementias such as Alzheimer's.

Scientists are investigating memory in a number of ways that will begin to interact in 1999. One approach uses the latest generation of brain scanners, which can create detailed, "real time" images of the brain as it works. This method shows which parts of the brain are involved in storing long-term or short-term memories. A team of American researchers announced in 1998 that it had pinned down the part of the brain responsible for the split-second job of deciding whether an experience should be encoded as a memory. "This is the first time we've been able to peer inside someone's brain and predict on average whether or not they will remember what they are now experiencing," said Dr Randy Buckner, a team member from Washington University, St Louis.

In Britain, scientists are looking at how memories are formed at the molecular level. They predict that in the coming years it may be possible to augment the process of memory formation by creating "smart drugs" to help the victims of memory decay. Professor Steven Rose, director of the brain and behaviour research group at the Open University in Milton Keynes, could be on the verge of understanding the precise way that memories are made. His group has found that special molecules hold the synapses together in a way not dissimilar to a Velcro strip. "When new lasting memories are made, the 'Velcro' molecules briefly detach so that the junctions can separate; new Velcro molecules are made and stick them together again in a novel pattern which forms a memory trace and which can be reactivated again when we remember what we have learned," says Mr Rose.

In the coming year, scientists such as Mr Buckner and Mr Rose, who have traditionally operated in relative isolation from one another, will be able to work more closely. The last year of the century should see the first fruits of this cross-fertilisation, with increasingly sophisticated brain scans showing memory-formation as it happens, enabling the molecular scientists to fit their experimental results into the patterns formed by a scanner as a living human brain captures a memory.

Such work means that brain functions such as memory are no longer the amorphous attributes of the human intellect they once were. They are becoming understandable, something that is physical and, ultimately, something that can be manipulated for human benefit. The next target will be consciousness itself, but nobody is under any illusion as to how difficult this will be. Nevertheless, some top scientists are beginning to talk seriously about the prospect that it may one day be possible to tackle consciousness in the way that memory is now beginning to be understood. When that day comes, it will be a truly historic moment in the study of human nature.

THE WORLD IN 1999 Dracula's sodapop: artificial blood becomes available in 1999, making transfusions safer, easier and cheaper.

Molecular medicine comes of age

Fiona Godlee

These little piggies went to hospital

There is, people say, a 40-year gap between a scientific discovery and its application. This was true of information technology, developed in the 1940s and applied on a wide scale only from the 1980s. True too of DNA, discovered in 1953 and applied in gene therapy in the early 1990s. And true of molecular medicine, which took off in the 1960s and will start to deliver real applications—particularly in the treatment of cancer—only over the next decade.

Detailed study of cancer cells over many years has shown us how they differ from normal cells. This knowledge can now be exploited in detecting cancers and treating them. Any cancer larger than 2mm in diameter needs its own blood supply to survive and continue to grow. But its blood vessels are more prolific and haphazard than those in normal tissue and carry different immunological markers on their surface. Diagnostic scans can spot these differences and can give information on how aggressive the tumour is. The more new blood vessels the tumour has, the faster it will grow. Drugs have been developed that attack the cancer's blood supply without damaging the blood vessels in normal tissue. Since the growth of abnormal blood supply is characteristic of all malignant tumours, these new antiangiogenic drugs could in theory attack all cancers alike. They are now being tested on a range of

different types of cancer.

Our understanding about the growth of new blood vessels, angiogenesis, will be put to use in another field of medicine. Some of the commonest disabling and fatal diseases are caused by poor blood supply to muscle, usually due to atherosclerosis, which causes narrowing of the arteries. Two such diseases are coronary artery disease, which can lead to heart attacks, and peripheral arterial disease, which can lead to gangrene and amputation. Patients with these problems are currently treated with drugs or surgery, both of which aim to improve the blood supply by widening existing arteries. Now researchers in Boston have developed another approach, using gene therapy to stimulate angiogenesis in the blood-starved muscles. The gene that produces vascular endothelial growth factor, a chemical that encourages new blood vessels to form, has been injected into the heart or leg muscles of patients. After several weeks, tests have shown a striking increase in the number of blood vessels to the area. In 1999, the long-term effects of the technique will be shown in clinical trials.

The manipulation of genes has opened new doors for patients awaiting organ transplants, by making it possible to use animal organs. Genetic engineering prevents initial rejection of the transplanted organ, and pig heart and kidney transplants are now technically feasible. Pig-liver transplants are further off be-

Fiona Godlee: assistant editor, *British Medical Journal*; executive editor, *Clinical Evidence*.

cause the liver is a much more complex organ. Against the idea of animal-to-human transplants is the fear that new viruses will cross the species barrier. In favour is the fact that for years humans have been exposed to pig tissue in the form of transplanted heart valves, spleens, and skin with no sign of cross-species infection. Studies aimed at resolving this issue are expected to report in 1999. If they find no significant risk, the year will see the first use of a pig's liver to keep a patient alive for a few days while awaiting a human-liver transplant. Pig kidney and heart transplants will follow. Only a few operations will be performed initially, under carefully controlled conditions. Animal organs will therefore make little immediate impact on the growing waiting lists for human organs, now estimated at 200,000 people worldwide, of whom fewer than one-third will receive a transplant in 1999.

Dishonest science

Philip Campbell

In several laboratories, scientific fraud, once regarded as quirky, isolated and ultimately absurd, will become a serious disruption to the advance of human knowledge in the year ahead.

Statistically, scientific misconduct is a minor but significant blemish. More than 1.3m scientific papers were published in 1997, whereas the number of cases of serious misconduct under consideration during that year ran only in the low hundreds. That still represents a significant growth from virtually zero over the past three decades, even though part of the increase could be attributed to a move

Philip Campbell: editor of *Nature* magazine.

away from institutional secrecy to greater openness.

There is comfort in the fact that misconduct has had a negligible effect on the strength of the edifice of scientific knowledge and its rate of growth. Unfortunately, the scientific impact of all too many publications is also negligible, so that the fruits of much misconduct—publications with fabricated data or results copied wholesale from others—can be well and truly buried in obscure journals. But scientists' confidence in their disciplines' resilience against fraud or, for that matter, honest mistakes rests on the assumption that important results—the stuff of textbooks—will get replicated ex-

Russia's other disease

Kate Mallinson

Russia's financial collapse in 1998 proved rapidly contagious. Expect a new and worse disease to come out of Russia in 1999: tuberculosis, once the scourge of Victorian Britain. Freely traversing international borders with business travellers, holidaymakers, immigrants, refugees and asylum seekers, it will be coming to a city near you in 1999.

Twenty of the 27 countries in Central and Eastern Europe and the former

Kate Mallinson: London bureau of Interfax, a Russian news agency.

Soviet Union are now seeing an uncontrollable resurgence of TB. However, it is Russia's far-eastern penal colonies which will be condemned as the world's incubator of a virtually incurable and highly contagious strain.

In these grim echoes of the Gulag, where only rudimentary medical standards are observed, a global problem is being distilled. More than 20,000 prisoners are reported to have died of TB in the past two years, and 100,000 are currently sick with TB.

Bad medical practice will make the

problem sharply worse. Incomplete treatment, when prisoners take only enough antibiotic to feel better but fail to finish the course, often bartering their remaining supply, leaves them with a highly contagious multi-drug resistant TB (MDR-TB). This is a hundred times more expensive to treat than standard TB. If it is to be contained, which it won't be, all new cases of this strain should be treated under the dots (Directly Observed Treatment Short-Course) protocol. DOTS has not yet been officially adopted by the Russian National Health Policy and is only being practised in pilot areas by the French aid agency Médecins Sans Frontières.

This is not simply a local problem. There has long been a correlation between sickly economies and the incidence of new endemic TB cases. The spread of contagion outside Russia's penal colonies is imminent; it will be borne rapidly along by Russia's present collapse. TB thrives on poverty. National frontiers are as porous to the bacilli as they are to a banker with a loan book. Up to 200m people worldwide could contract the disease by 2020. Some of the worst affected countries will be popular holiday and business destinations. They include regions of Brazil, India, Indonesia, Mexico and South Africa. The statisticians are not too upbeat about Britain either, where there will be some 6,000 new cases of TB in 1999. There has been a 100% increase in reported cases in London alone during the past decade.

No amount of bars will keep the bugs in

Your sales forecast just dropped.
Are sales management and the sales force giving you the same number?

Do you know ?

You can spend millions of dollars on application software and still not have the information you need to run your business. That's because most application software automates just the back office—or just the front office. Oracle® Applications integrate your entire business—sales, service, supply chain, manufacturing, accounting, projects, human resources. Everything. Our applications capture all the information needed to provide a complete view of what's going on in your business. Every decision you make is based on up-to-date information and impact on shareholder value. We call it business intelligence. And it's from Oracle. Now you know.

If you'd like to know even more—and who wouldn't—call Oracle.

+353 1803 9300, or visit www.oracle.com/info/6 today.

ORACLE®
Applications

plicitly, or checked implicitly, given that subsequent work will founder if based on falsehoods. And identified miscreants quickly find themselves out in the cold.

Fabricating falsehoods

Yet knowledge of that does not deter the major fraudsters, who may publish tens of wholly fallacious papers in prestigious journals before detection. Their motivation, it appears, is not so much personal gain, more impatience coupled with competitive pressure. More often than not, it seems, they appear genuinely to believe the result that they fabricate, but cannot be bothered with the laborious burden of painstakingly closing experimental or conceptual loopholes. And in today's biomedical research, where most scientific fraud occurs, the experiments are so finicky that exact replication of experiments in a different laboratory is sometimes impossible.

Even in minor cases, misconduct's impact can be hugely disruptive within a laboratory, smearing the reputations of all who come close to it. At its worst it can also bring science into grave disrepute with politicians and the media, waste large amounts of research funds, and divert significant energy into judicial investigation. In one celebrated case, the outcome hinged on FBI examination of laboratory notebooks, while a distinguished biologist, in supporting the accused, was forced to resign from his position at the head of a leading university. The accused was later exonerated.

Time was when fraudulent scientists were considered by their peers to be nothing short of deranged. Now increased competition has turned serious misconduct into a still tiny but inevitable part of what is, after all, a system made readily duplicitous thanks to the very values that have traditionally been at the heart of it: trust and openness. For example, papers and grant proposals are sent out to researchers for assessment on the assumption that they will behave honourably even if they are working in the same area. But realists know that peer review is all too easily abused by competitors. Plagiarism of ideas and deliberate delay are rare but are certainly tangible facts of life in the experience of *Nature*'s staff.

Slowly and somewhat grudgingly, sci-

Who needs a real body?

Shereen El Feki

For decades, virtual organs were one of medicine's pipe dreams. But powerful new computers, and a better understanding of how the heart and other body parts are made up cell by cell, are making such lifelike simulations a reality. In 1999 computerised models of the heart, lung and pancreas will be available for pharmaceutical companies to test their latest blockbuster drugs.

A computerised heart is already in action. An American company called Physiome Sciences has produced a virtual heart made not of flesh and blood but of thousands of mathematical equations which describe how the organ's biochemical, mechanical and electrical activities culminate in a heart beat. These equations are combined with a detailed blueprint of the heart's architecture to create a visual model which swells and surges on its own, just like a living heart.

The virtual heart is so real, and so reliable, that a Swiss drug company, Roche, has used it to test one of its new medicines for cardiovascular

---

Shereen El Feki: health-care correspondent, *The Economist*.

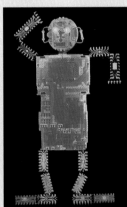

He's easier to operate on

disease. Scientists are also studying the model to understand how genetic mutations, which affect essential heart proteins, can cause lethal conditions such as cardiac arrhythmia and congestive heart failure. These are common disorders which drug companies would dearly like to treat with profitable new products. The virtual heart allows medicines to be tested and refined in cyberspace, boosting their benefits and reducing their nasty side-effects. The proof, of course, still lies in the patient.

Physiome is also building a virtual pancreas and lung, which will be ready for drug developers by the end of 1999. Other enterprising scientists are preparing computer models of the liver, kidney, immune system, circulatory system and gut. By early in the next century, scientists will have connected these and other models together into a virtual human body, which they can use to study physiology in ways simply not practical (or ethical) in living patients. One day click and drag, rather than cut and tear, will be all it takes to probe the body's inner workings.

---

entific institutions are facing up to the realities. The United States, until recently apparently holding a monopoly in contemporary scientific misconduct, has had a troubled history following controversial procedures in cases investigated by its Office of Research Integrity (ORI). Yet the ORI is valuable as a clearing house and a judge of serious cases which American laboratories are only too keen to see the back of.

With the exceptions of the Scandinavian countries and Australia, the world has been slow to tackle the problem at a national level. One of Britain's five research councils has generated guidelines for handling misconduct in its laboratories; the others are trailing behind but, under government pressure, are drafting guidelines. A recent scandal in France has highlighted a secretive defensiveness, although there is no reason to think that the country's research base has much to be ashamed of. Germany found itself having to move fast to catch up when a massive fraud hit the prestigious

Max Planck Society (MPS) of research institutes, an organisation famous for its focus on the purest of science. The MPS handled the problem promptly and with an appropriate balance of confidentiality and transparency, while Germany's principal funding agency has recently produced guidelines that other European organisations are finding invaluable.

There is another worry, far from the quasi-criminal end of the spectrum of misdemeanour, and closer to more humdrum human weaknesses. Two recent studies of applicants for scientific jobs discovered that a high proportion made false declarations about publications. And a study of undergraduate student tests in a prestigious American university uncovered a high level of cheating. It seems naive to have to teach students to be honest. But we must recognise that deceptively mild misdemeanours are creeping in at all levels of scientific endeavour. If allowed to continue unchecked these will poison the culture of honesty on which science has thrived.